Edexcel GCE History

The United States 1917–54: Boom, Bust and Recovery

Les Barker Geoff Stewart

Series editors: Martin Collier Rosemary Rees

Unit 3 Student Book

A PEARSON COMPANY

Published by Pearson Education Limited, a company incorporated in
England and Wales, having its registered office at Edinburgh Gate,
Harlow, Essex, CM20 2JE. Registered company number: 872828
www.pearsonschoolsandfecolleges.co.uk

Edexcel is a registered trademark of Edexcel Limited

Text © Pearson Education Limited 2010

First published 2010

15
10 9 8 7 6 5

British Library Cataloguing in Publication Data
A catalogue record for this book is available from the British Library

ISBN 978 1 846905 08 7

Edited by Elina Helenius, Bluenna Editorial
Designed by Florence Production Ltd, Stoodleigh, Devon
Typeset by Florence Production Ltd, Stoodleigh, Devon
Picture research by Susie Prescott
Cover image: Getty Images Time & Life Pictures/Margaret Bourke-White
Printed in Malaysia (CTP-PPSB)

Acknowledgements
The publisher would like to thank the following for their kind permission to reproduce:
Photographs:
(Key: b-bottom; c-centre; l-left; r-right; t-top)
Corbis: 108, Bettman Archive 76, 88, 147, 159, Vera Block 128; **Courtesy of the Jay. N. 'Ding' Wildlife Society:** 45;
Courtesy of University of Michigan: 58; **Getty Images:** Archive Photos/Buyenlarge 52, Archive Photos/Fotosearch 131,
Archive Photos/Jack Benton 63b; **John W Harman Center/Duke University Libraries:** Wayne P. Ellis Kodakiana Collection 26;
Library of Congress: Dorothea Lange 73, Motion Picture Division 6, National Photo Company 63t; **Magnum Photos Ltd:**
Elliot Erwitt 157; **Press Association Images:** AP 118; **Rex Features:** Everett Collection 133; **The Herb Block Foundation:**
160, Herbert Block 154; **TopFoto:** 152, The Granger Collection - New York 44; **US National Archives:** 144

All other images © Pearson Education

Written Sources:
p.8 Excerpt from THE ROBBER BARONS: THE GREAT AMERICAN CAPITALISTS 1861–1901, copyright 1934 and renewed 1961
by Matthew Josephson, reprinted by permission of Houghton Mifflin Harcourt Publishing Company; pp.70, 122, 173 Fiona Venn
The New Deal, BAAS Paperbacks, Edinburgh University Press, 1998; pp.54, 69, 124 From ANXIOUS DECADES: AMERICA IN
PROSPERITY AND DEPRESSION 1920-1941 by Michael E. Parrish. Copyright © 1992 by Michael E. Parrish. Used by permission
of W. W. Norton & Company Inc; p.69 From AMERICA: A NARRATIVE HISTORY, FOURTH EDITION by George Brown Tindall
and David E. Shi. Copyright © 1996, 1992, 1988, 1984 by W. W. Norton & Company, Inc. Used by permission of W. W. Norton &
Company, Inc; pp.70, 89, 100, 105, 173 From FDR'S FOLLY by Jim Powell, copyright © 2003 by Jim Powell. Used by permission
of Crown Forum, an imprint of Crown Publishers, a division of Random House, Inc; pp.80, 101 From David Reynolds *America:
Empire of Liberty* 2009. Reproduced by permission of Penguin Books Ltd; pp.80, 87, 100, 126, David M Kennedy *Freedom from Fear:
The American People in Depression and War 1929-45* 1999, By permission of Oxford University Press; pp.82, 113, 126 From Niall
Ferguson, *The Ascent of Money*, 2008. Reproduced by permission of Penguin Books Ltd; pp.89, 124, 126, 127 From Maldwyn A.
Jones, *The Limits of Liberty*, (second edition) 1995. By permission of Oxford University Press; pp.95, 109 From D.K. Adams,
Franklin D Roosevelt and the New Deal, Historical Association, 1979; pp.98, 121 From Hugh Brogan, 'The US 1900-1945' in *The
Oxford History of the 20th Century* ed. Michael Howard and W.M. Roger Louis. pp 128-139. 1998, By permission of Oxford
University Press; p.172 From *The Great Crash 1929 by* J.K. Galbraith, 1954. Reproduced by permission of Penguin Books Ltd

Every effort has been made to trace the copyright holders and we apologise in advance for any unintentional omissions. We would
be pleased to insert the appropriate acknowledgement in any subsequent edition of this publication.

Disclaimer
This material has been published on behalf of Edexcel and offers high-quality support for the delivery of Edexcel qualifications.
This does not mean that the material is essential to achieve any Edexcel qualification, nor does it mean that it is the only suitable
material available to support any Edexcel qualification. Edexcel material will not be used verbatim in setting any Edexcel
examination or assessment. Any resource lists produced by Edexcel shall include this and other appropriate resources.
Copies of official specifications for all Edexcel qualifications may be found on the Edexcel website: www.edexcel.com

Contents

Introduction

In 1917, the United States of America was the largest economy in the world. It could be taken as the growing point of humanity, a vision of what other countries might become. The fortunes of the new American business bosses dwarfed those of the European aristocracy. Andrew Carnegie, the poor lad from Scotland, was the first man to receive a cheque for a billion dollars when he sold his US steel companies. It was a land of opportunity. Even those who did not reach the elevated heights of a Carnegie could make fortunes. Poor Jewish immigrants from Eastern Europe were to become the movie moguls of the 1920s, men like Sam Goldwyn or Louis B. Mayer. Ordinary workers in Henry Ford's new car plant could earn $5 a day, a wage undreamed of in Europe. Cars were ceasing to be the preserve of the super-rich and in the subsequent decades the mass consumer society was born. Electricity made possible a new lifestyle, washing machines and vacuum cleaners eased the burden of domestic chores and radios and cinemas brightened the increasing hours of leisure.

However, this new 'earthly paradise' was not without its problems: The old America of farming and small towns, largely dominated by settlers from the British Isles and northern Europe and staunchly protestant in religion, faced an alien world of large cities teeming with recent immigrants from eastern and southern Europe or Ireland. Here, Jewish and Catholic immigrants gave rise to a different culture. Clashes in values were inevitable and possibly the most famous developed over Prohibition in the 1920s. Even deeper divisions existed over race. The cursed legacy of slavery poisoned society. Rigid segregation afflicted the old slave-owning centres of the South, but as black Americans moved north in their hundreds of thousands in the first two decades of the 20th century, new tensions developed in the big cities where they settled.

Between 1929 and the mid-1930s, the whole great experiment of ever expanding capitalist production seemed to have ground to a halt in the Great Depression. One of the central themes of this course is the need to come to terms with the causes of this major event. This is addressed in Unit 5. There are many interpretations of why this downturn took place and it is not intended here to advance one at the expense of others. It is intended to uphold the validity of several viewpoints, and the multi-causal complexity of the phenomena should be appreciated. The response of the new government of F.D. Roosevelt in 1933 to this 'Great Depression' became known as the New Deal and a second controversy is addressed in Unit 6, namely the impact of the New Deal on the USA. Did the policies of FDR's administration aid economic recovery, as many believe, or did it lengthen the Depression and hold up recovery, as others have argued? Certainly there was a massive expansion in the role of the Federal Government, which had grown during the USA's brief period of conflict during the First World War but which had then been sharply cut-back by the Republican governments of the 1920s. The tensions created by the slump and the Roosevelt's Administration's responses inevitably gave rise to bitter criticism from both those who felt that his government was doing too little and those who felt that he was doing too much.

In 1941, the United States became an active participant in the great global conflict which had broken out. The impact of the Second World War on the United States was to be far greater than that from its short and limited involvement in the First World War from 1917 to 1918. The Federal Government assumed responsibilities to an unparalleled extent, its power and authority symbolised by the construction of the Pentagon. The production of weapons and goods of all sorts multiplied to a hitherto unimagined extent. Henry Ford's corporation alone produced more armaments than Italy. Economic power was translated into military power leaving the US as the dominant nation on earth. At the same time her citizens enjoyed rising living standards, which continued long after the war ended. Bust had turned to boom. The post-war world, while being marked by economic expansion and rising living standards, was also marked by a new conflict with the Soviet Union. This 'Cold War,' as it was termed fuelled an internal search for hidden enemies in the United States – the 'Red Scare'. There were some genuine Soviet agents to be flushed out, but the process got out of hand and was exploited by the likes of Senator McCarthy. Prosperity and a degree of paranoia therefore marked the post-war United States.

The whole course under study is often referred to as 'Boom and Bust'. It should more accurately be known as Boom, Bust and Recovery. It is a study of the domestic affairs of the most powerful state of the 20th century, as it emerged into that role.

Exam tips

Do remember that there are two distinct sections to the Examination. Part A demands an essay based on the content in Units 2, 3, 4, 7 and 8. In this section no sources are involved in the assessment. Part B demands an essay using sources and own knowledge. There will always be a choice; one question will be based on Unit 5, the causes of the Great Depression, and one on Unit 6, the impact of the New Deal.

The USA in the early 20th century

What is this unit about?

This unit focuses on the situation that existed in the United States at the start of the period of study. In it you will find out about why the US economy was so successful and about some of the salient features of US society. There is, finally, a section on how the American political system developed, especially the role of the President. You may want to return to this section from time to time to be sure that you understand the issues fully.

In this unit you will:

- examine the background history of the USA leading up to the First World War
- cover the basics of the US political system.

Key questions

- What was the structure of the American economy before and during the First World War?
- What are the key features of the American political system?

Timeline

1783	Treaty of Paris gives independence to the 13 rebel colonies – now the United States
1787	New Constitution drafted for a better union of the 13 colonies
1789	New Constitution ratified
1861	A group of southern states seek to secede from the Union, precipitating the Civil War
1865	13th Amendment abolishes slavery throughout the Union
1890	Idaho and Wyoming become states, linking the Atlantic and Pacific coasts with fully organised and recognised states of the Union
1905	Peak year for immigration: nearly one million people arrive in the USA
1908	Henry Ford launches Model T motor car
1912	Woodrow Wilson elected President of USA

Please note

The Edexcel GCE History Specification Unit 3 Option C2 'The United States, 1917–54: Boom, Bust and Recovery' does not officially start until 1917, and you will never be set any questions that require a detailed knowledge of American history before that date. Nevertheless, it is important that you have a working knowledge of the background to the USA in 1917 in order properly to understand what was happening in the years after that date.

The Skillsbuilders included in this unit are designed to help practise your skills, rather than represent topics that you will be asked questions on in your examination.

Source A

O beautiful for spacious skies
For amber waves of grain
For purple mountain majesties
Above the fruited plain.
America! America!
God shed his grace on thee
And crown thy good with brotherhood
From sea to shining sea

From part of a poem written by Katherine Lea Bates, an American school teacher, in 1893 after a visit to Pikes Peak in Colarado.

The whole poem was set to music in 1904 and became a popular song, almost a second national anthem. By this time, several railway lines now linked the Atlantic coast, where the United States had begun its existence, to the Pacific, a distance of nearly 3,000 miles.

From colony to emerging superpower

The original 13 English colonies that had been established by the mid-18th century clung to the Atlantic seaboard and only slowly did first hunters and trappers and then settlers begin to push over the Appalachian Mountains into the great valley of the Mississippi and its tributaries. After the American War of Independence (1775–83) the 13 colonies became the first 13 states of the independent republic in 1783, remembered in the 13 stripes of the national flag.

As settlers moved westwards, new states, such as Kentucky and Tennessee, were created and joined the union of the original 13 states in the 1790s. By 1830, settlers had pushed across the Mississippi River and established states like Missouri on the western bank. From here up the valley of the Missouri River and its tributaries they began to move into the Great Plains and eventually through the majestic Rocky Mountains into the fertile Pacific coast. Their victims were the herds of buffalo and the Plains Indians, whose existence depended on them. In the same year that Katherine Bates wrote her poem of praise to America, an eminent historian, Frederick Jackson Turner, delivered an important lecture on 'The Significance of the Frontier in American History'. He argued that the presence of a shifting frontier of civilisation had shaped the American character and the new nation. It had provided endless opportunities and created a positive outlook and sense of self-reliance. Now, the frontier was closed, the last Indian threat had been defeated and the buffalo were nearly extinct. The era of expansion of the USA across North America was over and this experience had not only created one country 'from sea to shining sea', but had also ingrained a sense of individualism and endeavour into the American psyche.

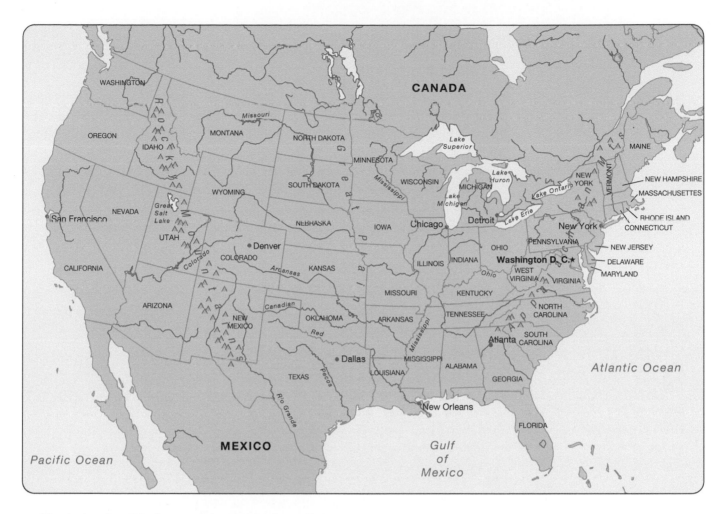

1.1 Physical and political map of the USA in the 20th century.

What were the main features of the American economy?

Bates' poem and Turner's lecture both point up key elements in America's economic success. Firstly, the United States was endowed with a wonderful range of natural resources. Rich farmlands and a variety of climates made possible a prosperous agriculture. Huge mineral deposits of coal, iron ore and oil were there to be exploited. However, other giant nations were equally well endowed by nature, such as Imperial Russia and the ex-Portuguese colony of Brazil, yet these did not develop vibrant economies during the 19th century. The dominant value system in the United States, the cult of freedom, aided and encouraged the exploitation of natural resources.

The first settlers in New England were fleeing religious persecution and established small independent colonies in the new world. They encouraged an ethic of hard work and a culture grew up which brilliantly combined self-reliance and community action.

The moving frontier kept these values alive. The victory of the northern states over the slave owning South in the civil war of 1861–65 ensured that it was the Northern vision of the Republic as a 'go-getting' industrial and commercial society that triumphed over the languid, aristocratic slave-owning society of the South.

One final ingredient of success was the legacy of the rule of law, inherited from the mother country, England. No profession was more respected than that of the lawyer, and lawyers played a crucial part in shaping the United States. The rule of law gave security to landowners and made possible the expansion of commerce and business. This was not simply the provision of law and order but the acceptance by all, including the government, that there was an agreed and respected method of settling disputes. Out of this came 'trust' and the possibility of a complex and sophisticated business culture.

The American economy experienced a sustained period of growth at the end of the 19th and start of the 20th centuries. Already, by the 1880s, shortly after the ending of the Civil War, the USA had the largest individual **Gross Domestic Product** in the world, having overtaken that of Great Britain. There were four main elements in this advance:

- application of new technology
- immigration
- transport
- development of large-scale business organisations, known as corporations.

Definition

Gross Domestic Product (GDP)
The total value of all the goods and services produced in a country.

Discussion Point

How could these four elements combine to enable the USA to become economically prosperous?

The development of new technology and methods of production

Labour had always tended to be in short supply in North America and wages consequently high. In the cotton states of the South, the problem had been solved by recourse to slavery. Slavery had brought its own problems and during the Civil War it was abolished, but it left a legacy of social division and bitterness. In the North and West, there was a premium on labour saving devices and technology. An engineering culture developed and one that, in view of the scattered nature of communities and farms, demanded toughness and ease of repair for its machinery. The interchangeable part was essential, rather than the singular crafted machine which needed to be taken back to the factory or workshop for fixing when it broke. Congress assisted the growth in engineering skills in 1862 by making funds available to the various states for the setting up of colleges for agriculture and the mechanical arts. By 1914, 4,300 people were graduating annually from 126 different colleges. Great Britain, which had led the first industrial revolution, was already dwarfed by this development.

American industry used a range of new inventions that impacted on many aspects of the American economy. The steel industry benefited from its extended use of the Bessemer process, a method of making steel that Andrew Carnegie had seen in practice on a visit to England in 1872. Steel production, and that of coal, both overtook that of the hitherto world leader, Great Britain. Food production benefited from improved technology in processes such as bottling, canning and the development of refrigeration and railway transport. The mass production of sewing machines was effectively implemented by the Singer Sewing Machine Company. All elements of industry took advantage of the longer working hours that were made possible by the invention of the light bulb, which became viable after Thomas Edison's work in 1879. Communications also improved in the last quarter of the 19th century with Alexander Graham Bell's invention of the telephone in 1876 – and by 1900 there were about 800,000 telephones in the USA.

With the development of electric lighting and telephones leading to the birth of the electrical industry, the USA became a world leader in what has been termed the second industrial revolution. This revolved around electrical goods, dominated by giants, such as General Electric and Westinghouse, chemicals (Du Pont) and the brand new motor car industry.

What was the importance of Henry Ford?

Henry Ford astonished the world by the scale and cheapness of his products. His Model T, launched in 1908, was sold at $825. By 1914 it cost $440 and one was being produced every 93 minutes. The cost was approximately six months' pay for a schoolteacher. Cars were no longer the playthings of the rich.

The secret of Ford's success was not just inventiveness in engineering, but the development of what became known as systems engineering. The whole process of production was rationalised and broken down into its component parts. Craftsmen were not required but attentive, rapidly trained labourers were. Ford paid well at $5 a day – a dream wage for most labouring men. Components were manufactured separately in subordinate shops and brought together rapidly in an assembly plant, to which they were transported automatically. The conveyor belt was born. Mass production on a large scale became possible and the **economies of scale** that resulted meant that production costs were reduced. The prophet and publicist of this system was Frederick Winslow Taylor, whose great book, *The Principles of Scientific Management* was published in 1911. What became known as 'Taylorism' was soon known and copied throughout the world, but none could initially equal the United States in the application of Taylor's and Ford's approaches.

Look at the photograph of the Westinghouse Factory near Pittsburgh Pennsylvania, in Source B on page 6, which was taken in 1904. This company started out providing air brake systems for the railway companies, but over time came to manufacture a range of products to support all aspects of the electricity industry from generation to application. This factory pictured employed 9,000 people in 1905.

Look at the photograph of the Westinghouse Factory near Pittsburgh Pennsylvania, in Source B on page 6

SKILLS BUILDER

In no more than 300 words, explain how the USA became an industrial world leader in the 19th century.

Definition

Economies of scale
The benefits gained by a business by creating a larger scale of production e.g. it may be possible to secure discounts by buying raw materials in larger quantities.

Source B

1.2 The engine room of the Westinghouse Factory in 1904 showing a production line.

Immigration

The significance of industry is demonstrated by the growing number of industrial workers who more than trebled from 885,000 in 1860 to over 3 million by 1900. For all the application of technology, industry required human workers and this was supplied by a flood of new American citizens pouring in from Europe. The United States before 1860 was very much populated by emigrants from the British Isles, with some pockets of Dutch and Germans. There was a shared culture between Great Britain and the USA in the first half of the 19th century that was cherished by many.

Yet it was during the 1870s and 1880s that emigrants poured in from new areas into North America. The Irish, Scottish and English continued to cross the Atlantic at the same rate as before, but thousands pouring in from Eastern Europe and Italy outnumbered them. The incoming human tide never dropped below 100,000 a year and in the peak year of 1905, immigration reached 974,000, of which 221,000 people came from Italy, 185,000 from Russia and 276,000 from the Austro-Hungarian Empire. This was to have enormous social and political consequences, but it also stimulated the economy and made possible the rapid expansion of industry. The USA was transforming into something different and this transformation was not without pain and protest. The old protestant United States found itself having to deal with an increasing minority of Roman Catholics from Italy, Poland and Ireland and Jews from Eastern Europe. Religious and ethnic tensions were inevitable and became a feature of the 1920s.

Transport

The flow of people into the great east coast ports of New York and Boston was made possible by a transport revolution in shipping. Coal-fired steam ships could cross the Atlantic faster than the sailing ships of previous decades. They could carry both more passengers to the USA and more US goods back to Europe. Grain from the West, meat either in cans or, after 1882, refrigerated ships could be transported from the New World to feed the Old World. The cities of Great Britain enjoyed a bonanza of cheap food and this demand stimulated both the agriculture and the processing industries of the United States.

Within the USA an even more important transport revolution was underway – railways. No sooner had they been developed in Great Britain, than they were copied on the other side of the Atlantic. The first line was chartered in 1827. By 1860 there were 30,000 miles of track. Railroad companies became huge employers. By the 1880s, the Pennsylvania Railroad was the single biggest employer in the country, with its 30,000 employees outstripping even the Federal Government. By 1900, several lines linked the east and west coast and by 1910, there were over 350,000 miles of rail, greater than in the whole of Europe. Railways stimulated the iron and steel industries and encouraged many others as well as helping agriculture. The steam trains brought barbed wire and utensils of all sorts for the farmers to use, and took away their cattle and grain to be sold in the eastern cities or loaded onto ships for transport to Europe. By 1914 the USA enjoyed the most advanced transport system of any country on Earth.

The growth of corporations

In the mid-19th century the economy of the United States was dominated by thousands of small family owned businesses. In the last quarter of the century this situation changed, as mergers and takeovers led to the creation of **corporations**. These had the added advantage for investors of having only **limited liability** in law. Small corporations then began to merge into larger corporations in order to benefit from economies of scale. These larger corporations were known as trusts. They had the advantage of being more efficient, but they also reduced the level of competition in the market, and often tried to fix prices. By many, they were regarded as unethical and corrupt. Those who owned these companies often became very wealthy. Famous examples of such trusts were the Standard Oil Company founded by John D. Rockefeller in 1870 and the United States Steel Corporation, put together by the banker J.P. Morgan. This latter corporation was largely based on the already giant steel business built up by Andrew Carnegie, a poor Scot immigrant to the States. When Morgan bought Carnegie's steel business he paid for it with the first cheque for a billion dollars. Carnegie proceeded to spend his wealth on a vast series of charitable bequests in the United States and Great Britain, an important reminder that all successful capitalist entrepreneurs are not simply greedy

SKILLS BUILDER

How far do you think religious and ethnic tensions were inevitable in the 1920s?

Discussion Point

Why was the railway system important to the USA's prosperity?

Definitions

Corporations

Corporations are groups of people legally empowered to act as individuals. These 'companies' had evolved in Great Britain and Western Europe as capitalism developed and were commercially advantageous compared to privately owned individual family businesses.

Limited liability

The principle of limited liability meant that only the assets put into the corporation by a shareholder were at risk in the event of bankruptcy and not other assets such as their corporations. They could therefore raise capital more easily than an individual.

self-seeking businessmen. Morgan's new giant steel trust, when it was created in 1901, controlled 80 per cent of America's steel production. Rockefeller's oil trust controlled 85 per cent of US production and Rockefeller acquired a reputation, not wholly unjustified, for ruthless business practice. For all his business brutality, Rockefeller gave $530 million away to charity in the last forty years of his life.

The great names at the head of the trusts were often pilloried in the press as 'robber barons'. The problem for many Americans was the sheer power that individuals like Morgan and Rockefeller exercised. This seemed to run counter to the American dream of a nation of small farmers and entrepreneurs with the possibility of every man making good if he worked hard. These new captains of industry and commerce appeared so powerful that they could fix everything, including prices and opportunities for others. At the time they were the subject of controversy and have remained so ever since. The farmers of the West resented the railroad bosses whom they suspected of exploiting their control of communication and transport. Farmers also resented the banks, to which they were often heavily in debt. Workers in some of the new trade unions resented the ability of their bosses to break strikes and refuse recognition to unions. These resentments were to surface with added vitriol during the slump of the 1930s, as the following extract makes clear.

Source C

When the group of men who form the subject of this history arrived upon the scene, the United States was a mercantile-agrarian democracy. When they departed or retired from active life, it was something else: a unified industrial society, the effective economic control of which was lodged in the hands of a hierarchy. In short, these men more or less knowingly played the leading roles in an age of industrial revolution. Under their hands the renovation of our economic life proceeded relentlessly: large-scale production replaced the scattered, decentralised mode of production; industrial enterprises became more concentrated, more 'efficient' technically, and essentially 'co-operative,' where they had been purely individualistic and lamentably wasteful. But all this revolutionising effort is branded with the motive of private gain on the part of the new captains of industry. To organise and exploit the resources of a nation upon a gigantic scale, to regiment its farmers and workers into harmonious corps of producers, and to do this only in the name of an uncontrolled appetite for private profit – here surely is the great inherent contradiction whence so much disaster, outrage and misery has flowed.

From M. Josephson, *The Robber Barons*, published in 1934

Other historians have seen Morgan, Rockefeller and their ilk as necessary agents of modernisation, as the following extracts show.

Source D

John D. Rockefeller and his colleagues engineered a radical new departure in the administration and operation of industrial activity. The oil combination constituted the first successful attempt to organise and operate, on a massive scale, the production and distribution of goods rather than services. Rockefeller and his associates were open to criticism as managers of a private business which maintained an overwhelming dominance of its industry, but many reactions stemmed from the fact that it was new and that it ran counter to the interests of some people and to many prevailing American ideals and fixed ideas. Inquiry reveals that Standard Oil men actually created an effective new behaviour pattern by merging new concepts with several business practices of long standing.

Ralph Hidy from an article in the Journal of Economic History, published in 1952. Three years after this article was published, Standard Oil chose Hidy to write a history of the company.

Source E

Rockefeller lived in a time of constant and rapid change and worked in an industry which in his day grew from an insignificant to an indispensable element in the worked economy. His capacity lay in planning and in organisation. He had both insight and foresight and the ability to choose competent and energetic subordinates. His greatest contribution to American business was his ability to integrate and to exercise effective control over the numerous and widespread functions of his enterprise. He also employed monopoly, ruthlessness secrecy, and, at times, even duplicity, to achieve his ends.

From Vincent Corossa's review of Allan Nevin's biography of John D. Rockefeller in The American Historical Review, published in 1953

SKILLS BUILDER

Read Sources C, D and E carefully, then consider these questions.

- On what points do they agree?
- On what points do they disagree?
- Are the disagreements about facts or opinions?
- How is it possible for modern historians to differ?

(**NOTE** – You will **not** be asked to assess contemporary source material, such as Source C, in your Unit 3 examination. However you will be asked to assess, cross-reference and evaluate historical claims.)

What were the main features of the American political system?

The Presidency

The American political system grew out of the British political system but is different in many crucial ways. This may be because the American Constitution was the product of a series of debates and compromises between some of the leading thinkers and practical activists of the American Revolution. The 'Founding Fathers' came together in Philadelphia in 1787 with the aim of drawing up a Constitution, which would provide an effective government for the new republic and yet prevent tyranny in the new nation, whether it was the tyranny of monarchs or the tyranny of the mob. They were heavily influenced by the system that they knew best, which was that of Great Britain. In place of a monarch they proposed an elected President to head the government. He would appoint ministers and civil servants and conduct the day-to-day running of the country.

A president was elected for four years, but there was nothing to prevent him from standing again. George Washington chose to stand down after his second term and this became the custom throughout the 19th century. Washington also established the rather informal nature of the US presidency. He preferred to be addressed simply as 'Mr President' and so it has remained. The president was in fact much less than a monarch with no grand court and few servants. It was possible that a visitor to the White House could find the door opened by the president himself.

The powers wielded by a president were hedged about by many constraints and the armed forces, of which he was commander in chief, were embarrassingly small with an army totalling just 26,000 in 1886. In fact the role of the Federal Government, of which he was the head, was minute, and many areas of public concern, such as law and order were left to the individual states to organise. The number of federal departments was small. Originally there had been:

- The State Department, handling foreign policy
- The Treasury
- The War Department, heading the tiny army
- The Department of the Navy
- The Postmaster General
- The Attorney General.

To these offices had been added a Secretary of the Interior in 1849, a Department of Agriculture in 1889 and one for Commerce in 1903. Appointments to all these posts were made by the President, but he required the approval of the Senate (see pages 11–12) for the chosen man to be appointed.

Although the President could stop a law being made by exercising his **veto**, it was very difficult for him to exercise initiative in making law. The president's personal staff was small and totally inadequate for launching complex legislative initiatives. He did not sit in either House of Congress as a British prime minister did in parliament, nor did any of his ministers. They were in fact forbidden to be members of Congress in line with the doctrine of the **separation of the powers** on which principle the Constitution was based. Congress was in consequence very difficult to control and manipulate. The Senate in particular was a notable block to initiatives. A single senator could 'filibuster' for hours, holding up a proposal by simply talking endlessly until there was no more time to take

Definitions

Veto

Latin for 'I forbid'. In constitutional terms the power given to an individual or group to stop a measure going through. The US President could stop a law he disapproved of, but this could be over-ridden by a two-thirds majority in both Houses of Congress. It can be a useful bargaining tool, the president threatening to veto a measure unless Congress lets through something else that the President favours.

Separation of the powers

An important political concept developed in the 18th century which came from a French study of the English Constitution, which was in part misunderstood. It came to believe that the greater liberty present in England when compared to France arose from the separation of Royal power (the executive) from the law-making power of parliament (the legislature) and the judges (the judicial power). The framers of the US Constitution in 1787 rigidly applied these ideas.

a vote. Only by mobilising public opinion, exercising personal charm and deploying the limited federal powers of patronage could a president hope to push through a new law. Even the formidable personality of Teddy Roosevelt, president from 1901–08, found many of his pet initiatives blocked by congressional indifference.

Roosevelt had become President by the easy route. He was elected Vice President in 1900 but William McKinley, the elected President, was promptly assassinated and under the Constitution, the Vice President took over. To secure the Presidency normally, most candidates had to undergo a gruelling ordeal. The first requirement was to secure the nomination of one of the two leading parties, **Republican** or **Democrat**. The nominee was selected at a party convention, where delegates from the different states settled on their man. The system of holding 'primaries', votes for presidential candidates within each state before the convention, was only just beginning. Florida was the first state to hold such votes in 1901 and Wisconsin followed in 1905. By 1916, 25 states held party primaries.

The successful party choice to emerge at the convention was likely to be a state governor or a senator. Almost all were drawn from the dominant white protestant elite, although a humble origin was no bar. The ability to raise large sums to pay for the campaign was, however, essential and big backers would – and could – expect a reward if their candidate won. Victory in the ultimate contest between the two party choices in November went to the one who secured a majority in **The Electoral College**. This could be very close. Woodrow Wilson won in 1916 by 277 votes to 254. The Vice President was elected at the same time as the President, standing on the same 'ticket', as it is known. Once elected the Vice President chairs the Senate but otherwise in L.B. Johnson's famous phrase, the position was 'not worth a bucket of warm spit' unless the President chose to consult his deputy or died, as happened in Johnson's case when John F. Kennedy was assassinated in 1963.

Congress and the Supreme Court

The equivalent of the British Parliament was Congress. Divided like the British Parliament into two houses, its function was to make laws. The upper house, the equivalent of the House of Lords, was to be the Senate. Each state, regardless of its population had two members and the senators were not directly elected by the people, but appointed by the various states for a period of six years. It was hoped they would be a check on popular democracy and act as defenders of property. The lower house, the equivalent of the House of Commons, was the House of Representatives. This was directly elected and each state had a number of representatives in line with its relative population. Thus, for example, tiny Rhode Island had only one representative, whereas Virginia, the most populous state in 1787 was given 14. In the 20th-century California, Texas and New York had the most members of the House of Representatives, or Congressmen as they are known. These Congressmen were elected for only two years.

Definitions

Democratic Party

One of the two main political parties in the US. The Democratic Party was the more 'liberal' or left-wing of the two parties, although white voters from the southern states were traditionally Democrat and anything but liberal or left-wing, being strongly opposed to black civil rights.

Republican Party

The Republicans were the party of big business and Western farmers. It was the party of Abraham Lincoln and associated with anti-slavery, so if black people in the South could vote it was likely to be Republican. This was to change between the 1930s and 1960s, with southern whites realigning with the Republicans and blacks becoming increasingly Democratic.

The Electoral College

This is the group of people selected to vote for the President. Each state has the number of Electors that is equivalent to the number of members of the House of Representatives (determined on the basis of the population of the state) plus the number of Senators (two per state, irrespective of population).

They were intended to be the 'democratic' element in the system, representing the popular will and they were crucially able to control taxation.

One of the most distinctive features of the US Constitution is the Supreme Court. This arose from the belief of the Founding Fathers in the doctrine of the separation of the powers. The Supreme Court was there as the guardian of the Constitution and as a permanent check on political abuse either by an over-powerful president or an over-enthusiastic democracy. The Supreme Court could pronounce an action by the President as unconstitutional and even overturn a law passed by Congress and approved by the President. One way round such a judgement was to change the Constitution, but this was a complex and lengthy process involving large, favourable majorities in both houses of Congress and the approval of the President, followed by approval in specially called state conventions. In the centuries since this Convention the Constitution has been amended twenty-seven times. The first ten amendments to the Constitution, known as the Bill of Rights, were passed in 1789 and guaranteed certain basic rights, such as the right to bear arms. In order to introduce Prohibition (see Unit 2 pages 21–22), the Constitution needed amending as it then did to end it, thus the 21st amendment repealed the 18th amendment.

The Supreme Court is also the arbiter of what individual states can and cannot do and judgements on various issues have proved vital over the years (see the Plessy vs Ferguson case on see page 61). Justices in the Supreme Court are nominated by the President and approved by the Senate. They then sit until death or resignation. It is a fortunate president who gets the chance of appointing several Justices, for by appointing men of his political persuasion he can influence politics for years to come after he has retired. It is important to note that the President would appoint men to be Justices, the first woman Justice was not appointed until 1981.

Conclusion

It is worth emphasising two key features embedded in the US Constitution that help us to understand the functioning of US government.

Firstly, the principle of 'Checks and Balances' is vital. The political system was split into three component branches – the Executive, the Legislature and the Judiciary. Each of these branches exists at every level of American politics – national government, state government and local government.

Secondly, the concept of federalism is important to grasp. When the Constitution was created in 1787 each of the thirteen states that existed at that time had to approve the Constitution for it to become law. As the states were not prepared to give up all their power, a compromise had to be reached. This led to the creation of a system known as federalism where power was divided between the state governments and the Federal Government. In the early years of the new country, the balance of power tended to lie with the states. It was unclear whether states could secede from the Union if they disagreed with the Federal Government. It was the attempt of several of the southern states to secede in 1861 that precipitated the US Civil War and finally settled the argument that States could not secede. This was part of a process that, over time, has changed the relationship between Federal and state governments, with the Federal Government acquiring more powers.

Table 1.1 The main branches of federal government.

	Executive	Legislature	Judiciary
Name of office	The President	Congress – divided into two houses, the Senate and the House of Representatives	The Supreme Court
Who can stand?	Natural born US citizen of at least 35 years of age who has lived in the US for the previous 14 years	Senate – at least 30 years of age and have been a citizen for 9 years House – at least 25 years of age and have been a citizen for 7 years Both must live in the state they represent	No formal requirements
Number of years elected for	4 years	Senate – 6 years (one-third re-elected every 2 years) House – 2 years	Life
Elected by?	The Electoral College	Senate – the people after 1913 House – the people	A total of nine judges appointed by the President. The Senate can veto (over-rule) the President's choice of judges
Responsibility?	Executes the laws	Enacts legislation	Rules on whether the laws enacted and executed are constitutional

SKILLS BUILDER

In not more than 300 words, identify the strengths and weaknesses of the US political system.

RESEARCH TOPIC

John D. Rockefeller

John D. Rockefeller is a person who has interested historians for many reasons. Was he a ruthless businessman or a philanthropist? A man who contributed to making the USA great or who was only interested in amassing a personal fortune – or all of these things?

Using books, articles and the Internet, try to find out as much as you can about John D. Rockefeller's career and personality. Then answer this question:

'John D. Rockefeller: robber baron'

How far would you agree with this view?

2 The impact of the First World War

What is this unit about?

This unit focuses on understanding why the USA at first refused to be involved in the First World War and why in 1917, it declared war on Imperial Germany. The war produced dramatic effects upon the USA – economic, social and political – and these are examined. Many of the key issues affecting the United States in the 1920s are products of the First World War.

In this unit you will:

- consider the changes to the US economy as a result of the First World War
- investigate the impact of the First World War on US society.

Key questions

- Why did the USA declare war on Imperial Germany in April 1917?
- What were the economic, social and political effects on the USA of the war?

Timeline

1914	Aug	Great Britain, France and Russia at war with Germany and Austria
1915		Tension with Germany rises as the *Lusitania* is sunk by a German U Boat with the loss of American lives
1916		Vast exports of war material from the USA to Great Britain and France Woodrow Wilson re-elected President of the USA Council of National Defence established
1917	Feb	Germany resumes unrestricted submarine warfare
	Apr	USA declares war on Germany
	Jun	*Espionage Act* restricts traditional individual freedoms
1918		Prohibition introduced for duration of war Hundreds of thousands of US troops reach France to play part in final victory
1919		US President Woodrow Wilson in France playing a leading role in the Treaty of Versailles

Please note

The Edexcel GCE History Specification Unit 3 Option C2 'The United States, 1917–54: Boom, Bust and Recovery' does not officially start until 1917, and you will never be set any questions that require a detailed knowledge of American history before that date, including the reasons why the USA joined the First World War.

Nevertheless, it is important that you have a working knowledge of the background to the USA in 1917 in order properly to understand what was happening in the years after that date.

When the First World War broke out in Europe in 1914, President Wilson declared that the United States would remain neutral. This was a policy that was supported by the majority of the American people. Indeed, it would have been difficult for a nation founded on immigration to decide what side to take: while many Americans were of British descent, many others were of German descent and many Irish-Americans also supported Germany because they thought that a British defeat might lead to Irish independence.

Despite the USA's avowed neutrality a policy called the 'preparedness programme' was implemented in 1915. This was an acknowledgement that the USA had to prepare for the possibility of war and involved the establishment of a regular army of 250,000, with enough officers to command an army of 1,500,000 if a crisis should arise. It also authorised immediate action to make the US Navy second only to that of Great Britain and the building of more permanent munitions. Congress lent its support to the notion of preparedness in 1916 when it created the Council of National Defence, a body to advise the President on how to prepare for a potential war.

Within five months of Wilson's victory in the 1916 Presidential election, the USA entered the war. The key factors involved in this decision were as follows:

- The USA retained close economic ties with Great Britain and France, despite the onset of the war. By April 1917, the USA had loaned them $2.3 billion compared with $27 million of loans to Germany. These links affected American views of the progress of the war and eventually helped lead to its intervention. This level of investment not only suggested which 'side' the USA would take, but was also a huge investment to be protected.

- German U-boats engaged in attacks on shipping around the British coast from February 1915. This culminated for the Americans in the attack on the British passenger liner, the *Lusitania*, in May 1915. Among the 1,198 dead were 128 Americans. Although many Americans now felt that the United States should enter the war, Wilson maintained peace by getting a guarantee from the Germans that they would stop unrestricted submarine warfare.

- In January 1917, Germany decided that the USA was effectively supporting the Allies, despite its declared position of neutrality because of the loans it was making and the fact that American industry was producing goods for the Allied war effort. The German High Command felt that the only way that Germany was going to win the war was to starve Great Britain by cutting off food supplies from abroad. The Germans therefore resumed the unrestricted U-boat campaign, which in turn led Wilson to break off diplomatic relations with Germany in February 1917.

- Wilson had grave concerns about the possibility of a German victory from the outset. He believed that it would undermine the liberal democracy on which the USA was based. He wanted the USA to be involved in determining the peace at the end of the war and for this reason believed the USA needed to be involved in fighting the war.

- The final factor was the Zimmermann Telegram. This was a telegram that was sent from the German Foreign Secretary Alfred Zimmermann

Discussion Point

In August 1914, President Wilson declared the USA to be a neutral country.

How far, by the end of 1915, was this still true?

to the German ambassador in Washington in mid January 1917. It was intercepted by the British who passed a copy to President Wilson. The telegram was the trigger for American entry into war.

Source A

We intend to begin on the first of February unrestricted submarine warfare. We shall endeavour in spite of this to keep the United States of America neutral. In the event of this not succeeding, we make Mexico a proposal of alliance on the following basis: make war together, make peace together, generous financial support and an understanding on our part that Mexico is to re-conquer the lost territory in Texas, New Mexico, and Arizona. The settlement in detail is left to you. You will inform the President (of Mexico) of the above most secretly as soon as the outbreak of war with the United States is certain and add the suggestion that he should, on his own initiative, invite Japan to immediate adherence and at the same time, mediate between Japan and ourselves. Please call the President's attention to the fact that the ruthless employment of our submarines now offers the prospect of compelling England in a few months to make peace.

Signed Zimmermann

The telegram sent by the Foreign Secretary of the German Empire, Arthur Zimmermann, to the German ambassador in Washington, Johann von Bernstoff, on 16 January 1917.

On 2 April 1917, President Wilson addressed both houses of Congress, outlining the reasons why he believed the USA could no longer remain neutral. One key point to note about the content of his speech is that Wilson made it very clear that he was not declaring war on the German people, only on the misguided actions of their government. This was because he was trying to ensure that Americans of German descent supported his policies.

Four days after this speech, both houses of Congress voted to declare war against Germany. They entered the war as an 'Associate Power' rather than as an 'Ally' to distinguish the aims that Wilson had identified in this speech from those of the other combatants.

Ever since April 1917, historians have debated and weighed the factors that they consider important in explaining why the USA went to war. Historians writing in the 1920s and 1930s saw economic explanations for US involvement as being the crucial factor for the USA's intervention. They argued that it was to protect the interests of the burgeoning US economy that Wilson finally decided to enter the war on the Allied side. This interpretation fell out of favour as the chief explanation for US intervention after 1945. The focus instead developed into an attempt to determine whether Wilson was more concerned with ideological (e.g. the defence of

SKILLS BUILDER

How far did President Wilson use the Zimmerman telegram as the reason to take the USA into the First World War?

liberty) or with strategic (e.g. preventing a German alliance with Mexico) considerations when he took the decision to address Congress in April 1917. Economic factors were acknowledged, but were no longer seen to be the main factor. As always, historians tend to disagree in explaining complex events and often disagree in explaining simple ones.

The First World War and the economy

The American economy, as has already been suggested, was in a strong state when the First World War broke out. Even before the United States' declaration of war in April 1917, the war in Europe had a considerable impact. Because of its neutrality, the USA continued to trade with Europe despite the war. Although there was some disruption of trade; the British and French, using their naval superiority, blockaded trade to Germany and Austria and the U-boat campaign waged by the Germans did sink some American shipping – the general trend of trade was upwards. War is a lucrative business; in 1913, the value of American trade was about $2 billion, but by 1916 it had risen to almost $6 billion. By late 1916, Great Britain was spending $10 million a day in the US purchasing war goods. Allied trade was initially financed by the sale of some of the extensive assets that the British held in the USA, but by 1915 Great Britain increasingly relied on loans raised in New York via the great US banks, to pay for the import of goods that were being used to sustain the British war effort. By 1916, loans were being raised at the rate of $4 million a day. Thus, as a result of the war, the USA increasingly replaced Great Britain as the most important creditor nation in the world. New York, rather than London, became the world's financial capital.

When war in Europe broke out in 1914, the size of the United States Army was relatively small at 120,000 strong. One of the first actions taken by the US government was to increase the size of the army through the *Selective Service Act*. This introduced conscription, via what became known as the **draft**. By the terms of the *Selective Service Act*, all men, in the first place those between the ages of twenty-one and thirty, had to register for the draft. They were given a number and those to be drafted were chosen by lottery. By the end of the war, nearly 3 million men had been drafted. The armed forces had to be supplied and equipped and this provided a considerable boost to all sectors of the economy. The Council of National Defence set up the War Industries Board in 1917 to organise supplies for the army. This was very effectively run under the leadership of Bernard Baruch, a Wall Street financier.

Up until the outbreak of war in 1917, the American government and its agencies had not taken a role in directing economic development. However, the War Industries Board changed that, taking a direct role and had a number of important functions. It established the priorities for war production and allocated raw materials to various industries. It also advised companies on how they might make efficiencies. As part of this process, it encouraged different companies which had previously been bitter rivals

Definition

Draft

A government order forcing people to join the armed forces in time of war. It was also known as conscription.

to work together. One such example was the greater uniformity in the manufacture of bicycles which saved two thousand tons of steel. The intervention of the War Industries Board marked a radical change but Americans were prepared to accept a degree of federal direction over the running of industry because it was needed to meet the military needs of the economy. The level of this involvement is demonstrated by the scale of the growth in Federal Government spending; in 1916 it amounted to 1.5 per cent of GNP; by 1918 it stood at 24.1 per cent. Despite the fact that the United States was only a participant in the war from April 1917 to November 1918; the cost of fighting a war was considerable. Indeed, it has been estimated that the United States government spent a total of $31.2 billion on the war in Europe.

Paying for the war

The Federal Government used two main methods to raise the money to finance the war effort, taxation and **liberty bonds**. Taxation raised about a third of the revenue needed to pay war costs. Americans had on occasions in their history been subject to income tax but it was not until the 16th Amendment was ratified in 1913 that Congress had the clear power to levy income tax. It was introduced at a very low rate (between 1 per cent and 7 per cent of income) and paid only by the wealthiest 1 per cent of the population who had an income above $500,000. The needs of the war led to a succession of rapid changes to this system which made a significant contribution to the financing of the war; revenue rose from $809 million in 1917 to $3.6 billion in 1918. By the 1916 *Revenue Act*, the rates were doubled to 2%–15% of income. The Act also introduced taxes on estates and business profits.

By the 1917 *War Revenue Act*, income tax was extended so that anyone earning more than $2,000 paid the lowest rate of 2 per cent. People earning $40,000 were now liable to a 16 per cent rate and the top rate rose to 67 per cent. Even with these extended rates the burden of taxation fell on only about 5 per cent of the population. The 1918 *Revenue Act* increased the lowest rate to 6 per cent and the top rate to 77 per cent. Liberty bonds were issued from May 1917. These were bonds that were sold to the public, so that they could support the war effort. They could be redeemed later with interest. In total there were five Liberty Loan campaigns between 1917 and 1919, which raised more than $21 billion. The launch of the campaigns was accompanied by much publicity and bond rallies where the public were urged to buy bonds by leading celebrities of the day, such as Charlie Chaplin and Mary Pickford. This was the Federal Government borrowing from the US public.

Definition

Liberty bonds

Like most combatants the USA paid for much of the war by borrowing off its own people. In return for their cash, citizens received a promisory piece of paper (bond) guaranteeing repayment and or a fixed rate of interest on the sum loaned. Such bonds could be traded and sold on or kept until the redemption date if there was one specified. Clearly foreign banks or wealthy individuals might buy such bonds.

SKILLS BUILDER

In what ways did the First World War lead to greater power for the Federal Government?

Definitions

Real wages

What the wages earned by a worker will buy. In other words, wages once the effects of inflation on purchasing power have been taken into account.

Debtor/creditor nation

In the 19th century there had been massive investment in the USA from Great Britain in particular. Many US businesses were partly or wholly owned by foreigners, largely British. This meant that more interest was paid from the USA than came in from US investments abroad thus making the USA a debtor nation. This was reversed as British investment in the USA was sold off and bought by American banks and citizens during the war and the USA became a creditor nation.

How important was the war to the American economy?

At the start of the First World War, the US economy was already developing rapidly, but it came out of the First World War even stronger. Because of the huge demand for war materials, imports from Europe fell and exports from the USA rose. As a result of this growing demand, industrial production increased between 1916 and 1918 by 39 per cent. Because of this vast growth in demand, the number employed in the civilian work force grew by 1.3 million and unemployment, that was already relatively low at 5 per cent, virtually disappeared. Not only did the workforce benefit from an absence of unemployment, but their living standards also increased. This was partly due to the fact that the level of **real wages** was higher in 1918 than in 1914. This was most significant for unskilled workers, who experienced a 20 per cent rise in this period. Not only did industrial production increase, American farmers increased their exports of food to Europe by 300 per cent. They also experienced a doubling of prices between 1913 and 1918.

The First World War damaged trade between Europe and the rest of the world. For example, the USA was now able to penetrate some of the UK's export markets, especially in Asia. US banks took advantage of the demand of European countries for money, for example, by lending large sums to Great Britain and Italy and earning high rates of interest on them. As a result, the USA shifted from being a **debtor nation** to a **creditor nation**. By 1919, the USA's overseas investments stood at nearly $10 billion and New York now rivaled London as the international community's main financial centre. Whole regions in Europe were devastated, whereas the USA experienced no war damage; industry had been able to develop and introduce standardised assembly lines, which reduced production costs dramatically.

However, there were also some negative consequences of the war for the United States. It was much less affected by both military and civilian casualty figures than the European countries who had taken part in the First World War. About 2 million German soldiers had been killed as had 1.8 million Russians, 1.4 million French and 885,000 soldiers from Great Britain and its Empire. However, around 112,500 Americans in military service died during the war, more than half of them from diseases, such as typhus and in 1918 the influenza pandemic. Even though the United States had now become a creditor nation, it had to borrow money to pay for the costs of war. As a result, the level of the national debt (the amount of money the nation borrows) increased by 658 per cent between 1916 and 1919 when it stood at just over $27 billion. In order to meet the cost of servicing the national debt, tax levels needed to remain at a higher level after the war than they had been before the war. They were however lower than the wartime levels.

As with all countries involved, when the war ended in 1918, there was a rapid de-mobilisation of troops and the cancellation of all wartime contracts. This led to an immediate post-war slow down in the economy, which appeared to return to normal in 1919, only to experience a further very brief recession in 1920–21. This period of uncertainty had come to an end in 1921, when the USA entered a phase of economic prosperity. While the slowdown went on, however, there was much disruption to the US economy. In 1919, for example, about a quarter of all workers went on strike at some point in the year.

The political and social consequences of the war

The war clearly strengthened the powers of the Federal Government in many fields. It raised and spent more money than ever before and was involved in the economy to an unprecedented extent. The railways were placed under federal control, and the Railroad Administration played a major part in promoting modernisation and creating a standardised national system with integrated timetables and a standardised track guage. The Fuel Administration set limits on the prices of oil and coal and even regulated time with the introduction of 'daylight saving time' as a conservation measure. The National War Labor Board worked closely with the unions who found their powers strengthened with guaranteed collective bargaining and acceptance of the **closed shop**. They secured improvements in wages and hours.

Perhaps the most dramatic area of the expansion of federal powers related to two federal acts, the *Espionage Act* of June 1917 and the *Sedition Act* of May 1918. These both amounted to a considerable limitation on personal freedom. Under the first it became illegal to attempt to obstruct military recruitment and to encourage disloyalty. A film producer was successfully prosecuted and given a ten-year jail sentence for making an allegedly anti-British film, which, it was felt, would injure the war effort by attacking an ally. The *Sedition Act* made it illegal to discourage people from buying war bonds or verbally attacking the Constitution and the war effort. Eugene Debs, a prominent socialist was given ten years of imprisonment for an anti-war speech and 1,500 people were locked up under the Act.

Another area of expansion, and perhaps the most famous infringement of personal liberty introduced by the war, was the triumph of **Prohibition**. There had been a powerful **temperance** movement, called the **Anti-Saloon League**, before war was declared. It drew its strength from Protestantism, women's organisations and small-town America. Now patriotism strengthened its appeal, as it was argued that banning alcohol would help the war effort. The business community also saw drink as a threat to the efficiency and reliability of their workforce. Finally, the fact that most breweries and distilleries happened to be owned by Americans of German descent, such as Ruppert, Pabst and Leibér, only served to help the Prohibitionists' cause. There was also the fear that the use of grain in alcohol production was impacting on food supply. The *Lever Act* curtailed the use of grain and reduced the alcohol content of beer in 1917, and stopped the sale of alcohol near army bases. In 1918, The *Prohibition Act* stopped the sale and manufacture of alcoholic drinks for the duration of the war. Congress also passed the 18th Amendment in December of 1917,

---

Definition

Closed shop
This was a business or company where a worker had to belong to a particular union or group of unions in order to be employed. It could be said to violate the freedom of the individual to choose whether to belong or not.

Discussion Point

Did the demands of wartime lead to serious and unjustified infringements of civil liberties?

Definitions

Prohibition
The banning of the sale of alcoholic drinks.

Temperance
Temperance was the abstention from drinking alcohol and had long been popular in the many protestant chapels of Great Britain and North America.

Definition

The Anti-Saloon League

The Anti-Saloon League emphasised the links between drink and violence that became the staple scene of western films when disputes over a woman or cheating at cards resulted in a mass brawl. It had been founded in 1895 and drew much of its strength from women activists, many of whom felt that alcohol was often linked to their oppression. They had a formidable champion in the six-foot tall Carry Nation who even expressed her view in verse:

'Drink will make the dark, dark blot.
Like an adder it will sting
And at last to ruin bring
They who tarry at the drink'

The dream of temperance reformers was Prohibition.

which would make the ban permanent. This was ratified by the several States by 1919. Following ratification, Congress passed the *Volstead Act* in October 1919, making illegal the sale, transportation and commercial manufacturing of any beverage containing over 0.5% alcohol, from 16 January 1920. Prohibition had become a peacetime reality, thanks to the war.

The war also strengthened intolerance of foreigners and any dissenters from the prevailing mood. Patriotism could quickly become prejudice. Those with German sounding names faced popular abuse and even 'sauerkraut' was renamed liberty cabbage. The war clearly encouraged the anti-immigrant movement and the Red Scares of the 1920s (see pages 55–61).

On a more positive note, as in Great Britain, the war gave a powerful push to the enfranchisement of women, whose contribution to the war effort was recognised. Only eleven states had female suffrage before the war, all in the West. In 1917, New York gave women the vote and then in January 1918, the 19th Amendment that would provide votes for women nationwide, began its progress. It finally passed through the House of Representatives in August 1920, after a long fight against it in the Senate from southern Senators.

SKILLS BUILDER

1. List all the advantages and all the disadvantages to the USA that resulted from entry into the First World War.
2. On a scale of 1–5, where 1 is the greatest and 5 the least impact, rate these advantages and disadvantages.

Unit summary

What have you learned in this unit?

The United States was already making considerable headway in its economic development when it decided to join the First World War in 1917. Although not all Americans agreed with Wilson's decision to declare war, he had the support of the majority of the country. When the war ended 19 months later, USA was – on balance – in an even stronger position economically than it had been at the start of the war.

What skills have you used in this unit?

You will have come to grips with a number of new ideas and concepts. Indeed, it might be quite good for you to have a 'definitions page' in your notes where you can write down some of the new concepts and words that you have picked up. You have discussed a number of issues and you have shown that you understand the significance of various events.

Exam style question

This is the sort of question you will find appearing on the examination paper as a Section A question:

How far do you agree that the impact of the First World War was beneficial to the economy and society of the USA?

Exam tips

The plan

A properly thought through plan is the key to success. In completing the plan you can fully think through your ideas and prepare yourself for completion of the response. In the plan you directly answer the question, using the words in the question. The purpose of the plan is for you to work out in your mind the argument in response to the question.

- The plan should take the form of two or three lines/strands of your argument.
- It is critical that the lines of argument in your plan refer to or cover all of the main issues in a series of bullet points.
- You should then very briefly highlight what you are going to put in each paragraph as a list of key sections and key points.

Writing analytically

In answering the question set you must ensure that:

- your answer is analytical throughout
- you show an explicit understanding of the question set. You will be credited for pursuing those issues that need to be addressed in relation to the set question
- a wide range of detail is precisely selected and used in your answer to support a developed evaluation of the issues. You will be credited for what you have found out in terms of the content relevant to the topic
- where there is a stated factor, it is dealt with for at least the first third of the essay. You should measure the stated factor against other factors, i.e. weighing the factors against each other
- you engage with other factors in your essay, using these factors to set up a *debate*. Top marks are awarded to candidates who can show that they can really get inside the debate
- your essay has a *substantial conclusion*. In your conclusion you should weigh the evidence one last time, judge how it stacks up against each other and make judgements on the basis of the evidence.

Structuring a response

Marks are easily thrown away because your essay technique is not as strong as it should be. The aim of this section is to give you guidance on how to write an assignment that is analytical throughout.

Introduction

Once you have written a plan you need to write an introduction that has a focus on the question and defines the key terms.

The introduction may involve writing out the main points from the plan.

It is essential that you attack the question directly in the introduction.

Your introduction should be straightforward, direct and delivers a focus on the question.

Paragraph structure

You need to structure your assignment into clear and sufficient paragraphs. To achieve the mark you want you need to stay linked to the argument throughout. This means that you *explicitly answer the question* throughout the essay. The best structure for every paragraph is suggested below.

- *Argue* – at the start of the paragraph you should present a line of argument. The best way to do this is to use the language of argument:

  One should argue that ...
  It is clear that ....
  Fundamentally ...
  Without doubt ...
  This most obviously ...

Try and avoid a descriptive start because this will often lead to a descriptive paragraph.

- *Link back* – at the start of the paragraph you should try to link back to other factors where appropriate, perhaps comparing their importance at the same time.
- *Explain* – the next section of each paragraph will explain that line of argument.
- *Evidence* – the next section of the paragraph should give and explain the relevance of detail that you have used to back up your argument, e.g. *'the clearest example of this point is the ...'*. This detail needs to be accurate, well selected and relevant. (What is meant by detail: facts, statistics, names, events and references to historians, for example.)
- *Reiterate* – the last half sentence of the paragraph should be a reiteration, going back to the main theme/ argument in the question.

RESEARCH TOPIC

Attitudes in the USA to the war

Despite legislation, some Americans did openly oppose the war. Examples of such Americans and groups of Americans were Senator Robert La Follette, the Women's Peace Party and socialist groups.

Choose one individual or group who opposed the war. Find out what they believed and what happened to them.

3 The years of prosperity, 1919–29

What is this unit about?

This unit focuses on the state of the US economy in the 1920s. This is a period that is often regarded as a period of considerable affluence, demonstrated in some of the nicknames that the period has been given such as the 'Jazz Age', the 'Boom Years' or the 'Roaring Twenties'. While these nicknames carry a large element of truth, there was a flipside to this outward 'glitz and glamour'. This unit also explores the reasons why not all the American people shared in this affluence. An economic upturn and associated prosperity doesn't come from nowhere, and this unit also focuses on the extent to which the policies of the Republican Party contributed to this prosperity.

In this unit you will:

- find out about the key features of the prosperity and the reasons for it
- discover the impact of government policies on the economy
- determine the extent of the prosperity across the USA.

Key questions

- Why was the USA experiencing a boom in the 1920s?
- How far did government policies create and perpetuate the boom?
- Did all Americans share in the effects of that boom?

Timeline

1919	Troops return
1920	First Radio Station begins broadcasting in Pittsburg
1921	Warren Harding takes over as President and Andrew Mellon becomes Treasury Secretary
1922	Fordney–McCumber Tariff
1923	Harding dies – replaced by his Vice President
1924	Peak year for manufacture of Ford's Model T
1926	NBC established as a nationwide broadcaster
1927	First Talkie
1928	23 million cars on the roads in the USA
1929	Herbert Hoover takes over as President

Source A

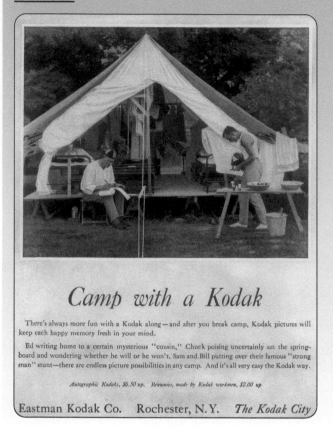

Camp with a Kodak

There's always more fun with a Kodak along—and after you break camp, Kodak pictures will keep each happy memory fresh in your mind.

Ed writing home to a certain mysterious "cousin," Chuck poising uncertainly on the spring-board and wondering whether he will or he won't, Sam and Bill putting over their famous "strong man" stunt—there are endless picture possibilities in any camp. And it's all very easy the Kodak way.

Autographic Kodaks, $6.50 up. Brownies, made by Kodak workmen, $2.00 up

Eastman Kodak Co.   Rochester, N.Y.   *The Kodak City*

3.1 This poster was part of a Kodak company advertising campaign in 1922 and epitomises the popular view of American prosperity in the 1920s.

Boom Years

There was a genuine mood of optimism in the period that followed the end of the First World War – a belief that life could only get better. At the heart of these changes lay the process of urbanisation.

Urban development

The USA was changing rapidly in terms of where people lived. The 1920 Census revealed that, for the first time in its history, more people were living in the USA's urban areas than in the country. But this valid piece of information reveals why it is necessary always to be careful when using statistics from a census. The census designated anyone living in a place with a population of more than 2,500 as living in an urban area. In fact one-third of those who were deemed to be living in urban areas lived in towns that had a population of less than 25,000. Despite this caveat, the large cities were growing rapidly. This same census shows that 15 per cent of the population were living in cities of more than half a million people. Chicago had topped two million and New York over five million people. Urban growth had been extraordinarily rapid. In 1833 Chicago, or Fort Dearborn as it was then known, had a population of just 350. Urban growth had been a marked feature already in the late 19th century. Kansas City in Missouri had reached over 200,000 by 1900 and San Francisco, the 'sin city' of the West Coast had reached 250,000 in the 1880s.

New features, however, marked the process of urbanisation in the 20th century and in particular the 1920s. The drive to build ever taller skyscrapers was the most visible of these features, especially in New York, the largest city in the country. The 1920s saw an ongoing competition to build ever higher, reaching its zenith at the very end of the decade and start of the following one with the completion of 40 Wall Street (today's Trump Building) at 282 metres, the Chrysler Building at 319 metres and the Empire State Building at 382 metres. City centres themselves were increasingly home to large numbers of black Americans migrating north from the southern states. The black population of New York City rose from 91,709 in 1910 to 327,706 in 1930. Many of these new citizens of New York were concentrated in the district of Harlem. In the 1920s, just over 118,000 whites left Harlem and just over 87,000 blacks arrived. The growth of a black urban population was thus linked to the third notable feature, the white population moving into suburbia.

There was a marked spread of suburbia, partly fuelled by the automobile revolution. Queens in New York City, for example, doubled in population and Elmwood Park in Chicago multiplied by a factor of seven. In the suburbs the quality of amenities that were offered markedly improved. Between 1920 and 1930, the percentage of families with inside flush toilets rose from 20 per cent to 51 per cent, those with central heating rose from 1 per cent to 42 per cent and electric lighting access rose from 35 per cent to 68 per cent. For those Americans who benefited from the boom, the development of consumer production in the 1920s meant that their standard of living saw a visible improvement. The lives that many Americans began to lead in the 1920s were to set the standard for many aspects of modern living the world over.

Urbanisation was also to have a dramatic impact on attitudes and one of the major themes in politics in the 1920s is the tension between rural and small-town America on the one hand and the big cities on the other. Lifestyles and value systems came into conflict with a largely white protestant rural America confronting an urban world dominated by recent immigrants and black industrial workers.

Growth in the production of consumer goods

The concentration of population in urban areas was one of the reasons why it became possible for more people to access the electrical consumer goods that came to characterise the vision of prosperity that is linked to this period. By 1930, 85 per cent of homes in the cities had access to electricity. The development of consumer goods was also aided by technological advances that saw the creation of new materials. Bakelite was effectively the first synthetic plastic and was patented in the United States in 1909. Its chemical properties meant that it could be used for containing many electrical products.

A range of domestic goods became available, which included vacuum cleaners – owned by 30 per cent of families in 1930, electric washing

Discussion Point

In what ways do you think urbanisation affected people's lifestyles and value systems?

machines – owned by 24 per cent of families in 1930, and electric refrigerators – owned by 8 per cent of families in 1930. There were many other items available too – toasters, waffle makers, hairdryers, to name but a few.

An American magazine of the 1920s, *Better Homes and Gardens*, paints a rosy picture of these developments:

Source B

It seems that the electrical industry has the entire family impartially in mind, for it provides comforts and conveniences for each and every member. From the baby up to the grandmother, there is the just-right electrical Christmas gift. Frequently the uses overlap, and Baby must share the immersion heater given him in order that he might have warm milk on demand, with Dad, who needs hot water for shaving early in the morning. But such 'loanership' is not all one-sided, by any means, because Mother's percolator will serve nicely as a bottle warmer in case Baby must pass his around among the other members of the family.

From an American magazine *Better Homes and Gardens*, published 1928

It is important to remember that most of rural America did not have electricity at this time. Indeed, it was not until the 1950s that most parts of the United States had their own electricity supply. The costs of supplying rural communities meant that it would take too long for the power companies to make a profit. In the few rural communities that did receive electricity, the prices that they were charged were generally at least twice as much as those charged in urban areas. There was a massive contrast in the lifestyles of the growing urban USA with its hustle and bustle, its consumerism and gadgetry and the old agricultural USA with its wood burning stoves, oil lamps and water from the well.

Source C

Look around your cabin, look at the dirt floor and the windows without glass! Then ask your folks already up north about the bathrooms with hot and cold water, the steam heat and the glistening hardwood floors. What chance has the average black to get these things down home? And if he does get them, how can he be sure that some poor white will not get his gang together and drive him out? Step on a train and ride for a night and a day to freedom. Your nickel is worth as much as the other fellow's nickel in the northern streetcars and you sit wherever you can find a seat.

From a black American newspaper in 1921, quoted in J.C. Furnas *Great Times: an Informal History of the United States 1914–29*, published in 1974

Discussion Point

How are the differences in lifestyle, described in sources B and C, best explained?

What potential for tension in American society can you detect here?

Stimulants to consumption

It was not merely that the supply of consumer goods increased because of greater efficiency in the methods used to produce them; it was also because of developments on the demand side that output increased. In order to encourage the consumer to buy the many new products that were available, developments began to take place in the ways in which they were advertised. Products began to display their brand name prominently on the advertisements they produced. They were displayed in a range of places. Large billboards were placed at the side of roads to catch the motorists' attention. Magazines, such as the *Good Housekeeping Magazine,* and especially those bought by women, presented an image of American life that all could aspire to. Advertising was also promoted on the new radio stations as they increased their audiences. Producers would link their products to particular programmes – thus, the first national advertising campaign on radio in 1928 for Pepsodent toothpaste was linked to the *Amos 'n' Andy* show. To make the advertising as effective as possible, the leading product producers employed psychologists to decide on the most appealing approach. By 1929, American companies were spending $3 billion every year on advertising their products – a five-fold increase on the amount that they had spent at the start of the decade.

Alongside new methods of advertising there were also new methods of distribution. The Sears Roebuck mail order catalogue had begun life in 1893 as a means of providing a range of goods, especially to farmers who found that their relative isolation made it hard to buy all the commodities that they might want. This gave them the opportunity of choosing things in the comfort of their own homes. Building on the success of the catalogue, the company opened its first retail department store in Chicago in 1925. During the 1920s, as part of the drive to greater efficiency, there was a sharp increase in the numbers of such stores. In New York City, Macy's expanded during the 1920s and introduced its Thanksgiving Day parade in 1924, demonstrating the creativity of American retailers in advertising their services.

One of the most important stimulants to demand was the use of **consumer credit**, which began in the motor industry. The motor manufacturers set up finance companies to help dealers buy their cars when demand was slow. From here, it was only a short step to make such loans directly available to the customer. In order to buy a car outright with cash, it would take a typical American family five years to save sufficient funds for the purchase. Using credit, the customer could literally buy now and pay later. By putting down an initial payment, and then making regular payments by instalment, the item could be purchased. From the finance company's perspective, if the customer defaulted on the loan, there was a commodity that could be repossessed. Such schemes had been available previously, but there had been something not quite reputable about buying in this way. That perception changed permanently in the 1920s and it became an acceptable method for buying expensive commodities. This is clearly evidenced by the fact that by the end of the decade 60 per cent of all furniture and 75 per cent of all radios were bought on hire purchase schemes.

Definition

Consumer credit

Consumer credit was a vital innovation in stimulating demand for products. Customers were provided with credit, in reality a loan by a credit company, which enabled them to have the article they desired immediately in return for a deposit and then a series of weekly or monthly payments, which of course included interest on the loan. In Great Britain it came to be known as the 'never-never' as final repayment seemed to take forever. The system worked well to everyone's advantage, as long as the purchaser retained his or her job and did not buy more than they could afford to repay.

SKILLS BUILDER

What were the social advantages and disadvantages of the three methods of stimulating sales?

Development of entertainment

New areas of entertainment were a key component in the prosperity of the 1920s, in terms of providing jobs, stimulating the stock market and the investment boom, and in promoting a feel-good factor. The 1920s – the 'Roaring Twenties' – were characterised by an increase in the range of leisure time pursuits that were available to all who could afford them. Most of these pursuits were dependent on technological advances, such as radios and the cinema, while others employed some of the new mass production techniques to create more effective methods of distribution, such as magazines. There was also a range of 'fads' that were encouraged by the use of the new methods of communication – this encompassed a range of activities from the sedentary crossword puzzles to the more energetic Black Bottom Dance, named after a district in Detroit.

The first radio station to receive a license to broadcast was KDKA in Pittsburgh. It began in 1920 and in that year broadcast the results of Harding's Presidential victory. The potential of this new medium was quickly realised and by the end of 1922 there were 556 radio stations broadcasting across the USA to three million radio sets. The growth continued through the decade, aided by improved quality of transmission and reception. The main element of programming was designed to entertain the listener – comedy sketches, drama and sports reporting were staples of the new phenomenon. After 1922 when WEAF, a New York station, was commercially sponsored, advertising became the norm on American radio. Using the business model of mergers, a process of enlargement began with larger companies taking over smaller radio stations and creating a national network. NBC (the National Broadcasting Company) was created in 1926 and CBS (the Columbia Broadcasting System) in 1927. As one recent US textbook put it; *'From Maine to California, Americans laughed at the same jokes, hummed the same tunes, and absorbed the same commercials at the same instant'*. The rapid growth of broadcasting companies was reflected in the rising value of their stocks and shares. RCA, Radio Corporation America, was the wonder stock of the decade. The company had been founded in 1919, and after steady growth the share price took off into the stratosphere, rising by 929 per cent between 1925 and 1929. Here was profit indeed for the shareholders.

SKILLS BUILDER

Was the growth of the radio industry a result of prosperity or a driver of prosperity? Consider the following factors when answering this question:

- radio production
- company and share growth
- radio ownership
- share ownership.

The birth of the modern cinema could be argued to have begun with D.W. Griffith's film *The Birth of a Nation* in 1915. Despite the controversy over its subject matter, which seemed to glorify the **Ku Klux Klan** (see Unit 4 on pages 61–64), this film is generally regarded as making the future of feature length films a viable undertaking. At roughly the same time, Cecil B. De Mille, writer and director in the new medium, rented a barn in a hitherto obscure place in California called Hollywood for $75 a month. He wrote to his backers, Jesse Lasky and Sam Goldwyn, hoping they would agree to the deal. Cinema tended to be dominated by Jewish immigrants from Eastern Europe: Goldwyn from Poland, Louis B. Mayer from Lithuania, William Fox from Hungary and the three Warner Brothers from Poland. They brought energy and imagination to the newly emerging technology – and in the process created the dominant art form of the 20th century.

By 1920, the number of cinemas stood at about 20,000 and the number kept rising until virtually every town in the USA had its own 'picture palace'. The largest was the Roxy Theatre in New York City, which opened in 1927 with a capacity of 6,200. By the end of the decade, the film studios were organised on the basis of the 'Big Five' of Metro-Goldwyn-Meyer, Paramount Pictures, Fox Film Corporation, Warner Brothers, and RKO Pictures. Between them, these five companies owned 90 per cent of the US film industry.

In the early part of the decade, the type of films being produced were silent movies. During this time a number of film stars emerged with a large fan base. Famous names included Charlie Chaplin (a comic star), Douglas Fairbanks (historical adventure hero), Rudolph Valentino (a romantic lead) and Mary Pickford ('America's sweetheart'). The first 'talkie' – film with accompanying sound – was aired in 1927. Starring Al Jolson, it was called *The Jazz Singer* and marked the end of the silent movie era.

Cinema-going is essentially a luxury pastime. It needs the disposable income that comes with prosperity to thrive – and thrive it did. The 1920s and the 1930s were the heyday of the American cinema with about 800 to 1,000 films being made each year, compared to about 500 a year today. By 1930, about one hundred million cinema tickets were being sold every week. In other words, statistically, just about every person in the USA was going to the cinema once a week. In reality, what this probably meant was that many people went to more than one film each week. Like the new radio, the cinema helped shape a common identity throughout the United States, breaking down the divisions between isolated communities and disparate regions. It helped to meld together the millions of immigrants into United States citizens, sharing a common set of values and sense of humour.

Definition

Ku Klux Klan
Originally a terrorist secret society organised in the South after the Civil War that used violence and murder to promote its white supremacist beliefs. It was re-founded in 1915 in the US State of Georgia with the same white supremacist beliefs and same techniques of terror and violence.

SKILLS BUILDER

What factors led to the development of cinema in the USA in these years?

What was the impact of cinema and radio on American society?

Definitions

Mass production

This involves the use of standardised parts on an assembly production line. By using standardised parts that can be machine manufactured, economies of scale can be achieved and by moving materials continuously through the production process it is possible to speed up that process. Both these elements have the effect of making the process faster and also cheaper as unskilled and semi-skilled workers can be used rather than craftsmen.

What were the reasons for the prosperity of the 1920s?

There were a number of reasons why the United States was so prosperous during the 1920s. By studying some of the key features of the prosperity, some of the reasons for that prosperity will emerge. In both Unit 1 and this unit, there has been extensive reference to technological change. The skills of US engineers drove the economy forward. As noted in Unit 1, (see pages 4–5) **mass production** and **scientific management** took hold during the early years of the 20th century and were well embedded by 1917. An important consequence of this greater efficiency in production was that the 1920s experienced almost a doubling of the USA's industrial output, although the size of the industrial workforce barely increased at all. The First World War contributed to this, as the following extract makes clear:

Source D

The consumer durables revolution produced a strong demand for industrial labour and, as a result, improvements in hours and wages. During World War I, many manufacturing industries accepted the 48 hour workweek, [and by the end of the 1920s this was standard for most occupations]. Another gain was the relative absence of cyclical unemployment. Unemployment averaged only 3.3% between 1923 and 1929. In short, the threat of unemployment was usually low. Real annual earnings of non-farm employees rose between 1919 and 1929 by about 23%.

From G. Walton and H. Rockoff *A History of the American Economy*, published 2005

Rising wages in the industrial sector could increase demand for goods and services and advertising and credit facilities could sharpen this demand.

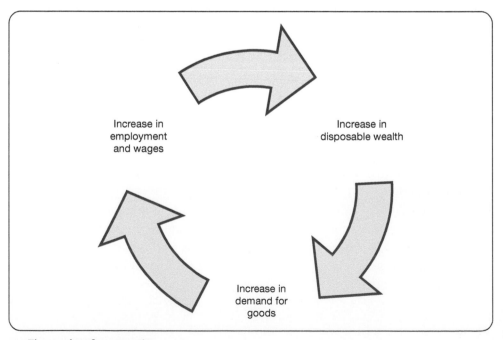

3.1 The cycle of prosperity.

Increase in employment and wages

Increase in disposable wealth

Increase in demand for goods

This diagram illustrates the basis of the American boom. It appeared that any increase in prosperity would lead to further prosperity. Americans believed that the good times stretched out towards infinity!

Definition

Scientific management
The brainchild of Frederick W. Taylor and deriving its name from his 1911 book *The Principles of Scientific Management*. Taylor established a set of principles that would improve the efficiency of industry. The key to his method was careful observation of all components of a task. Based on these observations, standards could be established which laid down the way in which the task should be performed and the amount of time it should take. By following these principles productivity would be increased. Workers who carried out their tasks in good time would be rewarded with bonus payments; so the application of scientific management had the tendency to raise real wages for the workers involved, even though the pace of change in the nature of the work was sometimes very rapid.

Henry Ford: a case study in 1920s industrial prosperity

Reference has already been made to the industrialist Henry Ford. He came almost to embody the prosperity of the 1920s. He had been born in 1863 in Dearborn, Michigan. He moved to Detroit in 1891 to become an engineer with the Edison Illuminating Company and was rapidly promoted to Chief Engineer in 1893. He experimented with building a vehicle that would be powered by the internal combustion engine and in 1896 he achieved this with his Quadricycle.

Henry Ford however is not really significant as an inventor – others in this field were more important. Nor was he the first person to manufacture mass-produced cars – the credit for that goes to Ransom Olds, who set up the Oldsmobile factory, which began mass production in 1901. Yet Ford's name became synonymous with the development of cheap and affordable cars. So, how did this come about?

In 1903, Ford opened a factory in Detroit. This was quite a small enterprise employing 125 workers and it did not use full mass-production methods, turning out fewer than 2,000 cars a year. The method used to make the cars was that two or three men would assemble one car in its entirety, moving around the factory to bring to the place of assembly the parts that they needed. After his financial backer pulled out of the business, Ford bought sufficient shares to have the majority control of the company. He then made what was to be the first of a number of crucial decisions – he reduced the production of expensive cars and started to develop a cheaper model; this was to be the Model T, popularly known as the 'Tin Lizzie', which first went on sale in 1908. In the first year of production over 10,000 were sold; all were still being produced using the same methods as before.

The business was being overwhelmed by the demand for its product. This led Ford to make a second momentous decision; in 1910 he transferred the production of the Model T to a new plant.

Source E

Henry Ford combined precision manufacturing, standardised and interchangeable parts, a division of labour, and, in 1913, a continuous moving assembly line. Workers remained in place, adding one component to each automobile as it moved past them on the line. Delivery of parts by conveyor belt to the workers was carefully timed to keep the assembly line moving smoothly and efficiently. The introduction of the moving assembly line revolutionized automobile production by significantly reducing assembly time per vehicle, thus lowering costs.

The Henry Ford Museum describes the process that was implemented in the new factory.

Discussion point

How justified do you feel Americans were in believing that the good times would last for ever?

Where it had taken 14 hours to produce a car in the old factory it was now taking about one and a half hours to produce each car. Prices dropped dramatically as a consequence, (see Unit 1 page 5) from $850 in 1908 to $360 by 1916. By 1925, Ford was producing more than 9,000 cars a day and the price had dropped still further – to less than $300. Part of the reason for the drop in price was that Ford was prepared to forego some of his profits per car in order to increase demand; this is a third example of his ability to make momentous decisions. He understood that increasing demand would ultimately lead to higher bottom line profits.

Ford and his workforce

These dramatic changes in the production methods had implications for the workforce that Ford employed. The tasks that they were engaged in were repetitive and not very well paid. This led to a high turnover of workers and increased the costs of production as so much had to be spent on training new employees to do the work. This led to a fourth momentous decision; Ford decided to dramatically change the conditions of employment in his factory. On 5 January 1914, Ford more than doubled the wages of his workforce, increasing them to $5 per eight-hour day. He also introduced a profit-sharing scheme. The impact of this was immediate: labour turnover was removed at a stroke and workers who were trained were now retained. This reduced Ford's costs of production as he no longer had to spend so much money on training new employees. Those workers who were employed were happy with their conditions of work and their productivity rose as a result of this. As a consequence of these high wages, Ford was able to prevent his factory from becoming unionised. He feared that the unions might challenge his managerial authority and could see no reason for his workforce to need unions in view of the high wages they received.

Between the introduction of the $5 day in 1914 and 1916, the profits of the Detroit factory doubled from $30 million to $60 million. By 1921, Ford was producing 60 per cent of all new cars being sold in the United States, with the peak year of production of the Model T being 1924 when 1.6 million cars were made. His influence was so profound that when he shut the factory down and laid off the workers in 1927 to change production from the Model T to the Model A, it was one of the factors contributing to a mild business recession at that time. His new factory, which opened in River Rouge in 1927, was a monument to Ford's desire to create the ultimate in mass production. He planned to own all the raw materials that were required to produce motor cars and the transport systems that were needed to convey them to the site. When they got there, the raw materials would be processed onsite before entering the production line. At its height in the 1930s, over 100,000 workers were employed at this 2,000 acre site.

There are different ways of perceiving Henry Ford's attitude to his work force. To some he was a considerate, **paternalistic** employer, but to others he was an unreasonable employer who adopted an authoritarian and even

Definition

Paternalistic

Meaning 'father-like'. When used for employers it implies that while looking after the material concerns of their employees, there is generally an expectation that in return the employees will give them due respect.

dictatorial approach to the men who worked for him. Ford put his own case in his autobiography published in 1922:

Source F

We expect the men to do what they are told. The organisation is so highly specialised and one part is so dependent upon another that we could not for a moment consider allowing men to have their own way. Without the most rigid discipline we would have the utmost confusion. I think it should not be otherwise in industry. The men are there to get the greatest possible amount of work done and to receive the highest possible pay. If each man were permitted to act in his own way, production would suffer and therefore pay would suffer. Any one who does not like to work in our way may always leave. The company's conduct toward the men is meant to be exact and impartial.

From Henry Ford *My Life and Work*, published in 1922

A recent writer on Ford takes a different view:

Source G

Henry Ford had lost his halo by the end of the thirties. Hate had come to fill his life. Ford factories remained spotlessly clean, their safety record was superb and company nutritionists still made sure that Ford box lunches contained at least 800 calories. But wages had dropped and fear had replaced the spirit of adventure. The man who once cared for every aspect of his empire abandoned its labour relations to Harry Bennett, a short, red-headed thug who ran a 'Service Department' of spies and goons. He fixed things for Ford, paying off servant girls he slept with and beating up 'troublemakers'. Violence was the answer to any form of grievance. In 1932 they crushed a Communist demonstration in a fracas at Dearborn's River Rouge Plant in which four were shot dead.

From H. Evans *The American Century*, published in 1998

Discussion Point

How far do you agree that the authoritarian approach of Ford's management style was justified by the high wages and good conditions offered to his workers?

What was the impact of the motor car on the United States?

The development of relatively cheap mass produced cars had two distinct types of effect – economic and social.

Economic effects

- The economic effects of the motor car industry were considerable. In 1918, there were 8 million cars on the roads of the USA. In 1920 around 9 million cars were registered. By 1929 it was nearly 27 million.

- The industry stimulated the economic development of a range of other industries. Cars needed:

  - steel – 15% of steel output went into cars
  - rubber – 80% of production went to the car industry
  - and 75% of plate glass went to cars.

In addition the paint, oil and electrical equipment industries were all stimulated.

- It also stimulated the servicing industries that supported it, such as sales and fuel stations.

- The increased mobility meant that more roads needed to be built. The total amount of roads across the nation rose from 387,000 miles in 1921 to 662,000 miles by 1929.

- On these routes were to be found restaurants and hotels (soon to be renamed motels – motor hotels) to meet the demands of drivers.

- By 1929 about 10% of the workforce were involved in either car manufacture or in the industries that supported car manufacturing.

- Car sales encouraged the growth of consumer credit as not everyone could afford to buy a car in cash, despite the ever lower prices.

The bottom line of all of this was that the production of motor cars created a huge number of jobs. The people in those jobs contributed to the growing consumer demand and the economic boom of the 1920s.

Not all effects were positive however. Agriculture, which was depressed as a result of over-production, suffered as a consequence of the growth of the motor industry. Fewer people used horses as a means of transport, so those farmers who bred horses and grew the fodder to feed them found the demand for their services reduced.

SKILLS BUILDER

Use the knowledge you have gained about motor cars to draw your own diagram showing their economic impact. Think about the general cycle of prosperity (Figure 3.1 on page 32) and try to build this into your diagram.

Social effects

The increase in car use created mobility on a scale not previously imagined. People were now able to travel far more easily, so the distance between urban and rural lives began to break down. It changed the way in which people spent their leisure time – more activities were opened up as people could travel more freely.

It increased the growth of suburbs as travel became so much easier.

These effects were clear, even at the time. In a study of Muncie, Indiana in 1929, Robert and Helen Lynd, two sociologists, noted such effects:

Source H

If the automobile touches the rest of Middletown's living at many points, it has revolutionised its leisure; more, perhaps, than the movies or any other intrusion new to Middletown since the (18)90s, it is making leisure-time enjoyment a regularly expected part of every day and week rather than an occasional event. The readily available leisure-time options of even the working class have been multiplied many-fold. As one working class housewife remarked, 'We just go to lots of things we couldn't go to if we didn't have a car'.

From Robert and Helen Lynd *Middletown: a Study in Contemporary American Culture*, published in 1929

Henry Ford was not only a commercial and engineering genius but also a master of self-publicity. He has become identified as the embodiment of the 1920s boom, and the best known example of capitalist mega-success. He did in reality embody much that was typical of 1920s America. He was the protestant farm boy made good through hard work and flare. He was bitterly opposed to alcohol and tobacco and devoted to the gospel of hard work. Yet there were many others who deserve to be remembered, and can stand as symbols of innovation and success in the 1920s.

- By 1929 Ford motor production output had been overtaken by General Motors under Alfred P. Sloan, who was president of the company from 1923. In a sense the less personalised General Motors Corporation represented the future much more than Ford did, dominated as it was by its founder.

- Clarence Birdseye was transforming food availability with new techniques of quick refrigeration.

- In the new movie industry, mention has already been made of Sam Goldwyn.

- Adolphe Zukor built up the Paramount Pictures empire, eventually controlling one tenth of all US cinemas.

- Every bit as important as Ford in the 1920s was the man known as the 'King of the Killowatts', Samuel Insull, who came to control vast swathes of electricity production in the USA. His complex system of holding companies controlled electricity production in 200 companies spread throughout 32 states. These were estimated to be worth $3 billion in the late 1920s. Perhaps more than Henry Ford, he deserves to stand as the representative of boom-time America.

These titans of business, as they were called, were much assisted by sympathetic politicians.

Republicans in power 1921–29

Four men were particularly influential in shaping economic, business and industrial events in this period: Warren Harding, President from 1921–23,

Calvin Coolidge, President from 1923–28, Andrew Mellon as Secretary of the Treasury throughout the decade and Herbert Hoover, Secretary of Commerce and the President in succession to Coolidge.

Warren Harding was conscious of his own shortcomings and appointed a number of outstanding individuals to his Cabinet. Among these men were: Charles Evans Hughes, a former governor of New York, as Secretary of State, Andrew Mellon, a leading Pittsburgh industrialist and financier, as Secretary of the Treasury and Herbert Hoover, who had run various wartime relief schemes, as Secretary of Commerce.

Biography

Warren Harding (1865–1923)

Selected as the Republican Party's candidate as a compromise when the two leading contenders for the nomination looked as if they were likely to become deadlocked, Harding was in marked contrast to the high minded academic, Woodrow Wilson, who had governed the USA since 1913. Harding's very ordinariness appealed to the voters. As the owner of a local newspaper in a small town in Ohio, happiest playing poker with his cronies or entertaining his girlfriends, he embodied small-town America. He felt quite under-qualified and his elevation to the presidency took him, and most informed observers, by surprise. Harding won the election by a large margin, winning over 60% of the popular vote (see pages 9–11 for details on presidential elections). A further critical reason for his success may be that he promised 'a return to normalcy' something that many Americans were very keen to do in the aftermath of the First World War. It also marked a massive rejection of Democratic Wilsonian liberalism, with its commitment to government intervention at home and a continuing involvement in world affairs through participation in the League of Nations.

Biography

Calvin Coolidge (1872–1933)

Similarly to Harding, Coolidge also came from a farming/small town background this time in Vermont. He progressed to study Law at Amherst College and was called to the bar. From here he progressed to a career in politics, holding a range of different positions starting as City Councillor in Northampton, Massachusetts 1899 and progressing through the Massachusetts State House of Representatives and then Senate to become Lieutenant Governor in 1916 and finally Governor in 1919. He was therefore a very experienced politician and was able to draw on this when he took over the Presidency. He was a taciturn man whose nickname was 'Silent Cal'. There were many tales and jokes told to illustrate this. In one, for example, a young woman who was sat next to him at a dinner party told him that she had bet a friend that she could make him say more than two words. 'You lose,' Coolidge replied. Despite this, he was aware of the need to communicate and held a record number of press conferences during his time in office.

Biography

Andrew Mellon (1855–1937)

A Pittsburgh banker of enormous wealth and served as Secretary of the Treasury from 1921 to 1932. He believed that a policy of tax cuts and lower government spending would encourage private effort and initiative. He gave his great art collection to the nation on his death in 1937 together with funds to establish the National Gallery of Art.

However, he also appointed some of his own friends and cronies who were less well-considered appointments. This included Harry Daugherty as Attorney-General, Albert Fall as Secretary of the Interior and Charles Fall as Director of the Veterans Association. By the time of Harding's death in August 1923, there were a number of enquiries into the activities of these men who were collectively known as the 'Ohio Gang', due to Harding's old position as Senator for Ohio. In the period 1923 to 1924 the following charges were brought against these associates of the President.

- Harry Daugherty: accused of being involved in taking bribes from **bootleggers**.

- Albert Fall: jailed for a year as a result of his involvement in the Teapot Dome Scandal. This related to his decision to lease naval oil reserves in two areas, Teapot Dome in Wyoming and Elk Hills in California, to two oil men Harry Sinclair and Edward Doheny. This arrangement was not put up for public bidding to achieve the best price. Furthermore, it was discovered that Fall had received 'loans' from both men in exchange for leasing them the reserves.

- Charles Forbes: jailed for two years for defrauding the government. During the three years that he worked at the Veterans' Bureau, it is estimated that he embezzled about $250 million.

These three men were only the tip of the iceberg. Other members of the administration were convicted of various charges relating to corruption and several committed suicide before they could be brought to trial. There is some debate as to the extent of Harding's knowledge of these events. It seems likely that he was not directly involved, although he must have been aware of the existence of corruption, as enquiries were beginning before his death from a heart attack in San Francisco on 2 August 1923.

Coolidge as President

Coolidge was Harding's Vice President and so on Harding's death he replaced him as President. In a rather charming tale, he was on a visit to his family home in Vermont and took the Presidential oath of office from his father, who was a local magistrate. As it was night and there was no electricity in his home, he had to take the oath by the flickering light of a kerosene lamp.

In view of the problems at the end of Harding's life, Coolidge had a major task in restoring the dignity of and respect for the Presidency. It was a task he carried out with silent efficiency. Initially, Coolidge kept all of Harding's Cabinet as he felt he had to respect Harding's choices, as it was he who the people had elected. However, he ran for office in his own right in 1924 and was elected with 54 per cent of the popular vote. This is an impressive result in view of the scandals that were associated with his predecessor. It seems to be the result of two key factors. Firstly, the country was in what appeared to be an economically sound position; indeed even by the time of the election, there were references to the 'Coolidge prosperity'. The pattern

Definition

Bootlegger
These people were responsible for the illegal production and transportation and sale of alcohol during Prohibition. Many showed great ingenuity in manufacturing 'medicinal alcohol' which exploited a loophole in the legislation. George Remus, the self-styled 'King of the Bootleggers', was reckoned to be making $5 million a year at one stage.

Table 3.1 *Index of Manufacturing Production in the USA.*

Year	Production (as a %)
1913	100.0
1920	122.2
1921	97.9
1925	148.0

of economic activity in the US reveals clearly why Coolidge won. There had been a sharp but short slump in 1921, followed by a dramatic period of economic growth (see Table 3.1).

Secondly, the Democrats were profoundly divided. At their National Convention in New York City, it took 103 ballots before they could finally decide on who their candidate to oppose Coolidge would be. However, given the prosperity and boom that marked 1924, it was unlikely that any Democratic challenger could have unseated Coolidge.

Coolidge generally supported business and only acted and legislated on what he believed to be absolutely necessary during his years in office. As the columnist Walter Lippmann wrote in 1926: *'This active inactivity suits the mood and certain of the needs of the country admirably. It suits all the business interests which want to be let alone. It suits all those who have become convinced that government in this country has become dangerously complicated and top-heavy.'* The years of the Coolidge presidency coincided with the height of the economic boom and happily for his reputation he decided not to seek a further term of office and informed the public about this decision in a suitably laconic way; he told reporters that *'I do not choose to run for President in 1928.'* The legacy that he left behind appeared to be fairly secure.

Economic policies in the 1920s

Although the characters of Harding and Coolidge were very different their actual policies were very similar, as the following extracts from the inaugural addresses made by both Harding and Coolidge indicate.

Source I

We can reduce the abnormal expenditures, and we will. We can strike at war taxation, and we must. We must face the grim necessity, with full knowledge that the task is to be solved, and we must proceed with a full realisation that no statute enacted by man can repeal the inexorable laws of nature. Our most dangerous tendency is to expect too much of government, and at the same time do for it too little ...

... All the penalties will not be light, nor evenly distributed. There is no way of making them so. There is no instant step from disorder to order ... No altered system will work a miracle. Any wild experiment will only add to the confusion. Our best assurance lies in efficient administration of our proven system.

Extracts from Warren Harding's Inaugural Address, March 1921

Source J

The policy that stands out with the greatest clearness is that of economy in public expenditure with reduction and reform of taxation. The principle involved in this effort is that of conservation ...

... I favour the policy of economy, not because I wish to save money, but because I wish to save people. The men and women of this country who toil are the ones who bear the cost of the Government. Every dollar that we carelessly waste means that their life will be so much the more meagre. Every dollar that we prudently save means that their life will be so much the more abundant. Economy is idealism in its most practical form.

Extracts from Calvin Coolidge's Inaugural Address, March 1925

Fundamentally both men agreed on the key issues that needed to be addressed in the United States.

Business interests

Business interests were of paramount importance within the Republican Party. Indeed, one of Coolidge's most famous statements was that 'the business of America is business'. To support business, both Presidents favoured limiting government activity in terms of taxation and foreign policy. They espoused a rejection of the League of Nations and a return to isolationism. It was felt by many Americans that the costs of the First World War had been too substantial, both in terms of money as well as lives, and the cost of funding this war had dramatically increased the National Debt. It therefore became a government priority to reduce this debt. Another priority of the Republicans was the reduction of federal taxes, which were seen as drag on incentives and initiatives. Money, it was believed, should be left in the pockets of the people, not taken by a wasteful government in Washington. There was also a feeling amongst many senior Republicans that Trade Union power had grown too much during the war and was now an obstacle to good business management and profitability. Their domestic policies, in other words, were underpinned by an approach that is known as 'laissez-faire'. This French phrase literally means to 'let alone'. It implies an approach to government that is minimalist; governments should intervene as little as possible and let the market determine how things progress. On the other hand, the Republicans accepted that government could assist the economy through tariffs and limiting immigration, which would protect American jobs.

The shared beliefs of the Republicans on the key issues, reflected the main concerns of much of the American public, and this explains the continuity in policy between the different Republican Presidents. This continuity is also explained by the long occupation of the post of Secretary of the Treasury by Andrew Mellon. Both Harding and Coolidge benefited from the fact that the Republicans did not merely control the Presidency but also had control of both Houses of Congress. Although this does not guarantee support in the American system, it does generally make it easier for the President to pursue the policies that he wishes to see enacted.

Taxation

The level of taxes had risen during the years 1916–18 in order to meet the burgeoning costs of the war. Now that peace had returned, Andrew Mellon, the Secretary of the Treasury, believed that taxes needed to be reduced in order to promote economic growth. He thought that if the wealthy retained more of their income they would use it to open new businesses and this would create new jobs. The wartime excess profits tax was repealed and Mellon wanted the maximum rate of income tax to be 25 per cent. It took three cuts in the rate – in 1921, 1924 and 1925 – but he achieved this aim in the last cut. Although the level of taxes dropped, the government actually increased its total income because of the prosperity of the 1920s. This seemed to show that reducing the burden of government or 'getting government off the back of the people', as many Republicans termed it, seemed to lead to prosperity. The increase in government income in the 1920s allowed the National Debt that had accrued during the First World War to be reduced.

One of Harding's key concerns was to reduce the cost of government and to make it more efficient. One policy that was introduced in the pursuit of this aim was the 1921 *Budget and Accounting Act*, which established a Bureau of the Budget. The President had to submit to Congress an estimate of federal income and expenditure annually. It made the whole process much simpler by centralising control of the budget rather than leaving the process in the hands of a number of different Congressional committees.

Tariffs

In 1913, the Democrats took control of Congress and introduced reductions in the levels of tariffs through the Underwood–Simmons Tariff. The Democrats tended to believe in the value of free trade, which Great Britain had adopted in the 19th century. Lower tariffs would mean lower prices for consumers but could leave American industries competing with cheaper foreign products. The economic effects of this went largely unnoticed as once the war started there were fewer imports. With the ending of the war, there were concerns, especially amongst Republican politicians, that higher levels of imports would threaten economic prosperity. These fears led to the passage of the *Emergency Tariff Act* in 1921 and the Fordney–McCumber Tariff a year later. The idea of **protectionism** that this embodied sat comfortably with the isolationism that withdrawing from the League of Nations involved.

The *Emergency Tariff Act* was first introduced at the very end of Wilson's administration, but Wilson was a Democrat and sympathised with free trade ideas and he vetoed its passage. However, it was reintroduced once Harding took office and this time was passed. It stated that there would be taxes on a range of imported agricultural products, such as wheat from Canada, in order to protect the prices that US farmers would receive. It was intended as a temporary measure until the Fordney–McCumber Tariff, which was under considerable debate in Congress, was implemented. The Fordney–McCumber Tariff was far broader, addressing a range of industrial products as well as food imports. Its passage through Congress was given a powerful boost by the sharp slump of 1921.

One of the key issues of controversy that held up the passage of the Fordney–McCumber Tariff was the American Valuation Plan, an aspect added to the Act by one of the many committees. This put forward the idea that the proposed tariff would be calculated on the basis of the cost of the item in the United States rather than in its country of manufacture. This

Definitions

Protectionism

This policy is one that restricts trade from abroad in order to limit competition.

Tariffs

These are duties on imported goods which raise revenue for the government, but also have the effect of making foreign goods dearer and thereby encouraging consumers to buy locally produced goods. In this sense they are often referred to as 'protective' tariffs since they protect native industries and jobs. They have the disadvantage of raising prices to consumers and could cause other countries to retaliate by putting duties on exports.

SKILLS BUILDER

What were the benefits of putting in place trade tariffs in this way?

would have tended to increase the level of the tariff. Even McCumber was against this element. Compromise was finally agreed by the creation of a Tariff Commission that would advise the President on tariff rates. The President was also given the power to vary the tariff rates by up to 50 per cent. A range of items were protected under these tariffs including foodstuffs, chemicals, rayon, china and toys.

There is a tendency to exaggerate the economic impact of the Fordney–McCumber Tariff. Although the level of duty was higher than it had been under the Underwood–Simmons Tariff of 1913 – an average rate of 38 per cent as compared to an average rate of 27 per cent, it was actually lower than the Payne Aldrich duty of 1909 (41 per cent).

In other words, there had been an increase of 11 per cent on selected products but even here this was far from the level desired by the real protectionist fanatics.

Despite this, the duty did have some potentially harmful effects. It led to counter measures being taken by other countries against American trade. Higher tariffs meant that American producers found it more difficult to sell their goods abroad. It also meant that prices rose for American consumers in a range of imported commodities. It did not increase prices for agricultural produce, which supporters of the tariff had claimed it would. As farmers sold their goods abroad, they too were damaged by the retaliatory duties imposed. Furthermore, the costs of equipment that they imported from abroad rose too. Some economic commentators have argued that on balance farmers were net losers. Clearly some industries gained from protection from foreign competition and during the 1920s the Tariff Commission, with Presidential approval, raised a series of duties to keep foreign products out. The US chemical industry probably benefited, but overall although tariffs were popular with big business they had a minimal effect in stimulating the boom.

In a sense, tariffs like the low taxation policy were symbolic of a business-friendly administration. It was what they didn't do that was probably most helpful and appreciated by the corporations. The Federal Trade Commission and the Interstate Commerce Commission, the two most important regulatory bodies, did very little. Harding and Coolidge appointed members to these bodies who had little interest in making them work. Coolidge appointed a lawyer, William E. Humphrey, as a member of the Federal Trade Commission. Humphrey, before his appointment, had described the FTC as 'an instrument of oppression and disturbance and injury instead of help to business'. With people like Humphrey running Federal agencies, businessmen could sleep undisturbed and rake in the profits. With regard to new industries like broadcasting, there was a clear acceptance of the free market. Unlike Great Britain, where a Conservative Government established a public corporation, the BBC, to control and manage all broadcasting, in the USA broadcasting was left entirely in the hands of private companies.

SKILLS BUILDER

How far would you agree that the trade tariffs introduced in the 1920s only hindered the economic growth of the USA?

Source K

3.3 'The Cash Register Chorus' by Fitzpatrick from 1924. Parodying a well-known hymn of the day, 'What a friend we have in Jesus', it shows business owners rejoicing under Coolidge's administration.

Government and trade unionism

In a similar way, the Republican government's attitude to trade unions and strikes was reassuring to big business. Trade unions had grown in power during the war, and the Wilson government had accepted the closed shop in the government-controlled railways and generally encouraged and fostered the growth of unions. This process was now reversed under the Republican presidents. The railways were handed back to their former private owners and in disputes between companies and the unions the Federal Government tended to throw its weight behind the companies. Federal troops were used to restore order in 1921 in a bitter coal mining dispute in West Virginia and in 1922 the Federal Government obtained a court injunction against pickets in a widespread railway strike involving 400,000 railway workers. The strike ended in failure for the union, and many railway companies reverted to being non-unionised.

The Supreme Court, with a conservative majority, handed down a whole series of judgements, which seemed to favour management at the expense of unions and workers. In 1921 the Supreme Court, under the newly appointed Chief Justice William Taft, overturned certain reforms that had improved conditions for workers. For example, he ruled that a federal law that had put punitive taxes on products manufactured by child labour was unconstitutional, as this was a matter for the states to determine, not Federal Government. He also ruled that a minimum wage Act that had been passed for women workers in Washington DC was unconstitutional.

Unsurprisingly, membership of trade unions fell during the 1920s. In 1920, 12 per cent of the labour force was in a trade union; by 1929 the figure had fallen to less than 8 per cent. The reasons for this were a mixture of 'carrots' such as the $5 day introduced by Henry Ford and 'sticks'. Among the 'sticks' was the use of the yellow dog contract – an agreement that the worker would not join a union as part of their conditions of employment.

An area of government intervention: agriculture

The one area where the Republican administration could not follow its instincts of adopting a non-interventionist policy was agriculture. The farmers of the North and West were traditionally Republican and they demanded action. Agriculture had done well out of the First World War. After the long fall in prices in the 1880s and 1890s as production had rocketed, the First World War witnessed a recovery, tempting farmers to produce even more by mechanising and bringing **marginal land** into production. After the war however, world prices once again began to fall as European production recovered. American farmers were competing in a

Source M

3.4 Cartoon by J. Darling, August 1921.

world market and their profit margins dropped quite dramatically. Between 1919 and 1921 the value of farm products more than halved, from $10 billion to just over $4 billion. Cotton slumped from 35 cents per pound during the war to 16 cents in 1920. Corn fell even more from wartime high of $1.50 to $0.52 per bushel. There was some recovery in prices in the early 1920s, but farming did not share in the boom and remained depressed. Debt and foreclosures by the banks on mortgaged farms became commonplace. In an attempt to deal with this problem, farmers increased production, but this proved to be a short-sighted policy as it merely increased supply and consequently drove prices down still further towards the end of the decade.

Tariffs were a policy with which most Republicans were comfortable, as they had been used since the mid-19th century to protect developing American industry from competition from their more developed British competitors. The result, as we have seen, were two tariffs, the *Emergency Tariff Act* of 1921 and the Fordney–McCumber Tariff of 1922. Both were intended to provide some help to farmers by restricting foreign competition, but they had only limited success. It was not the only legislation that was implemented during the 1920s in an attempt to help the farming community. Other measures included:

- 1921 The *Grain Futures Trading Act* was an attempt to prevent the manipulation of the grain market which it was believed was keeping grain prices artificially low.

- 1922 The *Capper-Volstead Act* enabled farmers to work together in co-operatives in order to facilitate the production and marketing of agricultural products. Although in theory, such organisations could be seen to be monopolies, they were exempted from the antitrust laws.

- 1923 The *Intermediate Credit Act* established a credit system to channel agricultural loans to farmers on easier terms than were currently available.

In 1924, a quite dramatic departure from *laissez-faire* was introduced. This was the McNary–Haugen bill, which proposed that the Federal Government should sell surplus supplies of corn and wheat abroad at the best price that could be achieved. Farmers would contribute to the costs of this through 'an equalisation fee'. The idea was that this would encourage a rise in the prices in the domestic market to a level that was equivalent to values at the start of the First World War, because supplies would be more restricted. The plan had some support from Coolidge's Secretary of Agriculture, Henry Wallace, but failed to pass Congress both in 1924 and again in 1926 when it was reintroduced. It was broadened in 1927 to include cotton and tobacco to gain the support of southern members of Congress. Despite now passing through Congress it was vetoed by Coolidge both in this year and again in 1928. It was a step too far for Coolidge and ran too counter to the ideas of *laissez-faire*, in which he believed so strongly. To set up a system like this would involve considerable government intervention, and in Coolidge's opinion, establish a complex and inefficient bureaucracy. Meanwhile farmers continued to suffer from falling incomes.

SKILLS BUILDER

How effective were the government's interventions in the economy during the 1920s?

Who were the losers in the 'boom' period and why could they not share in the general prosperity?

Conclusion: winners and losers

Overall, the 1920s were clearly a period of exceptional economic growth. Table 3.1 (on page 40) shows the growth of nearly 50 per cent in the years 1921–25. This is exceptional by any standards. In the next four years, the growth was slower but still impressive despite the slight setback in 1927 (see Table 3.2).

Clearly, the really big winners were the tycoons like Ford, Insull and Clarence Birdseye. They made their millions, or even billions, but many others gained as well. The trickle down theory of wealth creation and distribution really did work for much of the USA. Managers of all sorts prospered, as did salesmen and estate agents. The ordinary workers in Ford's plants or those of General Motors drawing their $5 a day were rich compared to their forefathers or their contemporaries in Europe. They may have been denied unionisation and had to accept mechanical obedience to foremen and managers but there were no shortage of volunteers for the generous pay on offer. In much of urban America the decade witnessed a degree of material prosperity unequalled in the history of humanity. The ownership of houses with flush toilets and labour-saving devices spread down from the middle classes into the ranks of the workers. Many still remained in crowded inner-city tenements but many were also joining the rush to the suburbs. More and more in urban environments were being linked to cheap electric power. Entertainment, either at the thousands of new cinemas, or in the privacy of the home with the radio was available to millions as never before. Perhaps most staggering of all was the increasing ownership of a car, once the plaything of the super-rich and still in Europe confined to a tiny percentage of the population. For a population of 123 million Americans in 1930, there were 27 million cars.

On the other hand much of rural America was suffering from falling agricultural prices and over-production. In many areas there was no electricity, the cost of bringing it to disparate rural communities was prohibitive. Here a grinding life of back-breaking toil for a declining return marked the decade. Worst served of all were the poor share-croppers of the South, most of whom were black. Many chose to leave and find a new life in the crowded ghettos of the North. The sad lot of these and the farming community as a whole is more fully dealt with in Unit 5 as are the other groups who did not share in the bonanza; the coal-miners of West Virginia and the textile workers of New England. Thus, it is important to remember that although the 1920s were predominantly a time of boom and prosperity, for many, the prosperity was merely a dream and in their misery lay some of the explanation of the 'bust' that was to come.

Table 3.2 *Index of Manufacturing Production in the USA.*

Year	Production (as a %)
1925	100
1926	106
1927	105
1928	110
1929	123

Unit summary

What have you learned in this unit?

The United States was experiencing a period of rapid industrial growth that was based on implementing new methods of production. Various new areas of technology came into play and perhaps the most important were those relating to motor transport although it is important to remember equally important developments associated with the application of electrical power. The Republican Presidents of this period pursued a policy of *laissez-faire* or minimal intervention. This was a sensible policy in the context of a booming American economy in the 1920s.

What skills have you used in this unit?

You will have come to grips with a number of new ideas and concepts relating to economics. It is important to grasp basic ideas such as the role of supply and demand in stimulating the boom and also how government policy might have impacted. It is vital to realise that at times there are no clear cut answers available to historians.

Exam style question

This is the sort of question you will find appearing on the examination paper as a Section A question.

How far does the application of new technologies explain the economic boom of the 1920s?

Exam tips

See the section at the end of Unit 2 for general tips relating to structure and approach, then consider the following:

There were a range of key factors that led to the prosperity in many areas of the USA of the 1920s. These factors included:

- the stated factor of new technologies – electrical/mechanical/chemical, etc.
- the economic impact of the First World War (refer to Unit 2 to remind yourself)
- the support of the Federal Government for big business
- changes in working practices, especially the development of mass production which led to an increase in worker productivity. The growth of interest in the strategies of scientific management such as 'Taylorism'
- changing attitudes towards consumption with the increased respectability of buying on credit and the development of advertising.

RESEARCH TOPIC

Read *The Great Gatsby*, a novel by the American author, F. Scott Fitzgerald.

How far does it accurately reflect American society of the time?

4 Political and social tensions, 1919–29

What is this unit about?

This unit explores the tensions and dominant political issues in American society during the 1920s. Much of the tension was around the fault line separating city and small town attitudes. Traditional, protestant, Anglo-Saxon America felt itself facing a number of perceived threats associated with alcohol, different ethnic groups and immigration, the possibility of a 'Red' revolution and the growing challenge to traditional religious beliefs.

In this unit you will:

- Examine the impact of differing religious and cultural beliefs on US society.
- Analyse the growing concern over immigration and race.

Key questions

- What impact did Prohibition have?
- Why did the Ku Klux Klan enjoy a revival and with what impact?
- Why did immigration become such a contentious issue?
- Why was there a Red Scare?

Timeline

1919	Red Scare
1920	Prohibition comes into force under the 18th Amendment
1921	*Emergency Quota Act* cuts back on immigration
1923	Calvin Coolidge restores respectability to Presidency
1924	*Quota Act* severely restricts immigration
1925	KKK membership reaches peak
	'Monkey Trial' in Tennessee
1927	Sacco and Vanzetti executed
1928	Al Smith, the Democratic Presidential candidate, campaigns against Prohibition
1929	St Valentine's Day Massacre in Chicago

Discussion point

What can be learned from Warren Harding's speech about attitudes in the USA at the end of the First World War?

Source A

My agenda is to safeguard America first. To exalt America first ... Let the Internationalists dream and the Bolsheviks destroy ... We proclaim Americanism and acclaim America.

Part of a campaigning speech in 1920 made by Warren Harding.

What tensions could be seen in American society after the First World War?

The First World War marked the USA's entry on world stage, transforming it into the world's most powerful country. Yet the war itself triggered a rabid nationalism and a real struggle as to what the national identity really was. Old-time rural America, largely white and protestant and connected with farming found itself at loggerheads in many different ways with a vibrant new urban and industrial USA, which added to existing tensions within US society. The growing cities teemed with immigrants whether Catholic Irish, Italians, Polish, or Jewish from Austria-Hungary and Russia, as well as blacks escaping from poverty in the South in increasing numbers. A clash in value systems was inevitable.

One of the most colourful and illuminating events of the decade took place in Dayton, Tennessee in 1925, the so-called 'Monkey Trial'. It embodied the clash between the big cities and old-fashioned settler America with its religious certainties and belief in that 'old-time religion'. It concerned the right to teach Darwinian natural selection in Biology lessons as opposed to creationism and the literal truth of the bible. At the centre was a young science teacher, John Scopes prosecuted for teaching Darwin's theory of evolution. A new state law made this a criminal offence with a fine of $500. The trial attracted two of the biggest names in US popular politics. William Jennings Bryan appearing for God and old-time religion and the atheist lawyer Clarence Darrow from Chicago, defended Scopes. Darrow, famously called Bryan to take the stand as an expert witness on the Bible, humiliating him by exposing his ignorance and old-fashioned credulity. Bryan asserted that Jonah had really been swallowed by a large fish and Joshua had made the sun stand still – 'fool ideas that no intelligent Christian on earth believes' according to Darrow. However, there was never any doubt that Scopes had taught evolution and he was fined $100, but the Tennessee Supreme Court quashed the fine on a technicality while still upholding the state law. The drama has attracted writers and filmmakers ever since. It remains one of the most interesting of the eruptions on the fault-lines separating the two Americas. However, perhaps the most famous of all the conflicts between the two related to alcohol.

The drive to Prohibition

Alcohol had long been a contentious moral issue in the United States dating back far into the 19th century. The saloon and its hard liquor had been seen as anti-chambers of hell by the protestant churches and chapels of the South and West. Within the new towns of the expanding settled areas, conflict tended to develop between the rival institutions of church and saloon. Many American citizens saw the saloons with their **80% proof strength spirits** as badges of shame, reminders of a primitive violent past to be eradicated as civilisation tamed the frontier. Powerful **anti-alcohol lobby groups** developed in many states to close saloons and limit the traffic in liquor. Protestant clergymen and women tended to be typical activists in the cause. They argued that liquor produced misery in the home through both drunken violence and poverty. A man's wages, it was said, would be better spent on his family than selfish and self-destructive inebriation. The cause made headway in many states and Kansas in the mid-west became dry in 1880. Often this was more in theory than in practice as most visitors to Kansas found it possible to get a drink if they wanted one.

Drink also became associated with the waves of poorer immigrants who flooded into the USA from the middle years of the 19th century, particularly the Irish. Respectable Protestants of English and Scots extraction saw booze as a root cause of feckless behaviour in their new compatriots Many of the new businessmen saw drink as the enemy of business efficiency. Henry Ford was a stern opponent as was Frederick Taylor (see chapter 1). Industrial efficiency and discipline, essential elements in the production line, required sobriety in the workforce. By the time war was declared in 1917, 18 states had adopted prohibition and 33 had done so by 1920 when the *Volstead Act* made the ban nation-wide (see chapter 2). The war fervour and anti-German sentiment made the national campaign unstoppable. The fact that many brewers were German in origin was a gift to the prohibitionists. In addition, the fact that both Houses of Congress, particularly the Senate, had an in-built bias to rural America made the cause of the prohibitionists that much easier. The 18th Amendment to the Constitution, making possible a federal ban on intoxicating drink, sailed through Congress with less than three days debate. By early 1919, the necessary 36 states had ratified the amendment making it constitutional to enforce prohibition. Only Rhode Island and Connecticut refused to ratify. Wilson tried to veto the *Volstead Act*, which provided the necessary definition of 'intoxicating' but the supporters of prohibition were able to summon the necessary two-thirds majority in Congress to override the presidential veto. Intoxicating liquor was defined as anything containing 0.5% alcohol. The USA was in theory dry. A broad alliance of groups, feminists, tee-totalling protestant preachers, patriots and proponents of business efficiency had swept the country along in a whirlwind crusade. Protests were surprisingly muted. There were some demonstrations of dissent in the bigger cities, a mass meeting in New York and a parade in Baltimore but in general the country accepted that prohibition seemed to represent the popular will. The keenest supporters were likely to live west of the Mississippi or south of the Mason–Dixon line, be self-employed and attend a Methodist or Baptist church. The opponents were likely to live in a large city and be Roman

Definitions

80% proof strength spirits

Distilled liquor from various sources with a high alcohol content. In Britain 70% proof or 40% by volume is the norm. Raw rum was the traditional spirit of the coastal states but in the west, corn whiskey and other spirits predominated.

anti-alcohol lobby groups

The Prohibition Party had been founded in 1869 and attracted over a quarter of a million votes by the 1890s. The Woman's Temperance Union was founded in 1874 and the very successful Anti-Saloon League in 1893.

Definition

Speakeasy

A place where illegal alcohol was sold and drunk.

Catholic. Many, who accepted it or nominally supported it, saw it as gesture politics – it would keep a noisy pressure group happy whilst not having any real effect on their own life-style. Senator Harding, soon to be President, voted in the senate to ratify the measure but had no intention of abandoning the whisky he so much enjoyed with his card-playing pals.

Prohibition and organised crime

Clearly many Americans felt that the legislation was an unwarranted and unnecessary intrusion on their liberties. Congress, although willing to pass Prohibition, was unwilling to find the funds to enforce it. There was, in fact, a serious lack of enforcement agents; 3,000 were meant to cover the whole country. There were huge logistical problems, too. The USA has 18,700 miles of coastline and land border. Bootlegging of alcohol between Canada and Detroit in the 1920s became common and was reckoned to be worth $215m a year. Whatever else it did, Prohibition did not end drinking. Washington DC, for example, had 300 bars before Prohibition, but by the mid-1920s it had 700 **speakeasies**. The state of Massachusetts had 1,000 licensed saloons before Prohibition, but in the 1920s had around 8,000 speakeasies, 4,000 in the city of Boston alone. Even far to the west of the cities on the East Coast drink was easily obtained. Kansas City in Missouri was famous for its nightlife and this came with a plentiful supply of alcoholic refreshment. Judge Harry Truman, later to become President, enjoyed a tipple with his friends over a card game in the respectable town of Independence, Missouri. Prohibition had simply handed over the sale and supply of alcoholic drinks to criminals.

In addition to smuggling alcohol into the USA, the new law was a great stimulus to the illegal manufacture of alcohol or 'moonshine'. Instead of

Source B

4.1 Police oversee the destruction of alcohol following a raid on a speakeasy during Prohibition.

the normal ethyl alcohol consumed in alcoholic drinks, methyl alcohol was often produced by accident and this could lead to blindness and even death. It was reported that over 30 people died in New York in one year. Much of the illicit liquor tasted so foul that it was necessary to mix it with various attractive drinks thereby giving a strong impetus to the taste for cocktails. Outlawing alcohol clearly did not abate the appetite for drinking and some even felt that the illegality gave drinking an added dash of excitement. It certainly pushed up prices, with the cost of a highball drink rocketing from 15 cents in 1914 to 3 dollars in 1920. The result was an unintended stimulus to organised crime as gangsters realised that there was serious money to be made. Thousands of speakeasies opened and millions of Americans defied the law. The money involved led to protection rackets and inevitable 'turf wars' as rival gangs struggled to control the supply of alcohol in an area and exclude rivals. Perhaps the most famous event linked with these gang wars was the St Valentine's Day massacre of 1929, when six people including members of the Irish Moran gang were gunned down by the Italian Capone gang. This was one notorious killing that hit the headlines, but there had been hundreds of gang murders before this in Chicago. Capone himself was reputedly enjoying an annual income of $60m by 1927. The vast profits to be made inevitably led to the bribery and corruption of police and officials. There were also cases of senior political leaders being bought off, including William Hale Thompson, the Mayor of Chicago.

The law triggered a significant rise in organised crime with Chicago alone experiencing at least 227 gangland murders. However, repeal of Prohibition did not end the crime wave, and racketeers moved on to new ventures with enhanced skills and know-how in organising big ventures. It can be argued that Prohibition provided a major stimulus to gang development. The vast sums made from supplying illicit booze could in part be pumped into fresh areas, notably drugs, gambling and prostitution. Clearly, organised crime pre-dated Prohibition, but it provided an excellent training opportunity to sharpen up skills and taught criminals to think big. The chief beneficiaries, in terms of the millions of dollars made, were drawn from the immigrant Irish, Italian and Jewish communities.

It is important to recognise that the diversity of American society is reflected in the impact of Prohibition. Rural areas often supported the ban on alcohol and certainly small-town America witnessed a marked decline in consumption, which was sustained after 1933 when Prohibition was ended. Only half the breweries in operation in 1920 in the USA, re-opened when allowed to do so. There was a clear shift from drinking hard liquor to wines and beer almost everywhere. The young and middle-class were particularly likely to visit speakeasies, more so than the working man who had supported his corner saloon, in the days before prohibition. Women entered speakeasies with their partners in a way saloons had never encouraged and the speakeasies and clubs selling liquor often became famous for their black Jazz musicians. In this way Prohibition promoted black musicians and gender equality. How far the decline and the shift in

Source C

We had one speakeasy in the basement of the Board of Education building, believe it or not. It was a real posh place, owned by Mr Capone. You used to go down a dark hall and rap on a steel door. There was a certain signal, and a peephole would open and a guy would identify you. Inside was a beautiful Gay Nineties bar. The bourbon was good, the scotch was excellent, and the prices were right, 75c a drink.

Verne Waley, a Chicago newspaperman in the 1920s, remembers a local speakeasy drinking patterns was a product of prohibition and how far a result of more complex social changes is impossible to assess. There was a marked decline in alcohol consumption in Britain in the same period, where there was no prohibition. Many areas also reported significant drops in figures for road traffic accidents. It is possible to argue that in some areas spare cash, previously spent in the saloon now went into consumer goods or family entertainment through the radio or cinema. In this sense prohibition stimulated a more wholesome prosperity, as its supporters had intended. There clearly were some positive benefits as indicated above but whatever prohibition did or did not do, it did not stop the drinking of intoxicating liquor.

In 1931, an eleven-member commission of enquiry into the working and enforcement of the *Volstead Act*, under a former attorney general, George Wickersham, reported to President Hoover that the social and political costs of prohibition outweighed the benefits, but they had no clear answer. Only two of the eleven actually favoured repeal and their report was satirised in the magazine, *New York World*:

> *Prohibition is an awful flop.*
> *We like it.*
> *It can't stop what its meant to stop.*
> *We like it.*
> *Its left a trail of graft and slime,*
> *Its filled our land with vice and crime.*
> *It don't prohibit worth a dime.*
> *Nevertheless we are for it.*

In general, most commentators have taken a negative view. In the words of Michael E. Parrish, author of the 1993 book *Anxious Decades*:

> *'In the short run prohibition proved a boon to boat operators, fire arms manufacturers, auto dealers, ethnic mobility and undertakers.'*

One of the supreme paradoxes about prohibition is that this policy, closely associated with traditional, white, Anglo-Saxon Protestant America, chiefly benefited the new immigrant communities and the entrepreneurs from their ranks – the Irish like Joseph Kennedy of Boston, the Italians like Al Capone and Johnny Torrio in Chicago and Jews like Meyer Lansky in New York. All emerged far richer as a result of Prohibition.

Some politicians began to come out openly against Prohibition in the 1920s. Al Smith the Democratic Presidential candidate in 1928, an Irish Catholic and governor of New York State campaigned openly for an end to Prohibition. There were 32,000 illegal speakeasies in New York City, twice the number of bars that had existed before the Prohibition. Now, it seemed to critics like Smith that the proceeds of alcohol had merely been handed over to the gangsters and mobsters and an important source of revenue had been lost to government. The Republican candidate, Herbert Hoover, stood by Prohibition and won the election with a landslide. Rural, protestant America rejected Smith – the big-city Catholic – and Hoover

SKILLS BUILDER

1. What were the goals of Prohibition?

2. How successfully did Prohibition achieve these goals?

won traditional Democrat areas like the Deep South. Prohibition was to remain until 1933, when a new Democratic President and Democratic Congress repealed it with little opposition. By then, the impact of the great depression had reinforced the arguments for repeal, particularly the importance of legalised drinking being a source of revenue to a cash-strapped government.

Immigration and the Imposition of Controls

The conflict between old and new America was most obvious in the attempts made in the 1920s to limit immigration. As indicated in Unit 1, the period 1880–1914 had been marked by a new flood of immigrants from eastern and southern Europe. Over 2.3 million Jews from Russia and Poland became US citizens, as did 2 million Catholic Poles. Between 1880 and 1920, 4 million Catholic Italians crossed the Atlantic to 'the land of the brave and the home of the free'. These new arrivals seemed to threaten the lifestyle of the old migrants who had come mainly from Great Britain, Germany and Scandinavia, all mainly Protestant in religion and culture. At various times in the past there had been 'nativist' protests against particular groups. The 'Know Nothing' Party in 1849 attacked the new wave of Irish immigrants brought about by the Irish potato famine of 1846–47, and the flood of Chinese labourers into California after the Civil War produced the Chinese Exclusion Act of 1882. Grumbles against the new wave varied in intensity according to the state of the economy but, in general, the expansion and buoyancy of the US economy in the years before 1917 made immigration not only tolerable but desirable to provide the new industries with workers.

There was a growing racialism even before the First World War with a series of books and articles emphasising the inferiority of the new immigrants compared to the old 'Nordic' stock. The most famous of these appeared in 1916, *The Passing of the Great Race*, by Madison Grant. A wealthy New Yorker, Grant believed in the new pseudo science of eugenics which divided the world up into a hierarchy of races with the 'Nordics' at the top. Congress had already set up a commission to study immigration in 1907 and it recommended literacy tests to limit the entry of 'inferior races'. Popular pressure and concern did produce the introduction in the 1917 of literacy tests, which required all immigrants to be able to read and write, although it did not necessarily need to be in English. This act was originally vetoed by President Wilson, but Congress re-passed it with the necessary two-thirds majority to overcome the veto. Thus even before the USA's entry into war there was growing pressure for restrictions. The First World War added significantly to the pressure. There was much talk of 'hyphenated Americans'. This mainly referred to German-Americans who in fact belonged to the older and acceptable Nordic group but the war stimulated nationalism and 'Americanism', which led to a backlash against recent immigrants who appeared so obviously different in their habits. There was a suspicion about their loyalty. President Wilson spoke of the

SKILLS BUILDER

How far do you agree with the view that Prohibition was a total disaster for the USA?

need for 100 per cent Americanism and ex-President Theodore Roosevelt demanded 'America for Americans'. Immigrants became associated with the threat of sabotage. The war in fact created an atmosphere of fear and intolerance which contributed to the anti-immigrant legislation in the early twenties. On the other hand, many thousands of recent immigrants served in the US forces during the war and absorbed the prevailing patriotism.

In many ways it was the post-war Red Scare, triggered by the Russian Revolution which was more directly responsible for the tightening of controls Racial prejudices became linked for some Americans to the fear that immigrants from southern and eastern Europe brought Bolshevik ideas with them that would lead to the spread of communism and undermine traditional American values.

The Red Scare, immigration policy and the case of Sacco and Vanzetti

Immigrants were increasingly linked with violent left-wing politics. In the cities there was also a worrying development as some of the labour unions began to ally themselves with international radical groups and, by the end of 1920, a series of strikes had involved over 4 million workers. Particularly disturbing was a police strike in Boston. This led to a feeling that communist agitators were at work. There was a growing fear of anarchy and a developing paranoia about a widespread plot to subvert the USA. The First World War had heightened nationalism and suspicion of foreigners and the **Bolshevik seizure of power** in Russia seemed to point to an international conspiracy of left-wing activists determined to overthrow capitalism. This was in part encouraged by propaganda coming from the new Bolshevik Russia, which openly proclaimed its support for World Revolution. Sixteen bombs were found in a New York post office, to be delivered to 'enemies of the revolution' and a further 18 were discovered elsewhere. In 1919, a bomber blew himself up on the steps of the home of the Attorney General, Mitchell Palmer. The bomber was an Italian anarchist who was a member of the radical movement inspired by Galleani, an Italian-American who edited an anarchist journal. This bombing and others led to the establishment of a new division of the Department of Justice dedicated to investigating and compiling lists of

Definition

Bolshevik seizure of power

In February 1917 the Tsarist regime had been overthrown by a popular revolution. After six months of mounting chaos and continuing defeat in the First World War, a Marxist minority group, known as the Bolsheviks, under the leadership of Vladimir Lenin, seized power in October and established 'a revolutionary dictatorship'. They won a brutal civil war, in which they were known as the **Reds** and their opponents as the Whites. Lenin and his colleagues saw their victory as merely the first step in the defeat of world capitalism. In reality, they unleashed on Russia a brutal and old-fashioned tyranny. Lenin killed more political opponents in the first year of his power than the last Tsar had in the whole of his 23-year reign.

Source D

My motto for the **Reds** is –
  'Ship or Shoot'
We should place them in a ship of stone with sails of lead and their first stopping place should be Hell.

From a speech made by Dr John Wesley Hill, an unsuccessful candidate for the Republican Presidential Nomination in 1920.

radicals. The group of agents was headed up by a relatively young civil servant, J. Edgar Hoover, who was later to become head of the FBI.

The investigators sought out anyone with even the most tenuous links to any form of radicalism. Subscription to a 'suspect' magazine or journal would be enough. Soon, 5,000 arrests were made, with over 1,000 prosecuted and 500 of these people deported. These raids of late 1919 and early 1920 were very quickly dubbed the Palmer Raids and were seemingly indiscriminate. Being in proximity to the wrong community would be enough to justify such a raid, and often led to extensive collateral damage with cases of tenement staircases being damaged almost beyond repair. The mood at the time bordered on hysteria with the Washington Post declaring: '*There is no time to waste on hair splitting over infringements of liberty*'.

Boston became a particular target for raids, with its Bay area containing a large Italian community. Over 800 arrests were made there. A member of this community was Bartolomeo Vanzetti who, as a subscriber to Galleani's journal, was already on the Hoover lists.

The Sacco and Vanzetti case

In the context of the social and political tension of the late 1910s and early 1920s, the Sacco and Vanzetti case erupted. It illustrates many of the fears present in American society. Two violent robberies took place in Massachusetts in late 1919 and early 1920. Shots were fired during a failed payroll raid on Christmas Eve 1919 and then in April 1920 two guards were killed in a raid at a shoe factory in South Braintree.

Suspicion centred on the immigrant community and pressure mounted on the police to make early arrests. Sacco and Vanzetti were reported to the police by a garage owner after they took a car in for repair – garages had been told to report all Italian car owners to the authorities. When arrested, they lied about possessing firearms and did not admit their anarchist connections. The police interpreted this as 'consciousness of guilt' and arrested them.

The conduct of the trial in 1921 aroused considerable disquiet which extended outside the United States. The evidence presented at the trial was often dubious and the conduct of the trial Judge Webster Thayer was criticised. He was an experienced judge, but his conduct of both the trial and the later appeal were open to criticism.

- During his summing up, he emphasised to the jury that the crime was very much in line with Vanzetti's radical ideas. Such a comment, in the atmosphere of the time, would have been very telling.

- He is reputed to have said: 'I want to see the Anarchist bastards hanged'.

Judge Thayer may have acted out of a genuine commitment to do what he felt to be in the public interest, but on this occasion it led to a lack of strict judicial impartiality.

Source E

'August 22, 1927

A cartoon from 1927 commenting on the outcome of the Sacco and Vanzetti case.

Furthermore:

- a 14-year-old boy was presented as a key witness, but he said he had not seen the face of a fleeing figure but 'could tell he was a foreigner by the way he ran'

- twenty-two out of the thirty-five eyewitnesses stated that Sacco and Vanzetti were not there. Seven were unable to identify them and the remainder were either discredited or changed their evidence during the trial

- Sacco and Vanzetti both produced evidence that they were elsewhere during the robberies but as their witnesses came from the immigrant community, it was seemingly disregarded by the jury.

Sacco and Vanzetti were sentenced to death in July 1921. During the six years they spent on Death Row, emotions raged inside and outside the USA, with the pair becoming icons for many socialist and anarchist groups. Many internationally known writers and intellectuals, such as Anatole France and H.G. Wells, expressed their horror at events. However, Sacco and Vanzetti were not released and the appeal process ground on. The final appeal came in 1927. Ominously, perhaps, Judge Thayer again presided. Since 1921 a fellow prisoner, Celestino Madeiros, had come forward and confessed to the South Braintree robbery, emphasising that Sacco and Vanzetti played no part in it. However, the court did not appear open to new arguments. An editorial in the *New York World* newspaper seemed to sum up the situation: *'The case is clouded and obscure. The fairness of their trial provokes doubt; doubt so deep that it can't be denied.'* Vanzetti's assessment after the appeal process failed was that *'Nick and I are anarchists, the black cats that are the terror of many. We are here for being the oppressed class.'* On Tuesday 23 August 1927 they were both executed.

Whether they were guilty of the charges or not the case caused widespread controversy, dividing left and right opinion. Those who went to the two men's defence were hardly less prejudiced than the presiding judge. Indeed, some new ballistic evidence emerged in 1961, which seemed to show that the murders had been committed with Sacco's gun, and indicated that he was guilty after all.

Other causes of immigration control

There was also support for anti-immigration measures in the southern states of the USA. Some of them were concerned that their political power was being undercut by the growth of population in northern cities through immigration. This population growth meant that the representation of the North in the House of Representatives would grow proportionately as the numbers of Representatives allocated to each state was linked to its total population.

Anti-immigrant feeling also operated amongst many wage earners. It was widely believed among working class people that unrestricted immigration led to wage reductions among those already resident in the country. This view even found some indirect mention in the case made for controls by President Coolidge.

Source F

American institutions rest solely on good citizenship. They were created by people who had a background of self-government. New arrivals should be limited to our capacity to absorb them into the ranks of good citizenship. America must be kept American. For this purpose, it is necessary to continue a policy of restricted immigration. It would be well to make such immigration of a selective nature with some inspection at the source, and based either on a prior census or upon the record of naturalization. Either method would insure the admission of those with the largest capacity and best intention of becoming citizens. I am convinced that our present economic and social conditions warrant a limitation of those to be admitted. We should find additional safety in a law requiring the immediate registration of all aliens. Those who do not want to be partakers of the American spirit ought not to settle in America.

State of the Union address made by Calvin Coolidge in 1923.

There were also strong racist arguments brought into the debate as Source G shows.

Source G

I think we now have sufficient population in our country for us to shut the door and to breed up a pure, unadulterated American citizenship. I recognize that there is a dangerous lack of distinction between people of a certain nationality and the breed of the dog. Who is an American? Is he an immigrant from Italy? Is he an immigrant from Germany? If you were to go abroad and some one were to meet you and say, "I met a typical American," what would flash into your mind as a typical American, the typical representative of that new Nation? Would it be the son of an Italian immigrant, the son of a German immigrant, the son of any of the breeds from the Orient, the son of the denizens of Africa? We must not get our ethnological distinctions mixed up with out anthropological distinctions. It is the breed of the dog in which I am interested. I would like for the Members of the Senate to read that book just recently published by Madison Grant, *The Passing of a Great Race*. Thank God we have in America perhaps the largest percentage of any country in the world of the pure, unadulterated Anglo-Saxon stock; certainly the greatest of any nation in the Nordic breed. It is for the preservation of that splendid stock that has characterized us that I would make this not an asylum for the oppressed of all countries, but a country to assimilate and perfect that splendid type of manhood that has made America the foremost Nation in her progress and in her power, and yet the youngest of all the nations. I myself believe that the preservation of her institutions depends upon us now taking counsel with our condition and our experience during the last World War.

From a speech made in Congress by Ellison Smith, Democrat Senator from South Carolina, in the debate on the 1924 *Quota Act*.

Discussion point

What do the two extracts indicate were the main reasons for curbing immigration in this period?

SKILLS BUILDER

What were the main reasons for the widespread support of anti-immigration policy?

The process of legislating against immigration went much further in the 1920s, arguably as another element in the Republican Party's policy of isolationism and protection. The 1921 *Emergency Quota Act* limited immigration to 3 per cent of the number of each nationality resident in the United States according to the 1910 census. This meant that immigration would be approximately 357,000 immigrants each year.

The 1924 *Quota Act* modified the terms of the earlier piece of legislation by making the base figure 2 per cent of the 1890 census. This obviously had the result of reducing immigration still further – to approximately 164,000 each year. This had the effect of significantly reducing immigration from southern and Eastern Europe. The legislation, however, went even further and completely stopped all immigration from East Asia. Although Senator Smith's comments, quoted in Source G, may be regarded as extreme, most Americans did believe that there was a need to restrict immigration and this law passed both the Senate and the House of Representatives by very large margins. There was some vocal opposition but it was very much in the minority.

Source H

The foreign born of my district writhe under the charge of being called 'hyphenates.' The people of my own family were all hyphenates – English-Americans, German-Americans, Irish-Americans. They began to come in the first ship or so after the Mayflower. But they did not come too early to miss the charge of anti-Americanism. Roger Williams was driven out of the Puritan colony of **Salem** to die in the wilderness because he objected 'violently' to the burning or hanging of rheumatic old women on witchcraft charges. He would not 'assimilate' and was 'a grave menace to American Institutions and democratic government.' My family put 11 men and boys into the Revolutionary War, and I am sure they and their women and children did not suffer so bitterly and sacrifice until it hurt to establish the autocracy of bigotry and intolerance which exists in many quarters to-day in this country.

The Detroit Democratic Congressman Robert Clancy's public criticism of the proposed law.

Clancy's eloquent plea for toleration and appeal to American history (Source H) was in vain. As far as many Americans were concerned, the country was full up or at least had more than was desirable of the wrong sort of Americans. This prejudice was to be particularly associated with the infamous hooded figures of 'the Klan'.

The Ku Klux Klan

The sinister Klan symbolise for many the bigotry and intolerance to which Congressman Clancy referred in Source H. The Klan had its roots in the small towns and rural communities of the southern states of the Confederacy. It began as a reaction of the defeated whites in the aftermath of the civil war, and the fears that their way of life was threatened by the black majority of newly freed slaves. After 1866, a number of armed white racist groups emerged in the South, the most enduring being the Ku Klux Klan, first established in Tennessee. Most members were ex-confederate soldiers and it grew to a membership of half a million spread across the southern states. The Klan practised terrorism against the black community, targeting especially schools and churches. Despite attempts by President Grant and the Federal Army to suppress it, many outrages occurred, including nearly 3,000 lynchings in the period to 1877. The first burst of activity died down as the triumphant North lost interest in the South and withdrew garrisons, leaving the southern whites to their own devices. With a subdued and terrorised black population there was less need for an active Klan. Lynchings still remained, however, as a means of terrorising blacks into docile submission. In 1892 alone, 155 African Americans were lynched. State Laws were passed, enforcing segregation and discrimination in various southern states and in a notorious judgement of the Supreme Court, (Plessy vs. Ferguson in 1896) these were accepted as not contrary to federal law. These developments strengthened the confidence and security of the white community and led to a decline in the activities of the Klan.

Definition

Salem

In 1692 there were infamous witch trials in Massachusetts, when hysteria gripped the small community of Salem and led to the execution of 19 citizens as witches. These trials were made famous in the 1950s by Arthur Miller's play 'The Crucible'.

Discussion point

On what basis did Clancy criticise the immigration laws?

The re-emergence of the Klan during and after the First World War was a complex phenomenon arising from a sense within rural protestant America of being on the defensive before an influx of new immigrants. The heightened nationalism engendered by the war also fed the growth of support for the Klan. One other reason for the Klan's re-emergence in 1915 was partly in response to the impact of D.W. Griffith's film *Birth of a Nation* which included graphic and inflammatory scenes depicting the threats blacks posed, especially to white women. The film seemed to glorify the Klan of the 1860s. It now influenced a new generation of fearful and prejudiced Americans portraying the revival of the South as being largely due to the patriotism and loyalty of the Klan. The key figure in re-founding the Klan was Doc Simmons a former Methodist preacher from Atlanta, Georgia. The foundation ceremony in 1915 was marked by the setting fire to a large cross on a hill just outside Atlanta. The Pledge was taken to save white, Christian civilisation. The *Fiery Cross* became the leading publication of the organisation.

By 1921 the movement had 100,000 members and it developed a structure which was funded by subscription. Each branch became a Klavern and several Klaverns a Klonklave. Klaverns were under a Kleagle and Klonklaves headed by a Grand Dragon. The National Chief was the Imperial Wizard, the title Simmons appropriated. The organisation claimed to have five million members in 1925.

The Klan put themselves forward as the defenders of the American way and Simmons spoke of defending 'Morality, Americanism, Protestantism and White Supremacy'. They felt this was challenged by African Americans, Jews and Catholics, and apparently all foreigners who did not arrive from north-west Europe. If its re-emergence owed something to *Birth of a Nation* ideals of 19th century social issues, it also reflected the fear of the more radical, especially Socialist, political ideas that came from East European immigrants in the early 20th century. The Red Scare (see pages 56–60) provided the perfect breeding ground for bigotry. The traditional view has been that the Klan prospered most in small communities often settled by the early pioneers where there was a fear of different ethnic groups, religions, political ideas and even cultural taste. The Klan had, for example, a particular aversion to jazz. These points reflected the fears of the farmers, artisans and shopkeepers of small-town America. However, misconceptions about Klan membership need addressing. The Klan was not just a feature of small-town America. Recent surveys, notably by Kathleen Blee, have shown that membership was not just restricted to the poor, downtrodden Americans who felt marginalised but increasingly involved middle-class citizens. Equally it was not an exclusively rural, southern organisation, as there were dramatic increases in membership from north central states, such as Indiana, Ohio and Illinois in particular. There were many places where the local police seemed Klan-dominated and even judges did not always seem to remain impartial.

Simmons had joined forces in 1920 with Elizabeth Tyler and Edgar Clark, two experienced southern publicists, who proved very effective fund-raisers and money poured in to the Atlanta HQ. Tyler and Clark pushed out

SKILLS BUILDER

How many reasons can you think of as to why Klansmen had such an aversion to Jazz?

Source I

4.3 The inaugaration of a new Klansman at a Ku Klux Klan meeting in the 1920s.

Simmons from day-to-day control, but in 1924 Tyler died and Clark was sent to jail for fraud. Power now came to the Exalted Cyclops of the Dallas Klan, a dentist by the name of Hiram Wesley Evans. He took over as Imperial Wizard and under his nominal leadership the Klan reached its greatest influence in 1925. However, the real driving force of the Klan's expansion lay in the North. Here the key figure was David Curtis Stephenson, Grand Dragon of Indiana Klans. Virtually the whole state fell under his control in 1924 when his nominee became governor and his followers dominated the state legislature. Indiana boasted the greatest number of Klaverns of any state. David Stephenson was a charismatic leader, but his private life undid him and helped to destroy the influence of the whole organisation. He was convicted of the rape of a 28-year-old secretary on an overnight train. The self-appointed guardians of American values were showing characteristics far removed from the ideals they publically espoused. Other scandals, usually financial, followed in other states' Klans and by 1930 membership had fallen back to 200,000, and they were no longer a player on the national stage, although their malicious influences endured in many individual communities.

It is difficult to assess the importance of the Klan. To the black victims of its violence it was supremely important and a source of real terror. However, its influence varied geographically to a considerable degree. In its peak year of 1925, 40 per cent of members were in three states, Indiana, Ohio and Illinois. Another 25 per cent were found in the old South. The Pacific coast and New England, except Maine, were largely untouched. Its point of greatest popular political influence was at the 1924 Democratic Convention and it had some Senators and Congressmen in its pocket in some of the Deep South states and Indiana. It, however, achieved

Source J

4.2 Ku Klux Klan members march down Pennsylvania Avenue, Washington DC in 1926. This was to be the high-water mark of their popularity.

SKILLS BUILDER

What was the significance of the growth in support for the KKK in the years 1915–25?

little at a national level. It was one among many pressure groups supporting Prohibition and restriction of immigration. To many members it was simply a social club like the 'Odd Fellows' or 'Woodmen'. Groups of white protestant males joined together with like-minded males and grumbled about how the world was changing. Parades and dressing up added some drama. But to others it was a way of terrorising those of a different ethnic origin under the cloak of respectability.

Women's suffrage and the role of women in this period

Women's suffrage had been achieved largely as a result of the First World War (see Unit 2). The necessary Amendment (19th) to the Constitution had been proposed in May 1919 and was finally ratified in August 1920. Southern concerns that this might be a first step to greater rights for blacks contributed to the delay in ratification. In practice, the enfranchisement of women produced few obvious results in the following ten years. There was to be no gender revolution in the period that could in any way be linked to the 19th Amendment. Women got the vote just in time for the 1920 Presidential election. Women appear to have voted more or less in line with their male relatives along regional, class, racial or religious lines. Women were slightly less likely to vote than men and very few sought to enter active politics. By 1928 there were 145 women in 38 state legislatures. Two women had been elected to the House of Representatives in Washington and two women had served as state governors in succession to their husbands. This hardly amounted to dramatic change.

The hopes of many of the suffragists who had campaigned during the First World War that the enfranchisement would lead to a much fairer deal for women all round, was not realised. By the early 1920s women could serve on juries in 20 states but the attempts to pass an *Equal Rights Amendment*, first introduced to Congress in 1923, repeatedly failed. It was finally passed in March 1972. Congress did pass the *Sheppard-Towner Act* in 1921, which provided federal money for the health care for pregnant women and women were given a major role in the administration of the local clinics set up under the Act . However funds were withdrawn in 1929.

Throughout the 1920s women made some progress in terms of their freedom in society but this had little to do with political reform. The spread of birth control reduced unwanted pregnancies. More women entered work than ever before. By 1930 there were 10,546,000 in a range of varied jobs. Nearly 3.5 million, it must be admitted, were in domestic service – the traditional area – but there was a growing number in clerical jobs and over a million in the professions. Women tended to be paid less than men, but there was growing female luxury trade catering to a new feminine affluence. The number of beauty parlours in New York leapt from 750 in 1920 to 3,000 by 1925. The cosmetics industry grew throughout the decade from being worth $17,000,000 per annum, to $200,000,000 per annum. Although women had not seized political power in the 1920s, they certainly used a lot more lipstick and face powder.

> **SKILLS BUILDER**
>
> Why did the role and position of women not become more of a contentious social issue?

Unit summary

What have you learned in this unit?

The United States was experiencing a period of rapid economic change that was bound to produce social and political consequences. You have seen how two Americas clashed in numerous areas: over religious beliefs and the teaching of science, the wickedness or desirability of alcohol, and the issue of race and immigration. The changing role and position of women has also been briefly addressed, although here it did not become a battleground between the two Americas.

What skills have you used in this unit?

You have been introduced to the complex web of social issues. These are often interconnected in a way that is difficult to disentangle. Prejudice then, and now, makes impartial, analytical judgements difficult. Attitudes amongst some groups in these years are often difficult to understand.

What made William Jennings Bryan deny the findings of much of modern science? What made many otherwise decent and respectable white men and women put on costumes and pointed hats and express racial intolerance? Why did the case of Sacco and Vanzetti so divide contemporaries and historians? In this case, recent evidence indicates that the contemporary liberal position was probably wrong.

Exam style question

This is the sort of question you will find appearing on the examination paper as a Section A question.

'How far do you agree that the clash between essentially rural and urban cultures was the fundamental cause of division and social conflict in the USA in the years 1919–29?'

Exam tips

See the section at the end of Unit 2 for general tips relating to structure and approach then consider the following:

There were a range of areas of conflict: Prohibition, race, immigration, religious teaching and the position and role of women.

- The stated factor of rural vs. urban is clearly important in Prohibition and over the issue of teaching Darwin in schools.
- Most members of the KKK were drawn from small town, or rural environments and condemned urban-based Jews and Catholics.
- There was a general fear of a growing big city immigrant community.

There were clearly, however, other factors.

- Fear of left-wing politics which were associated with the immigrant community.
- Racial prejudice – most African Americans lived in the rural south but had a growing presence in the large northern urban areas, more free from traditional southern white bigotry.
- Economic factors affected attitudes to Prohibition and immigration and the role and position of women.

RESEARCH TOPIC

The Monkey Trial

Find out more details of the roles of the following:

- John Scopes
- Clarence Darrow
- William Jennings Bryan

How far does the Trial mark a significant victory for urban America and its values over 'traditional rural' USA and its values?

5 Controversy: The coming of slump and the Depression, 1929–33

What is this unit about?

This unit focuses on the key historical controversy of why a depression developed in the United States. The relative importance of the causes that led to Depression has been a highly contentious issue and this unit seeks to help you explore the different interpretations offered by historians. Some, usually on the left of the political spectrum, have argued that wages lagged behind profits and consequently there was a lack of demand for the escalating production of consumer goods. Some, on the right of the political spectrum, have argued that unions had become too powerful during the First World War and wages too high, thus preventing business adjusting when circumstances became difficult. Some choose to see the root in the depressed state of agriculture and its failure consequently to provide a sufficient demand for goods. Others stress the international dimension and the failings of demand overseas. Most agree that the US banks were inadequate. There is controversy over the *laissez-faire* policies of the Republican governments and in particular the policies of Andrew Mellon, the Secretary of the Treasury. In general those on the left argue that they did too little and those on the right argue that they did too much and prevented recovery. The Monetarists are those who argue that the essential cause was too tight a control of the money supply. There are arguments over short-term factors involving both the domestic scene and the international situation. Was the infamous fall in the stock market in October 1929 merely a symptom or a cause? Finally, much ink has been spilled on why the slump turned into a prolonged depression and the role of the Hoover presidency in this will be explored.

In this unit you will:

- examine the nature of the Depression
- work with conflicting interpretations of how and why the USA moved from slump into depression and the reasons why it lasted so long.

Key questions

- How and why have historians' interpretations of the causes of the Depression differed?
- Why did the Depression last so long?

Timeline

1929	Oct	Great Crash in share values
		3.2% unemployed
1930	Jun	Hawley–Smoot Tariff damages international trade
	Nov–Dec	Major Banking Crisis
		8.7% unemployed
1931	Summer	International banking crisis develops
	Sep	Great Britain leaves gold standard
	Oct	522 US banks collapse
		15.9% unemployed
1932	Jan	Reconstruction Finance Corporation established
		Big increase in taxes to cut large Federal deficit
	Nov	Roosevelt defeats Hoover in Presidential election
		23.6% unemployed
1933	Mar	Roosevelt takes over from Hoover
		24.9% unemployed

Using Sources in the Controversy Section B

Unlike the units that you have studied so far, which are tested by straightforward essay questions, in the controversy section you will be faced with a series of extracts from secondary sources. These will offer differing interpretations of the causes of the slump and depression and you will be asked to use these with your own knowledge to explore a particular opinion. The sources should drive your answer, but additional material should be introduced to develop, challenge or supplement the extracts. It is vital to try to understand the essential viewpoint of a source and to be able to appreciate similarities and differences between the extracts. What distinguishes a good answer is the ability to appreciate, not only the central thrust of the case being made, but also the subtle nuances that the author is trying to convey. The extracts, therefore, need reading and interpreting with care. You will not be, in general, asked to comment on the provenance and reliability of the extract, but to recognise that it is an interpretation. The following three extracts deal with the rapid rise in the stock market which pre-dated the crash of October 1929.

SKILLS BUILDER

What explanation is offered in Source A for the rise in stock market values in 1928–29?

Source A

Walter Chrysler commissioned the Chrysler Building at precisely the moment the great 'Bull Market' of the late 1920s was rising to its frenzied peak. It was no accident that the era's monument to success should have been raised by a car manufacturer. The stock market's dramatic rise in 1928 and 1929 was fuelled by ever-increasing profits and expansion of companies like General Motors and Chrysler Motors.

From Lucy Moore 'Anything Goes': A Biography of the Roaring Twenties, published 2008

Source B

There were sound reasons for stock prices to rise after 1926, including the steady growth in GNP and per capita income, rising productivity and higher corporate profits. But the magnitude of the increases that took place, especially in 1928 and 1929, remained out of all proportion to these rational indicators. Fantasy not facts ruled the market. Although it had not paid a single dividend, for example, the stock of the Radio Corporation of America zoomed from 85 to 420 in the course of 1928. Montgomery Ward, another of the decade's glamour stocks, shot up in the same period from 117 to 440, and Du Pont from 310 to 525. In the frantic summer of 1929, according to one estimate the securities of Insull's vast utilities empire appreciated at a rate of $7,000 a minute during one fifty day period.

From Michael E. Parrish, *Anxious Decades: America in Prosperity and Depression 1920–41*, published 1992

SKILLS BUILDER

How does Source B differ from Source A in the explanation it offers for the rise in stock values in 1928–29?

Source C

Until 1927 stock values had gone up with profits, but they began to soar on wings of pure speculation. Mellon's tax reductions had released money that, with the help of aggressive brokerage houses, found its way to Wall Street. One could buy stock on margin – that is, make a small down payment (the margin) and borrow the rest from a broker who held the stock as security against a down market. If the stock declined and the buyer failed to meet a margin call for more money, the broker could sell the stock to cover his loan. Brokers' loans more than doubled from 1927 to 1929.

From George Brown Tindall and David E. Shi, *America: A Narrative History Vol. II* published 1984

SKILLS BUILDER

1. In what ways does Source C agree with Source B in the explanation it offers for the rise in stock values in 1928–29?

2. How does Source C differ from Source B in the explanation it offers for the rise in stock values in 1928–29?

Nature of the crash and Depression and differing interpretations

The great economic crisis of 1929–33, which some would argue continued until 1939, is the subject of massive controversy because of its initial causes and its longevity. For most Americans it meant two related unfortunate developments: rising unemployment and banks collapsing. Between 1929 and 1932, the number without work leapt from one and half million to over twelve million. In the same period, 20 per cent of US banks collapsed bringing ruin to those unlucky enough to have their savings invested therein. Unemployment did not return to the 1929 level until 1943.

It was a complex interplay of various factors that were at work. At one level it was simply a healthy correction to an overheated economy. It had overheated because production had simply outstripped demand as technology produced a flood of goods the like of which humanity had never seen before. The demands of the market simply could not keep up with the amount of goods being produced. Such corrections had been a feature of the developing industrial economies of the 19th century. The stock market fall of 1929 was also a healthy correction to a share market, which had risen well beyond sensible values; the assets and income of companies simply did not warrant such high share prices. There had been a sharp short slump in 1921, then production had dropped, shares and wages had fallen, the government had made massive cuts in its overblown spending, and by 1922 growth was resumed. The economy had re-balanced quickly and efficiently following market principles. This did not happen in 1929–33.

Great parts of the US economy, notably agriculture, were overmanned and economically rotten. An economic shake-out was inevitable and the small-scale tenant farmers and sharecroppers of the old south were facing economic oblivion, like the handloom weavers in early 19th-century Great Britain. A serious banking crisis, partly American in origin and partly international, intensified the more general economic crisis. There were too many too small banks in the United States. Those tied into the depressed rural economy were particularly vulnerable. The US policy of protection by raising tariffs, intensified in 1930, hit international trade. Finally US government policy got it wrong in other ways. To some, the Hoover administration of 1929–33 did too little too late. To others, he did too much, undermining business confidence, stopping wages falling and pursuing a tight money policy at the wrong time. A combination of all these factors produced the worst economic downturn in American history.

One recent short study of the New Deal lays out the issues simply:

Source D

The exact causes of the Depression are hotly debated particularly between the monetarists and the Keynesians, but whatever they were, the impact they had on the American economy was devastating.

From Fiona Venn, *The New Deal*, published 1998

Essentially, monetarists see the root of the problem in a shortage of money and credit brought about by a 'dear money' policy pursued by the Federal Reserve. This involved the Federal Reserve attempting to stem the wild speculation in shares in the autumn of 1929 by raising interest rates. Banks and brokers could not lend as easily as money became more expensive. The monetarists argue that they overdid this course of action and persisted with it, leading to bank collapses as banks could not borrow cheaply and could not lend. An example of a monetarist explanation lies in the following:

Source E

The Federal Reserve polices began a monetary contraction. As the contraction became more severe, it brought on a depression in output, employment and income. If nothing else had happened there would have been a depression because of the severe monetary contraction.

From Jim Powell *FDR's Folly, How Roosevelt and His New Deal Prolonged the Great Depression*, published 2003

By comparison, the traditional explanations have tended to be Keynesian. They were influenced by the contemporary economic thinking of the great British economist John Maynard Keynes (1883–1946), who argued that the root of the problem lay in lack of sufficient demand. A well-respected British historian, who, like Keynes, teaches at Cambridge University, offers a typically Keynesian explanation in the following extract.

Source F

Economists for a long time highlighted the structural weaknesses of the American economy in the 1920s. Because of mal-distribution of income and the flaws of the banking system and the operation of the stock market, there was insufficient demand in the American economy to sustain the great gains made in productivity by American industry and agriculture. This lack of demand was not offset in the early years of the Depression by any compensatory government spending.

Extract from Anthony J. Badger, *The New Deal: The Depression Years 1933–40*,
published 1989

SKILLS BUILDER

Read Source F carefully and make sure that you understand all the words, phrases and economic concepts raised in this short passage, for example, structural weaknesses, insufficient demand, stock market, productivity, compensatory government spending.

Source F highlights several of the key issues related to the onset and continuation of the Depression and might be said to reflect the consensus 'liberal' position, particularly in its emphasis on the failure of government to increase demand by spending more. The key structural weakness relates particularly to agriculture. It is significant that the world's two leading industrial economies of the time, the USA and Germany, had large agricultural sectors, far larger, proportionally, than in the world's third largest industrial economy, Great Britain. The slump in both Germany and the USA was far worse than in Great Britain, possibly indicating the role of a large but depressed agricultural sector.

Summary of factors leading to the Depression

- Insufficient demand
  - Depressed agriculture
  - Declining old industries
  - Wages even in the new industries not rising fast enough to encourage greater consumption
  - Overseas demand discouraged by high tariffs

SKILLS BUILDER

Using the information you have studied in this unit so far, create a diagram showing how the key factors of the slump interacted with each other to create the Depression.

- Government failed to increase demand by increasing spending sufficiently
- Shortage of money and credit
  - Banking crisis – too many small banks and as they collapse they pull down others (20% collapse).
  - Government follows a dear money policy from 1929 i.e. keeps interest rates high – adds to the banking crisis and discourages consumption.
- A victim of its own success

The technological revolution and mass production techniques were so successful in producing goods and services that they could not be absorbed within the USA and the rest of the world hit by tariffs and war debts could not afford them.

What part did agriculture play?

In 1929, American farmers' annual income stood at an average of $273 a year, well below the national average of $750 and their hard times as well as lack of purchasing power was an important factor in the Depression. In the 1920s, farmers did not share in the boom. They had benefited from the demand for agricultural produce during the First World War, but the 1920s brought severe problems. Investment in new equipment had loaded many farmers with high levels of debt. The debt level of $3.2 billion in 1910, rose to $8.4 billion in 1920 with annual interest payments alone totalling $574 million.

As European agriculture recovered from the ravages of war, the 1920s became a period of overproduction which put smaller farmers under intense pressure. Their unit cost of production could not compete with the larger operators who had been able to invest in superior technology. Price levels fell and the mid-West was hit especially hard. A bushel of wheat cost $2.19 in 1919 but had gone down to 90c in 1922.

Natural disasters, notably drought, also hit the rural communities of the mid-West and in some instances eliminated already declining income completely. Net farm income fell from $6.1 billion in 1929 to $2 billion in 1932. In Oklahoma, the wheat harvest which had an average annual yield of $1 million produced only $7,000 in 1933. Farmers felt the repercussions very badly. As incomes fell, they fell behind with mortgage repayments and their tax debts increased. Many also owed huge sums to cover the interest on equipment they had bought to improve their efficiency. The cotton and tobacco plantations suffered particularly badly. Again, natural disasters exacerbated an already desperate situation. The boll weevil hit cotton crops in the early 1920s, but then two good years produced record low prices. It seemed that whatever happened was bad for the producer. Many farms, for example, were devastated by the Mississippi flood of 1927. In the state of Mississippi income fell from $239 peer head in 1928 to $117 in 1933. Over a third of the banks in the state failed. There were 3,500 **foreclosures** out of 5,280 farms.

Definition

Foreclosures

Foreclosures refers to banks who have lent money to farms or businesses on the security of the property and who are refusing to lend more or extend the period of the loan, taking over the property in compensation for the 'bad debt'.

The fate of the agricultural 'under classes' must not be forgotten. Farm labourers lost their jobs, **sharecroppers** became destitute and the smaller farmer had no opportunities as markets shrank. Many black people made their way from the South to the northern cities. It is important to realise that, for rural America, the Depression began well before the Wall Street crash in October 1929. The value of farmland dropped 30 per cent between 1920 and 1929. Already, by 1928–29, agriculture was in serious trouble throughout much of the South and West.

There are many evocative sources concerning the plight of rural America. The poverty of the rural South is vividly illustrated in literature of the time. The journalism of John Steinbeck is very powerful, as is the book *Let Us Now Praise Famous Men* by James Agee, which includes a large collection of photographs taken by Walker Evans.

Definition

Sharecroppers
These were tenant farmers who paid part of their crops as rent to the land owner.

SKILLS BUILDER

Explain how agriculture was hit by – and helped to create – the slump.

Source G

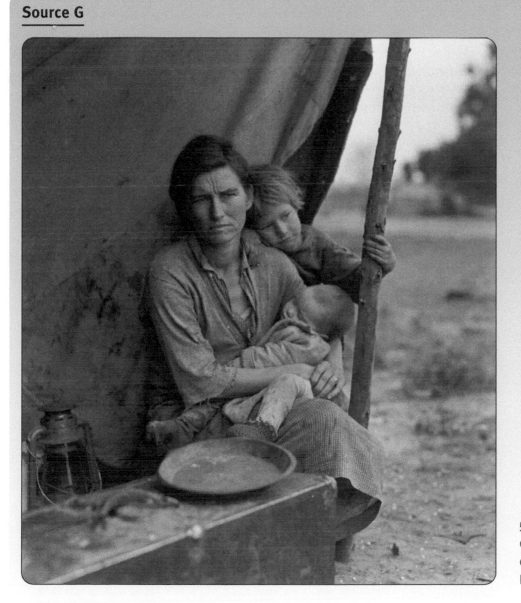

5.1 A woman and her children in rural America during the Great Depression.

Source H

The New England textile industry collapsed under competition from mills in the South, where labour costs, because of the general poverty, were low: bankruptcies were commonplace, and in ten years (1923–33) the workforce employed in the industry shrank from 190,000 to less than 100,000

From Hugh Brogan, *The Penguin History of the USA*, published 1999 (second edition)

Source I

At the root of stagnation was uneven distribution of income. While real wages of workers in manufacturing were increasing by 12% between 1921 and 1929, corporate profits jumped by 62%. In 1929 the richest 5% of the population received 33.5% of disposable income; the richest 1% got 19%.

From Anthony J. Badger, *The New Deal: The Depression Years 1933–40*, published in 1989

Problems in Industry

In the industrial sector there were depressed black-spots even in the early 1920s. Traditional industries, like coalmining and textiles, began to decline because of overproduction and falling demand. The restoration of European production and exports after the First World War, competition from new fuels like oil, and the ending of the great railroad boom, all brought problems to coalmining in the USA. Prices fell and mine owners responded with attempts to cut wages, leading to vicious labour disputes. In 1931, 2.2 million man days were lost in strikes. In textiles, again, new technologies had a considerable impact with the introduction of fibres like rayon, hitting traditional cotton producers.

However, the essence of the problem was not a result of old, mature industries entering decline. It was the very success and dynamism of the new consumer industries that generated the problem. Too much was being produced and it could not all be absorbed by the consumers. The new technology and production techniques were saturating the market and even with the extensive use of credit purchases and all the skills of the advertiser, there was a limit to what could be absorbed in a free-market economy. Production simply outstripped demand. There was bound to be a downturn, as the expanding textile industry in early 19th-century Great Britain found, with its repeated slumps and booms. Usually, the bigger the boom, the bigger the slump, and the boom of the 1920s had been massive.

It is clear that there was insufficient purchasing power in the economy to sustain the growth of the 1920s, particularly in consumer durables, such as cars and radios. By 1927, the majority of those who could afford to buy such goods had done so, and demand began to level off leading to decline. Increased consumer demand had not been universal even in the 1920s. At the end of that decade, 16 million families, approximately 60 per cent of the population, lived below the line which it had been calculated was 'sufficient to supply only basic necessities'.

Source J

Another myth that has grown up about these times is that the Twenties boom was a mere drunken spending spree, bound to end in disaster, and beneath a veneer of prosperity was an abyss of poverty. That is not true. The prosperity was very widespread. It was not universal. In the farming community it was patchy, and it largely eluded certain older industrial communities, such as the New England textile trade. But growth was spectacular. On a 1933–8 index of 100, it was 58 in 1921 and passed 110 in 1929.

The Twenties marked the biggest advance for American women of any decade, before or since. By 1930 there were 10,546,000 women 'gainfully employed' outside the home; the largest number, as before, were in domestic/personal service (3,483,000) but there were now nearly 2 million in clerical work, 1,860,000 in manufacturing and most encouraging of all, 1,226,000 in the professions.

From Paul Johnson, *A History of the American People*, published in 1997

As indicated above, part of the problem lay with the large depressed agricultural sector and most historians agree that this depressed agricultural sector was a factor in the slump. Many historians also choose to stress the uneven share in the prosperity of wages and profits. Wages did not rise fast enough, even in the prosperous parts of the economy, to enable workers to be adequate consumers of the plethora of goods produced.

However other historians stress the very real and widespread prosperity of the 1920s. In other words, the problems of under consumption lay largely in the depressed state of agriculture and the essence of the problem was over-production not under consumption in the urban areas.

However, once the downturn began, the growing unemployment in the new industries added to the problem. The new consumers stopped consuming and thereby threw themselves and others out of work. Unemployment in urban areas was a key sign of economic malaise and its impact on consumer spending was a vital factor in deepening the slump. In 1931, 15.9 per cent of the urban workforce lost their jobs. By 1933, this had risen to 25 per cent and even those in work were victims of declining income, which went down by 32 per cent in terms of what they could buy. For an economy depending so much on consumer spending, this was a dire situation.

Notably, this was seen dramatically in the automobile and electrical manufacturing industries. Their combined sales shrank by over two thirds between 1929 and 1932. The automobile industry provides an instructive case study. Average numbers employed in Detroit fell by over 20 per cent. Ford employed 120,000 workers in the spring of 1929. By late 1931 this had shrunk to 37,000. Ford tried to increase efficiency and meet competition from his great rival General Motors, but no matter how hard he tried, profits were still down. The electrical industry had brought higher standards to people's lives with its fridges, vacuum cleaners and so on, but the consumers had no money for replacements and there was no market of new buyers. The two giants were General Electric and Westinghouse, which originally had symbolised prosperity and enterprise. But General Electric's income fell from $60.5m in 1930 to $14.17m in 1932. Its workforce fell from 88,000 to 41,000.

The decline in the construction industry is often cited as a mirror of the slump. Contracts awarded dropped from $6.6bn in 1929 to $1.3bn in 1932. This had ramifications leading to job losses in the timber industry as well as civil engineering and architecture. By 1931 three quarters of iron and steel workers were on short time. Those out of work or escaping from rural poverty made their way to other cities and sometimes were forced to live in ill-constructed shanty towns as they searched for a livelihood. These were soon dubbed 'Hoovervilles', and provided some of the most poignant images of the Depression.

SKILLS BUILDER

Using Sources H, I and J and your own knowledge, do you agree with the view that the American economy of the 1920s contained the seeds of its own destruction?

Source K

5.2 A 'Hooverville' community in Central Park, New York in 1932

The Great Crash in share values, October 1929

In popular opinion, the Great Depression is often tied closely to 'the Great Crash' in share values that took place in October 1929, yet its importance in the chain of events that produced the great economic downturn is much disputed amongst historians. The drama of October 1929 has entered the collective historical memory of the Western world and much of this is due to an excellent little book written in 1931, entitled *Only Yesterday*. It conjured up the human misery associated with the disaster and gave an impression of widespread involvement.

Definition

Big Bull Market

An *expression* used in share dealing, meaning a period when there are more buyers than sellers and share prices are rising.

Source L

The **Big Bull Market** was dead. Billions of dollars worth of profits – and paper profits – had disappeared. The grocer, the window cleaner, and the seamstress had lost their capital. In every town there were families which had suddenly dropped from showy affluence into debt. Investors who had dreamed of retiring to live on their fortunes now found themselves back once more at the very beginning of the long road to riches. Day by day the newspapers printed the grim reports of suicides.

From Frederick Lewis Allen *Only Yesterday*, published in 1931

Source M

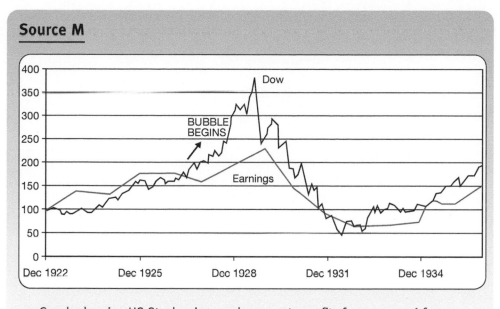

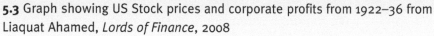

5.3 Graph showing US Stock prices and corporate profits from 1922–36 from Liaquat Ahamed, *Lords of Finance*, 2008

The bubble began in the autumn of 1927. There seemed to be an almost religious belief in the market and anyone who expressed any reservations found themselves being treated as if they were a blasphemer. Investment in the market became increasingly widespread, although anecdotes exaggerate how widespread it was. In reality only a tiny percentage of the population owned shares.

All of this seemed to suggest that the United States had developed into a society in which all shared in the wealth and prosperity generated by the ultimate free market consumer-orientated society. However, the reality was somewhat different. Millions lived below the poverty line and much of the investment by 'ordinary people' was bought '**on the margin**'. When the bubble burst the vulnerability of the whole edifice began to be exposed. There had been a vast amount of unregulated speculation with investors running up huge debts which they assumed would become easily repayable as their stocks rose in value. But the increases in stock prices far outran real economic growth. When confidence snapped and panic selling began, investors anxious to minimise losses sold as fast as possible. This quickened the fall in share prices. Between September and November 1929 industrial stock fell by 50 per cent. This dwarfed any previous panics in the United States. While speculating could bring high returns from stock when the market was in the ascendant, the consequences of the slide were enormous. The lender (often including large banks) called in their money and the market which had appeared to be moving only upwards, collapsed.

Definition

On the margin
This involved buying shares through a stockbroker without putting up the money for their purchase. The broker bought on your behalf and then when the stock rose, sold it, making a profit for the purchaser and money for himself through a commission. The banks charged up to 12% to underwrite the purchase i.e. to guarantee the stockbroker would not lose out. The system worked fine with everyone a winner while share prices were rising.

Definition

Insider dealing

This involved the buying or selling of shares by those privy to crucial information on the company not available to the general public, e.g. it was subject to a takeover bid not yet publicised.

SKILLS BUILDER

How far does Source N explain the Stock Market bubble revealed in Source M?

There were also many examples of exploitation through what would later be termed '**insider dealing**':

Source N

Stock Market geniuses like Michael J. Meehan, armed with investment capital from a variety of individuals, manipulated the hopes of the amateurs; during one week in March 1928, for example, Meehan drove the price of the Radio Corporation of America up from $90 to $109 a share, then quickly sold out, netting the investors a total of $5m and himself a handler's fee of $500,000. The rest of the buyers faced a handsome loss, as RCA's shares dribbled back down to $87 before those not on the inside understood what was happening.

Extract from T. H. Watkins, *The Great Depression*, published 1993

Apparent experts gave the impression that investors could only win. John J. Raskob is the Wall Street mogul most frequently quoted:

'Anyone could be worth $80,000 in 10 years time if they invested $15 a week in the Stock Market.'

Ironically, at the moment these words appeared in a financial journal, Raskob was quietly selling off his own stock.

The collapse required a trigger, and this was provided by the collapse of the financial empire built by the British slot machine king, Clarence Hatry. Many British investors liquidated their stock holdings, including those held in New York. A pattern of selling began to emerge. The immediate dip did not raise general alarm. Indeed, many still felt favourable conditions could and would endure, one pundit Irving Fisher saying: *'The Stock Market has reached a permanently high plateau'.*

There was a feeling that the Big Bull Market would go on forever. However, warning signs were there as in the first two weeks in October when stocks had dipped by 20 per cent. Wednesday 23 October was a turning point when significant slippage in the stock market turned into an avalanche. The next day became known as Black Thursday, as panic hit the markets and the Index fell by 20 per cent in one day's trading. Freak weather conditions added to the uncertainty, but perhaps even held up the market as some sellers were unable to communicate their decisions to sell to their brokers because so many telephone lines were down. Crowds began to gather outside the Exchange Building and the Chief of Police drafted in 600 extra men. A crisis meeting was convened at 23 Wall Street, the headquarters of JP Morgan, perhaps the most established US banking firm. The calming statement, *'There has been a little distress selling'* issued by a Morgan Director, Thomas Lamont, did little to steady nerves. Perhaps more appropriate was the remark of another financial journalist: *'It was like bailing Niagara Falls with a bucket'.* Richard Whitney of JP Morgan showed his intent by purchasing 10,000 shares in US Steel and then repeated the process buying other stocks. Overall, the six banks spent $30m. There was a rally, but the bankers knew it would only be temporary. One of their committee summed it up: '*There is no man or group of men who can buy all the stock the public can sell*'.

Even though a consortium of six big banks had intervened, it is significant that the Federal Reserve Bank did not give a clear lead. They were bitterly divided and 'decisions' they made, including revision of interest rates, were very quickly countermanded. Even the Apostle of Affluence, Treasury Secretary Andrew Mellon, confessed himself uncertain what to do.

The second and decisive crisis hit on Monday 28 October. This came from all directions and J.K. Galbraith, the author of perhaps the most famous book on the crash, entitled *The Great Crash*, characterised it thus:

'*The most devastating day in the history of New York's Stock Market, it may have been the most devastating in the history of Markets*'.

The figures speak for themselves:

- 9 million shares changed hands.
- 14% drop in Market.
- 14 billion dollars wiped off share values.
- By the end of Tuesday 29 the market had shrunk by 50% in just six weeks.

There were proposals to close the Exchange but these were resisted and perhaps this was just as well, because in retrospect many analysts think this would have stored up tension and led to a later and even more dramatic decline. The **Federal Reserve Board** gained resolve largely because of the energy provided by its new Director Frederick Harrison. Harrison managed to coordinate a response from the major New York banks that they would take over a large proportion of brokers' loans to head off another bout of panic selling. Harrison summed up his reasoning: '*Aim to squeeze the froth out and return the Market to fair values*'. Even at this stage there was still debate among financial journalists. The *New York Evening News* still reckoned the underlying situation was sound and that what had been experienced was a mere 'prosperity panic'. However, *Business Week* was not so sanguine:

'*For 6 years, American business has been diverting a substantial part of its attention to the speculation game. It is now clear it has lost.*'

Different viewpoints on the importance of the crash can be gleaned from the following two extracts and Source L, quoted on page 76.

Definition

Federal Reserve Board
A body established under an Act of 1913 to regulate the national banking system. It established a bank for banks with the intention of stabilising them – the Federal Reserve Bank. Its chief instrument of control was varying interest rates. The usual charge against it is that it kept interest rates too low until 1929, thus fuelling the boom in shares and then raised it too much causing a shortage of money and a 'liquidity' crisis, causing many banks to fail and adding to the seriousness of the downturn.

Source O

In itself the stock market crash of October 1929 was not decisive. Share prices had become vastly inflated and were ripe for corrections; in any case only about 1% of the population owned securities in 1929. But millions of Americans had come to see the stock market as a barometer of the economy as a whole; with the future economic climate uncertain, they cut back on more spending and new debts. The result was a massive contraction of the whole economy, but particularly affected were boom industries such as cars and electrical goods and in turn the rubber and steel manufacturers that supplied them. In 1930, spending on consumer durables fell by a catastrophic 20%.

From David Reynolds, *America: Empire of Liberty*, published in 2009

Source P

The average American – a description that in this case encompasses at least 97.5% of the population – owned no stock in 1929. Even indirect ownership of stock must have been minimal in this age before the creation of pension funds gave millions of workers a financial stake in capitalism. Accordingly, the crash in itself had little direct or immediate economic effect on the typical American.

From David M. Kennedy, *Freedom from Fear: The American People in Depression and War 1929–45*, published in 1999

SKILLS BUILDER

Using Sources N, O and P and your own knowledge, do you agree with the view that the Great Crash in share values in October 1929 had very limited impact?

How far were weaknesses in the banking system responsible for the Depression?

The banking system in the United States was fragile in the extreme. Unlike Great Britain, there had not been the consolidation of small local banks into a few giants who could withstand a tempest. The majority of rural banks were small and lacked sufficient reserves to cope with pressure when it came. The lack of regulation before 1933 was astonishing; no federal deposit insurance system existed to provide security and the majority of state banks operated entirely independently. This often led them to use depositors' money for speculation. The management of the banks was often very poor and the granting of unsecured loans for speculative enterprises was a manifestation of the feeling that the United States was in an unending boom. David M. Kennedy, in his magisterial study of the USA in the years 1929–45, emphasises the weaknesses of the banking system in the USA.

Source Q

American banks were rotten even in good times. They failed at a rate of well over 500 per year throughout the 1920s. 1929 saw 659 bank suspensions, a figure easily within the normal range for the decade. 1930 witnessed about the same number of collapses through October. Then with sickening swiftness, six hundred banks closed their doors in the last sixty days of the year, bringing the annual total to 1,352.

Underlying the weakness of the American banking system was the sheer number of banks and the muddled structure that held them together – or failed to. There were some 25,000 banks in 1929, operating under fifty two different regulatory regimes. Many institutions were pitifully undercapitalised.

From David M. Kennedy, *Freedom from Fear: The American People in Depression and War 1929–45*, published 1999

The difficulties of the United States' banking system became enmeshed with the international financial crisis in 1931 and it is a complex combination of US domestic banking weaknesses and international pressures that turned the downturn of 1929–30 into the Great Depression. In this slide into a depression of lengthening misery, the behaviour of the Federal Government had a crucial role. The key institution was the Federal Reserve Bank, which could vary interest rates to control the amounts of money in circulation, and therefore curb speculation – or by lowering them, increase **liquidity** in the system, which was necessary from 1930 onwards. However, the Federal Reserve Bank had inherent weaknesses. The bank itself was based in New York and not Washington, where the Federal Reserve Board that controlled the bank met. In the pre-electronic communication age, the two branches did not always work effectively together and the bank in New York tended to be more detached from the political decision making in Washington. The Federal Reserve Board was essentially made up of private bankers. These men were essentially believers in the system that had created prosperity. It is not, therefore, surprising that they were slow to react to the speculative mania of 1928 and 1929 by curbing the money supply and even more importantly, increasing the money supply from 1930 onwards. Some controversy surrounds their role in the speculative mania of 1927–29 and some critics point up this failure as a contribution to the crash. Their actions to control the frenzied buying proved ineffectual. There were interest rate hikes, but the impact was minimal. Most analysts believe that by the late 1920s, fine tuning interest rates had only a limited effect. Hugh Brogan is highly critical.

Definitions

Liquidity
This refers to the availability of money. Interest rates reflect the dearness or cheapness of money. High interest rates mean dear money: it costs more to borrow and this can lead to a liquidity crisis (i.e. shortage of cash).

Gold Standard
Currencies are given a fixed value in terms of gold for which they can be exchanged. This gives stability and confidence in international trade. The *Gold Standard Act* of 1900 had fixed the dollar at $20.67 per ounce of gold.

Source R

The Federal Reserve Board made a last timid attempt to discourage the gamblers by raising the rate charged for their bank loans by 1%, and by suggesting that anyway FRS banks ought not to lend their clients money for stock market operations. Unfortunately, Charles E. Mitchell, head of the National City Bank and a director of the Federal Reserve Bank in New York, the chief component of the system, was deeply involved in the speculation; he used every ounce of power and influence at his command, and forced the Board to eat its words.

From Hugh Brogan, *The Penguin History of The USA*, published 1989

Others disagree and feel that the mistakes of the Federal Reserve, or the Fed as it was known, lay not so much in the failure to curb the boom but in not reacting to the downturn. Much of this is based on the research and writings of Milton Friedman and Anna Schwartz, to whom reference is made in Source T. During the great stock market boom of 1927–29, the Federal Reserve was primarily concerned with defending the restored international **Gold Standard** and this meant protecting pound sterling by keeping rates low in the US to avoid attracting too much gold from London. Low interest rates had a knock-on effect on the US economy by making money cheap and therefore partly fuelling the boom.

Source S

In perhaps the most important work of American economic history ever published, Milton Friedman and Anna Schwartz argued that it was the Federal Reserve System that bore the primary responsibility for turning the crisis of 1929 into a Great Depression. They did not blame the Fed for the bubble itself, arguing that with Benjamin Strong at the Federal Reserve Bank of New York a reasonable balance had been struck between the international obligation of the united States to maintain the restored gold standard and its domestic obligation to maintain price stability. By sterilising the large gold inflows to the United States (preventing them generating monetary expansion), the Fed may even have prevented the bubble from growing even larger. However after Strong's death from tuberculosis in October 1928, the Federal Reserve Board in Washington came to dominate monetary policy, with disastrous results. First too little was done to counteract the credit contraction caused by banking failures.

From Niall Ferguson, *The Ascent of Money*, published 2008

SKILLS BUILDER

Using Sources Q, R and S and your own knowledge, explain the weaknesses in the US Banking system.

The great crash in share values certainly hit many fragile banks but it did not lead immediately to a complete or widespread collapse. In fact, by the spring of 1930 many felt that the worst was over. Share values were recovering and bank failures lessened. However renewed problems developed at the end of the year. The Fed kept money tight. It made it difficult to borrow by maintaining high interest rates. Banks were forced to call in loans and sell assets to maintain liquidity. Prices of property and shares therefore experienced renewed falls, and in November the Banking crisis deepened. The Bank of Kentucky failed, triggering other bank collapses in the agricultural areas of the mid-West, and then on 11 December 1930 the Bank of the United States in New York City collapsed. It had 400,000 depositors and $286m on deposit. This was a different scale of disaster to anything that had happened before. Nevertheless, once again, by early 1931 many believed that the worst was over. Bank failures declined and President Hoover, like many, expressed optimism. Then a new international dimension came into play.

The international dimension

Hoover, in his memoirs, was later to argue that from 1931 the real heart of the economic crisis was not in the USA but in the international situation, which he largely blamed on the First World War. There were several interlocking problems.

- There were the problems of war debts that Great Britain and France owed to the USA. These involved regular payments to Washington, and weakened both the French and British currencies and the capacity of these countries to buy US goods.

- Germany, the most important economy in Europe, was damaged by reparation payments to Great Britain and France, but until 1928 borrowed heavily from the USA. When US loans dried up, or were called in (in 1929), this had a devastating effect on the German economy, which plunged into recession.

In other ways the whole international trading system had been weakened by the war. Prior to 1914, the pound sterling fixed to gold functioned as a world currency to which other currencies could relate. The weakening of Great Britain in the war removed a key prop, as the following source makes clear.

Source T

The world economic system was unstable unless some country stabilised it, as Britain had done in the nineteenth century and up to 1913. In 1929, the British couldn't, and the United States wouldn't. When every country turned to protect its own interest, the world public interest went down the drain, and with it the private interests of all.

From Charles P. Kindleberger, *The World in Depression, 1929–39*, published 1973

Europe as a market for American goods declined and this was made worse by the US putting tariff barriers still higher in 1930. They had been relatively high throughout the 1920s, in an attempt to protect its own market. Most countries throughout the world followed suit. Even the traditionally free trade British eventually introduced tariffs. The result was that world trade contracted to a devastating extent. In 1929 it had been worth $36 billion, but by 1932 it was $12 billion.

In the spring of 1931 the European banking system appeared close to collapse and the whole world trading system based on the gold standard imploded. The biggest bank in Austria, Kreditanstalt, collapsed in May and this triggered a rash of failures across central Europe and Germany. In September, Great Britain abandoned the gold standard for sterling, effectively **devaluing** the pound. The Fed raised interest rates to stop an outflow of gold from the United States and this had a further depressing effect on an already depressed US economy. Money was now more expensive to borrow. More bank failures followed, with 528 failing in October alone. By the end of the year, 2,294 banks had closed their doors (i.e. they had collapsed). Depositors lost their savings and companies could not borrow. To many it seemed safer to keep money under the mattress. Money, the lifeblood of capitalism was draining from the system. Hoover's raising of taxes in the autumn of 1931 added to the terrible monetary squeeze on the economy.

SKILLS BUILDER

Why was money in short supply in the US economy in 1931?

Definition

Devaluing

Since the pound sterling was no longer tied to gold at a fixed rate, its international value fell in relation to the dollar. In 1925, Great Britain returned to the gold standard at the pre-war value, which gave a dollar parity of $4.76. In September 1931, it fell to $3.60.

The Role of Herbert Hoover

Herbert Hoover has proved a tragic political figure, criticised by both left and right for his handling of the economic crisis. He had been the 'wonder boy' of the two previous Republican administrations. Various measures to address the problems of agriculture referred to in Unit 3 were his work, as was the new regulatory frameworks for air transport and broadcasting.

Biography

Herbert Hoover (1874–1964)

In his origins he was typical of those who backed the Republicans in the 1920s. He was born of Quaker stock into a farming community in the mid-Western state of Iowa. He became a self-made millionaire through his work as a mining engineer, but in his extensive overseas travel, his high intelligence and energy he was very different from his two Republican predecessors. In a sense he was not a politician and this was probably his greatest weakness. He was almost a non-party bureaucrat. He believed, like most Americans, in self-help or as he put it 'rugged individualism'. He worked happily and effectively for the Wilson Administration and headed the relief operation to devastated Europe in the aftermath of the First World War. He was appointed Secretary for Commerce by Harding and held the post under Coolidge who did not really like the 'Wonder Boy'. In contrast to Coolidge, Hoover was a doer who believed in constructive government.

Many in the Republican Party had doubts about his Republican credentials and opposed his selection in 1928 as the successor to Coolidge but his reputation for intelligence, energy and honesty gained him the nomination and he comfortably beat the Democrat Al Smith in the November Presidential election.

Definition

Voluntarism

The use of – or dependence on – voluntary contributions rather than government funds.

This was the first election for public office that Hoover had ever fought. Most Presidents were either senators like Harding, or important State Governors like Wilson and Franklin Roosevelt. Hoover lacked political experience. His promises and self-assurance of 1928 were to seem horribly inappropriate in 1932. Many commentators have identified personal weaknesses in Hoover. There appeared to be a stubborn belief in his own correctness and an inflexible conviction that **voluntarism** would be enough to relieve the situation. He lacked communication skills, especially when compared with F.D. Roosevelt, and William Allen White described him as: '*Constitutionally gloomy. A congenital pessimist*'.

It must be remembered, however, that Hoover did not know, as most Americans did not know, what the scale of the problem was. The last recession, in 1921, had been severe but short-lived, and most people imagined that 1929 would be a repeat performance. It is also important to realise the small scale of the White House staff serving the President and, indeed, the small scale of the Federal Government. Much criticism is made from the left of the political spectrum, that Hoover should have launched more federal initiatives to bring down the rising unemployment. In reality, Federal expenditure in 1929 was only 3 per cent of GNP compared with 20 per cent by the 1990s. State and local government budgets were five times greater than that of the Federal Government in 1929, and therefore it is not surprising that Hoover sought initially to work through local government initiatives.

Furthermore, Hoover did not have effective control over Congress. This was partly a result of his failings as a politician in the arts of wheeling and dealing, but it was also a result of facing an increasingly hostile Congress after the elections of 1930. The Democrats made gains but many on the Republican right disliked Hoover and his initiatives.

Whatever restraints were imposed by his views and Congress, Hoover did recognise there was a real problem and in April 1929 he called a special session of Congress. This was aimed especially at the issues facing the farming community. However, it is important to emphasise that Hoover was not prepared to countenance any form of export subsidies. He did, however, support the development of an *Agricultural Marketing Act* that allocated up to half a billion dollars which could be used to help establish farmer owned cooperatives. The potential of this is recognised by Badger in his 1989 book *The New Deal: The Depression Years 1933–40*, as:

> 'A massive effort by Government which was funded on an unprecedented scale'.

However, despite its good intentions, the measures proved inadequate and the waves of grain imports from countries such as Argentina and Canada drove prices down and further undermined the farming community. This in part lead to Hoover's biggest mistake: the acceptance of the **Hawley Smoot Tariff Act of 1930**. Successions of commentators, at the time and since, have focused on this measure as 'choking off international trade'. The measure resulted from Hoover's inability to deal with a well-organised protectionist lobby in Congress, led by Senator Joseph Grundy. Hoover wanted some protection for agriculture but ended up with a much more protectionist measure than he intended. A prominent banker, Thomas Lamont, said at the time: *I almost went down on my knees to beg Hoover to veto the asinine Tariff measure. That Act intensified economic nationalism all over the world'.*

Hoover tried to mobilise the country behind a programme of economic expansion. He called a conference at the White House and addressed key groups. Leading businessmen were implored to sustain wage rates and maintain levels of employment. Union leaders were asked to foster industrial harmony and encourage their members to spend money. Mayors and governors were told to develop spending programmes on roads, schools, etc. But the reality did not match up to the expectations. By the spring of 1931, wage cuts in key industries were reaching epidemic proportions, as were job losses. For example, US Steel instituted a 10 per cent wage cut and within ten days this meant that 1.7 million workers had less money in their pockets.

The President tried to tackle the banking crisis by establishing the National Credit Corporation in October 1931. A capital fund of 500 million dollars was established and the words of the measure sound familiar to us today: *The aim is to break the liquidity crisis by purchasing dubious assets held by banks on the verge of insolvency. Fears will be checked and depositors reassured'.*

Definition

Hawley Smoot Tariff Act of 1930
This raised duties on a range of farming products and manufactured goods to an average level of 42%. It produced retaliation from other countries and even free-trade Great Britain adopted tariffs in 1931. It contributed to the downward spiral in world trade.

However, the outcome of the measure fell short of the expectation. The revenue available was controlled by a group of ultra-conservative bankers who only spent ten million dollars of the available funding. The banks were not saved and many, especially in the rural mid-West and South collapsed. Bank failures in the year 1931 (see page 82) were running at record levels. Hoover was opposed to direct federal aid to individuals, but the exceptional droughts put this to the test. The crisis in Arkansas, where crops withered in the fields and livestock died from starvation confronted the authorities with a vast social as well as economic problem. This acted as a catalyst and – by introducing the Reconstruction Finance Corporation in January 1932 – Hoover was recognising that voluntarism had not worked. Two billion dollars was made available to rescue banks, trusts, credit unions and other financial institutions. However, there was a clear feeling that most aid went to the larger banks and companies.

Pressure began to build in congress from Senators like Robert La Follette of Wisconsin. La Follette, and his chief ally Senator Wagner, argued for large-scale spending on public works and direct federal grants for unemployment relief. Hoover could not swallow the whole pill but did agree to support proposals for $1.5 billion to be given to States to finance local public works, a positive example being the development of the Boulder Dam project which provided hydro electric power, better flood control and irrigation to the Imperial Valley in Southern California.

But nothing dissuaded Hoover from his central economic belief that a balanced budget was crucial. Increased Federal expenditure, which he increasingly supported, would necessitate a tax rise. Hoover, like most of his contemporaries, believed that increased spending should be paid for by increased taxes. He did not accept deficit financing and neither did Roosevelt. The fact that private borrowing remained stagnant, and that a tax increase would dampen consumer spending, did not weaken Hoover's resolve. On 6 June 1932 the largest peace-time tax rise in US history was introduced.

In general, Hoover is criticised from a left-wing perspective for doing too little too late and clinging to *laissez-faire* attitudes and volunteerism, by simply exhorting individuals or companies to take action.

Source U

However noble Hoover's aspirations the fact remains that his anti-Depression policies failed. The President was eventually forced to abandon his voluntary principles. But in the main, Hoover clung doggedly to his anti-State control policies, often wilfully refusing to acknowledge the extent of the failure of his policies.

From Anthony Badger, *The New Deal*, published 1989

Such views are partly echoed in the essay by Stephen Graubard on Hoover.

Source V

Under the most trying circumstances Hoover failed as a political leader. His domestic policies, lame and limited, gave scant satisfaction to a society reeling from the effects of mass unemployment and huge losses of income and savings. Though he had once boasted a great reputation as a publicist – able to advertise his own accomplishments – he appeared to have lost even that ability. The sheer magnitude of the nation's economic distress made all his accomplishments seem insubstantial.

From Stephen Graubard, *The Presidents*, published 2004

Other historians have emphasised just how much Hoover did do and that in the most difficult circumstances he was a constructive politician.

Source W

Given the constraints under which he laboured, Hoover made impressively aggressive countercyclical use of fiscal policy. Measured against either past or future performance, his accomplishment was remarkable. He nearly doubled federal public works expenditure in three years. Thanks to his prodding, the net stimulating effect of federal, state and local fiscal policy was larger in 1931 than in any subsequent year of the decade.

From David Kennedy, *Freedom From Fear*, published 1999

SKILLS BUILDER

Using Sources U, V and W and your own knowledge, do you agree with the view that Hoover's responses to the Depression were lame and limited?

To his right-wing critics Hoover did too much not too little. His initiatives harmed the morale of big business and his tax increases tightened the monetary squeeze. His other great failure was his inability to control the Federal Reserve System and force it to increase liquidity in the economy by reducing interest rates. Few politicians have been criticised from so many points of view. Perhaps he was simply unlucky.

One of the most politically disastrous developments for Hoover arose from the decision he made towards the end of July 1932. 15,000 First World War veterans had assembled in Washington demanding the payment of a promised bonus scheduled for 1945. They had set up temporary camp in the capital and some of the unemployed had their wives and children with them. Hoover ordered General Douglas MacArthur to clear the camp, but to use restraint. It was a word not known to Macarthur and the following scenes of brutality injured Hoover's reputation beyond repair. The sight of troops so thoroughly routing helpless, unemployed veterans, women and children froze Hoover's uncaring image in ice.

Source X

5.4 The shanty town of the bonus marchers at Anacostia Flats burns after troops have cleared the protestors. In the background the top of the Capitol building, where Congress meets, can be seen.

Combined with his presiding over an unprecedented economic disaster, Hoover's reputation is perhaps irredeemably sullied by the images of the Hoovervilles, and the precipitate, insubordinate acts of McArthur against the Bonus Army Veterans at Anacostia Flats.

Unit summary

What have you learned in this unit?

The sheer complexity of the slump and depression has been presented and you should appreciate the interconnectivity of various strands: the depressed state of agriculture, the presence of declining old industries in the North East, the overproduction in the new consumer industries, which for various reasons could not be absorbed, the weakness of the American banks, the international dimension and the responses of the Federal Government.

What skills have you used in this unit?

It is essential to appreciate the range of explanations of the slump offered by different historians. Some of this is merely a question of emphasis rather than fundamental disagreement. Most agree on the weakness of the US banking system but the role of both the Great Crash of October 1929 and of the responses of the Hoover presidency has attracted much debate and differing interpretations. It is important to understand why historians have come to such widely differing conclusions and it is important to avoid simplistic black and white judgements.

Exam style question

This is the sort of question you will find appearing on the examination paper as a Section B question.

> *'The Great Depression was a government failure'*

How far do you agree with this opinion? Explain your answer using the evidence of sources AA, BB and CC and your own knowledge of the issues relating to the controversy.

Source AA

The world economic system was unstable unless some country stabilised it, as Britain had done in the nineteenth century and up to 1913. In 1929, the British couldn't and the United States wouldn't. When every country turned to protect its own interest the world public interest went down the drain, and with it the private interests of all.

From Charles P. Kindleberger, *The World in Depression 1929–39*, published in 1973

Source BB

The Great Depression was a government failure, brought on principally by Federal Reserve policies that abruptly cut the money supply; unit banking laws that made thousands of banks more vulnerable to failure; Hoover's tariffs, which throttled trade; Hoover's taxes which took unprecedented amounts of money out of people's pockets at the worst possible time and Hoover's other policies which made it more difficult for the economy to recover.

From Jim Powell, *FDR's Folly*, published in 2003

Source CC

The most serious underlying weakness of the economy was that the capacity to produce had outrun the capacity to consume. One reason for this was that a substantial part of the population – farmers, for example, and workers in declining industries like coal and textiles – had not shared in the general prosperity. Another was that income was maldistributed. Profits and dividends had risen faster than wages, while Republican tax policies favoured the wealthy. By 1929, 5% of the population received a third of the income. On the other hand, 71% of the population received incomes of less than $2,500 a year, the minimum generally thought necessary for decent comfort. The mass of the people though better off than before were unable to buy their share of consumer goods and thus sustain the prevailing level of mass production. In addition, the American banking system was inherently unsound.

From Maldwyn A. Jones, *The Limits of Liberty* (second edition), published in 1995

Before you start, please read the advice below.

Exam tips

- *Plan* your answer before you start. You can use the advice about planning and structure which is given at the end of Unit 2 on pages 23–24.
- You will need to *analyse* throughout the response, supporting your arguments with well chosen own knowledge.
- Be very sure you know what '*view*' is being expressed in all three sources.
- You should show that you understand the nature of the *debate* which lies at the heart of the question.
- *Cross-reference* between the sources by focusing on support and challenge.
- Use your *wider knowledge* both to reinforce and to challenge the points derived from the sources
- *Synthesise* the arguments and points presented in the sources into your analysis.
- Present a *substantiated judgement* as to the validity of the stated view and/or any alternatives in the light of your understanding of the issues of interpretation and controversy.

RESEARCH TOPIC

Try to find a copy of *An Oral History of the Great Depression*, written by Studs Terkel, first published in 1970. It is a compilation of first-hand accounts of the impact of the crash and slump on ordinary Americans. Find the two contrasting stories of Arthur A. Robertson, a successful businessman and Oscar Heline, a farmer.

What do the stories of these two men illustrate about the difficulties faced in the Depression?

6 Controversy: The New Deal and its impact

What is this unit about?

This unit offers a survey of the reforms introduced by the Roosevelt Administration to the United States entry into the Second World War at the end of 1941, and seeks to assess the success of these reforms in dealing with the problems created by the relentless slump. It will examine whether they assisted or slowed down recovery and if they provided effective relief. It will also question if the measures transformed the USA in any way and provide an opportunity to consider if the New Deal was a radical departure or a pragmatic series of responses to an intractable crisis. Historians, following on from contemporary commentators, have argued bitterly about all these points and there is a perfectly respectable viewpoint that it was rearmament and then the war that really transformed the USA. This latter point is examined in Unit 8 (pages 141–163).

In this unit you will:

- Examine the nature of the New Deal
- Look at different interpretations of the impact of the New Deal on the US economy and society.

Key questions

- What were Roosevelt's background and beliefs?
- What were the distinctive characteristics of Roosevelt Administration?
- How successful was the New Deal legislation?
- In what ways and to what extent was the USA transformed in this period?

Timeline

1932	Nov	Roosevelt elected by a landslide
1933	Mar	Roosevelt's Inauguration
	Mar–Jun	The Hundred Days
	9 Mar	*Emergency Banking Act*
	12 Mar	President's first 'fireside chat'
	20 Mar	*Economy Act*, making it clear that Roosevelt determined to keep Federal Budget under control
	31 Mar	Civilian Conservation Corps
	19 Apr	United States leaves Gold Standard
	12 May	Federal Emergency Relief Administration
		Agricultural Adjustment Administration

	18 May	Tennessee Valley Authority
	13 Jun	Home Owners Refinancing Act
	16 Jun	Glass Steagall Banking Act
		Farm Credit Act
		National Industrial Recovery Act, which involved:
		– Public Works Administration
		– National Recovery Administration
1934	**Jan**	Farm Mortgaging Refinancing Act
	Feb	Crop Loan Act
	April	Jones–Connally Farm Relief Act
	June	Federal Farm Bankruptcy Act
	Aug	Securities Exchange Commission set up regulating stock market
	Nov	Congressional elections reinforce radical Democrats
1935	**Apr**	Soil Erosion Act
	May	Works Progress Administration established
	May	Rural Electrification Act
	July	Social Security Act
	July	National Labor Relations Act (Wagner Act)
	Aug	Wealth Tax Act
1936	**Feb**	Soil Conservation and Domestic Allotment Act
	Nov	Roosevelt wins second term with a landslide
1937	**April**	Wagner–Steagall Act establishes US Housing Authority
1938	**Feb**	Agricultural Adjustment Act
	Jun	Fair Labor Standards Act – Minimum Wage
	Nov	Federal National Mortgage Association set up (Fannie Mae)
1939	**Sep**	Outbreak of war in Europe – heavy demand from Great Britain and France helps stimulate the US economy
1940		US begins rearmament
1941	**Dec**	Outbreak of war with Japan and Germany

Franklin D. Roosevelt was once described as having a second-rate mind but a first-class personality. In contrast to the serious-minded and gloomy Hoover, he radiated charm, happiness and confidence. Where Hoover had fought poverty and family adversity to make his millions, Roosevelt was born with the proverbial silver spoon in his mouth. He was part of the New York State ruling elite, dating back many generations. The family home was Hyde Park, a large estate and mansion on the Hudson River. He attended the exclusive private school of Groton and then Harvard, the US equivalents of Eton and Oxford. He was not particularly academic, nor interested in theories of government, but loved riding and the sea. Teddy Roosevelt, the charismatic President at the beginning of the 20th century, was a distant relative of Franklin D. Roosevelt who married Teddy's niece Eleanor. Although charming and affable to all and a born political campaigner, in private he was something of a snob and very much a product of the exclusive class into which he was so lucky to be born.

After a brief stint in New York State politics, he was offered the post of Assistant Secretary to the Navy by President Wilson in 1913 and learned the business of Federal Government politics from the inside. His growing popularity with Democratic Politicians earned him a place on the 1920 Presidential Ticket as the Vice Presidential candidate. His rise, so far, had been almost effortless. The Republicans swept to power but Roosevelt had put down a marker for the future. A year later his career seemed in ruins when he was permanently crippled by polio. Thereafter and after years of struggle, he was only able to move with great difficulty and the help of others. The experience toughened him and he was determined to continue his public career. When Al Smith stood as the Democratic candidate in 1928, Roosevelt was elected to replace him as Governor of New York State. Here he began to encounter some of the problems created by the recession. He developed no grand theory in answer, and later a British economist John Maynard Keynes described him as an 'economic illiterate', but Roosevelt was willing to experiment. In contrast to Hoover, who was eventually willing to embrace more and more initiatives, Roosevelt readily accepted the idea of direct government help to provide employment and this was one of the key, and perhaps only, major difference between them in terms of policy. FDR was re-elected as State Governor in 1930 and came to the presidential race of 1932 as a favourite to win the Democratic nomination, which he duly did. In his acceptance speech in Chicago, he pledged himself to create a 'New Deal' for the American people.

The election in November turned into a landslide victory for Roosevelt. Hoover was damned by the treatment of the bonus marchers and the shanty towns of the unemployed named 'Hoovervilles' (see pages 75–76). He never enjoyed campaigning, in contrast to Roosevelt, who thrived in the bustle and bonhomie of electioneering. Roosevelt appeared to have no specific answer to the slump, any more than Hoover had and, like Hoover, he stressed the need for a balanced Federal Budget. Nevertheless, he concentrated on Hoover's negativity and simply exuded charm and happiness. He loved the press and they loved him. Roosevelt carried all but six states in November. Under the existing rules he then had to wait until March to take over. The result was an interim period of drift when the banking crisis assumed new proportions of disaster.

The style and approach of the new administration

F.D. Roosevelt had no fixed ideas or recipe for recovery, nor had he any idea as to what would work. The incoherence of his thinking had been

Discussion Point

Were the differences between Hoover and FD Roosevelt more imagined than real?

Definition

Brains Trust

A group of academics that advised Roosevelt during his campaign in 1932, and he referred to as his 'privy council'. They continued to exercise influence when FDR took office. The New York Times christened it his 'Brains Trust' in September 1933. The founding member was Raymond Moley of Columbia University, and also two others from Columbia, Rexford Tugwell and Adolf A. Berle. Vienna-born Felix Frankfurter, of Harvard Law School, was also important. The ideas of the group often conflicted and they in no way monopolised policy formulation. They were a new feature in American public life and, as such, attracted media attention, which probably exaggerated their influence.

revealed by his approach to the issue of tariffs during the campaign. Half the Democrat Party were for high tariffs and half for low ones. One of his speechwriters asked for guidance on what line to take on the subject. Roosevelt suggested weaving the two contradictory policies together. He tended to vary the message according to where and to whom he was speaking, and this was to be typical of Roosevelt's approach when in power. Politics was everything: consistency did not matter if you could get away with being inconsistent. He was undoubtedly duplicitous, inclined even to lie. By comparison, people were to find his successor Harry S. Truman, refreshingly honest to deal with. Beneath a surface charm and bonhomie was a secretive and ruthless political operator. For example, he used the Federal Tax Department to hound opponents whilst at the same time stifling their enquiries into his friends and supporters like the young Lyndon Baines Johnson of Texas.

Roosevelt was adept at handling the press and appreciated its power. He went out of his way to charm the 125 accredited journalists and held many more press briefings than Hoover did. Initially, he held two press conferences a week. He did away with the need for written questions in advance, but divided information given out into 'attributable', 'background' and 'off the record'. He realised the need to feed the press, to give them something even if the information was often misleading. He also developed a mastery of the radio broadcast or 'fireside chat', getting effectively into the homes of ordinary Americans. He also proved a skilful manipulator of Congress. He was helped by having a Democratic majority to work with, in both the Senate and House of Representatives, but he also understood the black arts of how to achieve legislative success by charming and manipulating Congressmen and Senators with appropriate promises.

Roosevelt was no revolutionary and his aim was simply to preserve American society and capitalism, but he was willing to experiment and try almost anything. He surrounded himself with a **Brains Trust** of academic experts and gave an impression of energy and direction, which gave hope to many. The incoherence, duplication and waste that all historians agree were present in much of the New Deal programme were secondary, in his view, to the need to give hope in a time of despair. Typical of the impression of dynamic action were the spate of initiatives, which became known as 'The Hundred Days'.

Source A

At the heart of the New Deal there was not a philosophy but a temperament. The essence of this temperament was Roosevelt's confidence that even when he was operating in unfamiliar territory he could do no wrong, commit no serious mistakes. From the standpoint of an economic technician this assurance seemed almost mad at times. Hoover had never been able to convey to the masses a clear picture of what he was trying to do; Roosevelt was often able to suggest a clear and forceful line when none in fact existed.

From Richards Hofstadter, *The American Political Tradition*, published 1962

SKILLS BUILDER

In what ways is Source A complimentary about Roosevelt and in what sense is it critical?

Source B

When questioned about his political philosophy Roosevelt, on one famous occasion, replied simply that he was a Christian and a democrat; that was the response of an intelligent but non-intellectual man accustomed to express his ideas in homely metaphor and unadorned phrase. He liked to talk to intellectuals and talk with politicians. The latter understood him: the former were frequently puzzled, including John Maynard Keynes, who was disappointed that a man who seemed to be following Keynsian policies could apparently be economically illiterate. Roosevelt was, moreover, said Keynes, like a 'big fluffy pillow. He bears the imprint of the last person who sat on him'. The President did have an absorbent mind, and ideas came from many sources but sometimes his amiable receptivity was a device consciously developed by a man who had lost the use of his legs. He could not stand to terminate an interview, but he could send his caller on his way believing that his case had been well put.

From D.K. Adams, *Franklin D. Roosevelt and the New Deal*, published 1979

Source C

FDR had a knack of coining or causing others to coin, useful catchy phrases. The term the 'New Deal' was resurrected for his acceptance speech at the Democratic convention by Sam Rosenman. It had been used before, more than once, but FDR made it seem his alone. In his March 1933 inaugural address, he had a splendid line; 'Let me assert my firm belief that the only thing we have to fear is fear itself'. That had a useful impact. And FDR was lucky. A weak recovery, which had been underway during Hoover's last six months, became visible in the spring and was promptly dubbed the 'Roosevelt Market'. Luck is a very important element in political success, and FDR usually had it.

From Paul Johnson, *A History of the American People*, published 1997

SKILLS BUILDER

In what ways do Sources B and C suggest that Roosevelt's most important political asset was in presenting the ideas and words of others?

Biography

John Maynard Keynes 1883–1946

Keynes was an important British economist who established an international reputation, criticising the economic consequences of the Treaty of Versailles in 1919. His great work was *The General Theory of Employment, Interest and Money*, which was published in 1936. He appeared to offer a means of controlling the vagaries of the market by government policy, thereby offering an alternative to the two opposed viewpoints of the period, namely free market capitalism and state socialism. He urged governments to spend more during recessions, not less. This of course meant an unbalanced budget often described as 'deficit financing'.

What was the scale of the crisis?

By 1933, the **GNP** had halved compared to that in 1929. Unemployment had grown to devastating levels, from 4 million in 1930 to 7 million in 1931 and somewhere between 12 and 15 million in early 1933. Possibly 25 per cent of the workforce were out of work and there was no dole money to ease the pain. In some areas charity payments were made, but there was real hunger and signs of malnutrition began to appear. Homeless, unemployed men wandered the country and the cardboard slums on the edge of cities stood as pathetic symbols of how the greatest economy in the world was faring. In rural areas, poor farmers and sharecroppers were not technically unemployed but had hardly any income. The black population – whether sharecroppers, labourers in the South or unemployed ex-factory workers in the North – seemed to bear the brunt of the downturn. Queues of job seekers became a feature of American life, as the following extract makes clear. It also gives an insight into the operation of the political system and the key role of Democratic Party bosses like **T.J. Prendergast** in Kansas City.

Definition

GNP (Gross National Product)

A measure of the total value of goods and services produced in a country and its overseas earnings. Divided by the number of people, GNP will give an approximate indication of the standard of living. It is a useful way of comparing the relative economic importance of different countries.

Discussion Point

How fair was the 'system' used by Tom Prendergast in helping to find work for the unemployed?

Was it really one big scam?

Source D

The lines began gathering before dawn most weekdays, and by mid-morning stretched two or three blocks. TJ saw as many people as possible, on a first come first served basis, no matter who they were, keeping the interviews to a few minutes at most, beginning about nine and ending promptly at noon, when he stopped for lunch. Rarely was anyone sent away feeling empty handed. Invariably courteous, Prendergast would listen attentively, ask a few questions then scrawl a note on a slip of paper requesting somebody somewhere in one or other city or county organisation, or in one of his own enterprises, to consider the needs of the bearer 'and oblige'. These final two words seeming to carry the full weight of his command. Actually, it all depended on which color pencil he used. If the note was written in red, his 'and oblige,' meant the applicant should be given a job, or granted a favour, without delay. If, however, the Big Boss wrote in blue, then this was only someone to keep in mind should anything turn up. If the note was written with an ordinary lead pencil, the bearer was nobody to bother with.

From David Mc Cullough, *Truman*, published 1992

Biography

Tom J. (TJ) Prendergast (1873–1945)

As the colourful boss of the Democratic Party machine in Kansas City, he was one of the most powerful men in the state of Missouri. His support was vital for any aspiring candidate like the young Harry S. Truman who became a senator for Missouri with Prendergast support. He was always known as TJ and his power and wealth came from a series of illegal rackets involving bars, clubs and brothels. Kansas City was one of the liveliest entertainment centres in the USA, even during the bleakest period of the recession.

There were, however, plenty of white workers also suffering. Even the middle classes found their lives devastated. In Chicago teachers were unpaid for a year as the city ran out of money. Thousands of elementary schools, often in rural areas, simply shut down. The bank failures ruined many who had thought themselves well off in 1929. By the time Roosevelt was inaugurated the fresh wave of bank failures had led 32 states to close their banks for 'extended bank holidays' to avoid open collapse. Six other states had closed almost all their banks and another ten had limited withdrawals. In Texas it was $10 a day. Some $7bn of depositors' money had been wiped out. A quarter of a million Americans lost their homes in 1932 alone. This was on top of the 350,000 who had lost homes over the two previous years. Capitalist USA seemed to be approaching meltdown.

The social consequences of slump and depression were deeply troubling, as the brief extract from the biography of Lyndon B. Johnson, Vice President 1960–63 and President 1963–69, by Robert A Caro makes clear.

Source E

'Lost generation' was a phrase occurring with increasing frequency in discussions of American youth. Attendance at the nation's colleges had begun falling in 1931, with more and more parents unable to afford tuition and with students having a steadily more difficult time obtaining part-time jobs to help pay their way. High school attendance had begun falling in 1932 because steadily increasing numbers of teenagers had to drop out and go to work to help support their families, often at a dime an hour – the prevailing Depression wage for teen-age workers.

From Robert A. Caro, *The Years of Lyndon Johnson; The Path To Power*, published 1981

Crime escalated, an index of the rising level of human misery, and the prison population increased by 40 per cent. As David Kennedy puts it 'gloom seeped even into the nation's bedrooms' as marriages and births declined. Some young skilled men sought refuge in the 'socialist paradise' that was Stalin's Russia. An advert placed by the USSR government for 6,000 skilled men to go to work in Russia in 1932, attracted 100,000 applicants. It was true there was no unemployment there, but knowledge of the millions of corpses brought about by forcible collectivisation did not surface in the Western press. Russia appeared to many to enjoy a superior political system to Western capitalist democracies. Others could see the attractions of fascism. Hitler came to power in Germany in January 1933 when democracy seemed to have failed in **Weimar Germany**. Some began to question its continuation in the USA. Roosevelt saw the danger and set out determinedly to preserve democracy within the United States. His words in an early interview are not just political melodramatics; *I will go down in history either as a great American President or the last American President'*.

Definition

Weimar Germany
Term used to describe the new Republican Germany established in 1919. The name comes from the town of Weimar where the new republican Constitution was drafted.

Discussion Point

What did Roosevelt mean by saying he might be the 'last American president'?

Few incoming Presidents had faced such a battery of challenges. Roosevelt would need all his charm and sunny disposition to meet them, but it was a disposition that was tuned to the American psyche, which was naturally optimistic.

Source F

In the United States in 1932–33, when things were worst, unemployment stood at 24% of the labour force of 53.2 million people. It was the sort of challenge which simultaneously brought down the Weimar Republic in Germany, making way for the Nazi dictatorship; but the immense and ancient structure of American party democracy was not to be swept aside in a year or two, however long the breadlines. There were serious disturbances in the mining areas and the farm states, but as a whole the Americans stood fast. As the depression deepened, they did not entirely despair or turn to communism; simply they abandoned President Herbert Hoover and his Republicans, who had shown themselves unable to attack the country's problems effectively, and in 1932 elected Franklin D. Roosevelt to the White House, and a large Democratic majority to Congress.

From Hugh Brogan, *The Oxford History of the Twentieth Century*, published 1998

The Hundred Days

In his inaugural speech Roosevelt asked Congress for a hundred days of total cooperation. This lasted from 19 March to 16 June. During this period, 16 significant measures were put through. Initially, the emergency session of Congress was meant to deal with the banking crisis but Roosevelt rapidly decided to capitalise upon the support and enthusiasm of the new Congress and extend the special session to address some of the other pressing problems facing the nation. These could be summarised as follows:

- **The Banking System and the Markets.** Roosevelt felt re-establishing stability in these was an essential precondition for recovery.

- **Agricultural issues.** Roosevelt knew the importance of rural America and was acutely aware that its problems needed to be tackled. He also felt that agricultural recovery was an essential requirement if the United States economy was to revive generally.

- **Providing jobs in a revived industry.** Roosevelt realised that to ensure the future political, economic and social stability and prosperity of the United States the urban economy had to be revived.

- **Providing relief** for the victims of the slump. Roosevelt knew that society and its political leaders had to take more responsibility for those who were the victims of social and economic distress.

Banking and the markets

Roosevelt was very clear in his 1933 inaugural address to the nation about his views of the financial world:

> *'The rulers of the exchange of mankind's goods have failed through their own stubbornness and incompetence ... There must be supervision of all banking ... and there must be an end to speculation with other people's money.'*

It is clear that the President felt that the bankers and brokers had a major share in the responsibility for the Depression. His words revealed an ability to articulate a popularly held feeling and possibly a personal contempt for the bank's betrayal of financial trust. However, it is equally clear that he had no agenda for radical change. His intention was to overhaul the system and make it work, not to build a new structure based, for instance, on public ownership of the banks. Many were disappointed that Roosevelt was so conservative. There was a feeling on the left of the political spectrum that he should have seized the moment when he had a popular majority behind him (58 per cent of popular vote) and a compliant congress. Senator Cutting of New Mexico made the point:

> *'The nationalisation of the banks could have been accomplished without a word of protest.'*

It is, however, highly debatable whether or not this could have been done, and Roosevelt remained content to strengthen the existing system. On the day following his inauguration, Roosevelt took emergency action using powers granted in the 1917 *Trading with the Enemy Act*. He declared a four-day national bank holiday (in practice, by this time over 32 States had already shut their banks).

It was essential that when the banks reopened, confidence had been restored. Therefore, an *Emergency Banking Act* had been prepared. This relied on the active support of several members of the outgoing Republican Treasury team, notably Treasury Secretary Ogden Mills. The Act also used Hoover's **Reconstruction Finance Corporation** (RFC) to buy stock and, if necessary, to buy up bank debts in order to make the institutions financially sound when they reopened. The legislation also banned the export of gold and suspended dollar convertibility to gold. The Administration then concentrated on sanctioning the reopening of the maximum number of banks. In fact, 70 per cent were able to do so and by the beginning of April one billion dollars had been registered as bank deposits. In other words, savings were moving from under the mattress where they were inert, to entering the financial system again. A vital element of recovery had been achieved.

President Roosevelt played a key part in the recovery the day before the banks reopened. He delivered the first of his 'fireside chats' and struck exactly the right note. His words exuded confidence as he explained the significance of the banking system and stressed the need for a national partnership based on trust to restore first stability then prosperity. The result was a resounding success with deposits far outweighing withdrawals. This was a significant economic boost as well as a sign of the President's rising prestige.

Definition

Reconstruction Finance Corporation

An organisation established in 1932 to dispense federal funds and fight the recession. See Unit 5 (pages 67–90) for more detail.

Definitions

Securities Exchange Commission

Securities Exchange Commission had five members and its task was to administer the *Federal Securities Act* of 1933 and the *Securities Exchange Act* of 1934. It was given strong legal powers to enforce rules on stockbrokers, and in the process stopping the widespread practice of buying shares 'on the margin'.

Underwriting

This banking practice took a percentage of profits in return for guaranteeing that a stockbroker would not lose out on their 'on the margin' trading. The system worked fine with everyone a winner while share prices were rising.

The *Emergency Banking Act* was followed by two further significant banking measures. Under the *Glass–Steagall Act*, ordinary high street banks were no longer allowed to be involved in investment. This was designed to remove conflicts of interest created when commercial banks were allowed to **underwrite** stock. The Federal Deposit Insurance Corporation was also established to provide a system of Federal guarantees of bank deposits. This was an essential instrument in the restoration of financial confidence.

In 1934, tighter regulation was introduced to the Stock Market. The **Securities Exchange Commission** provided control and a much needed framework which tackled speculation by outlawing insider dealing and banning purchasing of shares '**on the margin**'. Its first chairman was Joseph Kennedy, father of the future President. He himself knew all the tricks and had made a fortune in the 1920s. Somebody said at the time that it was rather like putting a fox into a henhouse, but he proved a very effective regulator.

Some felt that Roosevelt should have gone much further in promoting the rationalisation of the banking system by removing the small banks that lay at the heart of the weakness of the American banking system. The problem was not the large banks like JP Morgan, which often attracted the criticism of the ignorant, but the under-funded town and country banks. Roosevelt, however, took a pragmatic line, doing what seemed both popular and at the same time promoted some degree of financial stability, which needed to be re-established as a matter of urgency. The same argument applied to the markets. The following three extracts reflect the debate on Roosevelt's achievement and the missed opportunities.

Source G

On Monday the thirteenth the banks reopened, and the results of Roosevelt's magic with the Congress and the people were immediately apparent. Deposits and gold began to flow back into the banking system. The prolonged banking crisis, acute since at least 1930, with roots reaching back through the 1920s and even into the days of Andrew Jackson (1830s), was at last over.

From David M. Kennedy, *Freedom From Fear*, published 1999

Source H

While breaking up big universal banks, the *Glass–Steagall Act* had no impact on the small unit banks that failed by the thousands. These banks typically didn't engage in corporate underwriting. Incredibly, as George J. Benston noted in his detailed 1995 study of the *Glass–Steagall Act*, the *Glass–Steagall Act* 'did not change the most important weakness of the American banking system – unit banking within states and the prohibition of nationwide banking'. In fact, he says, 'This structure is considered the principal reason for the failure of so many US banks, some 90% of which were unit banks with under $2m of assets'.

From Jim Powell, *FDR's Folly*, published 2003

Source I

In reforming the banks, Roosevelt and the Congress failed to take the opportunity to create a system of branch banking of the sort that protected neighbouring Canada and Britain from an American style banking crisis. And the new deposit insurance system helped keep in business many small banks that should have been rationalised.

From David Reynolds, *America: Empire of Liberty*, published 2009

SKILLS BUILDER

1. Study Source G. Who does Kennedy give credit to for resolving the banking crisis?

2. Examine Source H. To what extent does Powell agree with Kennedy that the banking crisis had been resolved?

3. Using sources G, H and I and your own knowledge, how far do you agree with the view that Roosevelt's reform of the banking system in 1933–34 was marked more by what it failed to do rather than what it achieved?

Definition

On the margin
This involved buying shares through a stockbroker without putting up the money for their purchase. The broker bought on your behalf and then when the stock rose, sold it, making a profit for the purchaser and money for himself through a commission. The banks charged up to 12% to underwrite the purchase i.e. to guarantee the stockbroker would not lose out. The system worked fine with everyone a winner while share prices were rising.

Agriculture

Source J

Farm prices, in steady decline since the Coolidge years, had gone from bad to worse. Eggs that normally sold for 25c a dozen were bringing in 5c. Since 1930, more than 18,000 Missouri farms had been foreclosed. Abandoned houses, their windows boarded, fences falling, dotted the landscape. Sharecroppers were living in two-room, dirt floor shacks, walls insulated with old newspapers. The look of the land and in the faces of farm families in this summer of 1934 was as bleak as in anyone's memory. It was both the worst of the Depression and the year dust storms on the western plains began making headlines.

From David Mc Cullough, *Truman*, published 1992

The agricultural community was of great importance to the United States. Farm workers in the 1930s made up 30 per cent of the workforce and the agricultural associations were past masters at lobbying in Washington. Traditionally, farmers had formed the backbone of the United States. There were growing signs of farmer militancy in 1933 and the spring planting season was rapidly approaching. Roosevelt also had his own reasons for giving agriculture a high priority. He had a genuine interest in conservation and rural affairs, but he also had gained his first significant political support from the rural states of the South and the West. This had helped tip the balance in his battle against Al Smith for the Democratic Nomination in 1932. Politics was never to be treated separately from economics in FDR's mind.

The President believed that tackling the problems of agriculture was central to restoring the United States economy. He felt strongly that a more prosperous farming community would help to stimulate demand and, therefore, industry. The importance of agriculture was paramount but many felt that Roosevelt's methods were misguided and that he approached the issue from the wrong angle. The emphasis, they feel, should have been on stimulating demand for agricultural produce in the urban areas rather than focusing on reducing agricultural production. Critics who held this view felt that the problem was not one of overproduction, but of under-consumption.

Roosevelt was certainly aware of the social issues in the farming areas. Tens of thousands of families had lost, or were in danger of losing, their homes and livelihoods. There was a need to rescue farmers from rock bottom prices and crushing indebtedness. The *Farm Credit Act* began to tackle this issue and loan funds were made available. Government agencies arranged for $100m to be available to re-finance mortgages. The central reform, though, was the *Agricultural Adjustment Act* introduced on 12 May 1933. This made it clear that, in the eyes of the Administration, the key issue was overproduction. The Act subsidised farmers to cut production in order to increase prices and raise income. Farmers owning their own land were paid to take land out of production in certain crops. A subordinate agency set up later in the year, The Commodity Credit Agency, made loans to farmers to store their products and the loans only had to be repaid when a certain price for the crop was reached. The targets would be principally: corn, cotton, milk, pigs, tobacco and wheat. Payment was to be financed by a tax on food processing. This, in turn, would mean the cost being passed on to the consumer.

Both at the time and since, there has been criticism that the interests of the rural poor were neglected and the chief beneficiaries were the large-scale producers. Payments went to the landowner and in the South it was the owners of the big estates who gained, much to the dismay of the radicals in the Agricultural Adjustment Administration (AAA), the body set up to apply the terms of the *Agricultural Adjustment Act*. In particular, the sharecroppers and the migrant workers who were suffering very badly gained little help from the Federal Government. It became clear that the more prosperous members of the rural community had achieved the biggest influence in formulating policies. It was wealthier Southern whites, who dominated the Democrat Party in the South and Roosevelt needed their votes and cooperation in Congress. The leader of the majority party in the Senate was Democratic Senator Joseph Robinson of Arkansas and he was much more important to the President than radical protestors associated with the Southern Tenant Farmers Union or STFU. Roosevelt closed his eyes and ears to complaints from AAA activists against the violent repression of STFU meetings. Jim Powell a recent critic of the New Deal in his book *FDR's Folly* castigates the *Agricultural Adjustment Act* for a lack of social fairness:

> 'The more acres one owned and kept out of production the greater the subsidies. Big farmers got rich whilst the small farmers and sharecroppers became destitute.'

Many critics, then and since, believed that the crisis was being tackled from the wrong end. The problem was not overproduction but under-consumption. If every American family consumed an adequate diet, farmers would need to increase, not curtail, production. A million cotton farmers were paid to plough under some 10 million acres of farmland; 6 million pigs were slaughtered and 12,000 acres of tobacco were ploughed under. In California, peaches were left to rot. Powell quotes the economic correspondent John Flynn, who produced a series of scathing attacks on the economic policies of Roosevelt:

> 'We had men burning oats when we were importing oats, killing pigs when we were increasing our imports of lard.'

It seemed a classic example of the incoherence of much of the New Deal legislation.

The AAA did, of course, succeed in raising farm prices for the landowners but most others were worse off, particularly the millions of unemployed industrial workers, who now had to pay more for their food, but that would not be the concern of the Department of Agriculture.

SKILLS BUILDER

1. How was reducing agricultural production supposed to help farmers?
2. How far do you agree with Powell that reducing agricultural production did nothing to help those farmers struggling with economic hardship?

The reforms were produced in emergency conditions where farmers faced a desperate plight. There was a lack of any national administrative apparatus and even at its height, the AAA never employed more than 3,000 people. The production control programme was designed to work in the short term, to enable desperate farmers to stay on the land. It is understandable, but it does illustrate a common issue with many aspects of the New Deal: a lack of coherent, overall thinking about the needs of the United States economy and society as a whole. The implementation was difficult, as no bureaucratic structure existed and the Administration needed to gain the cooperation of farmers. The hierarchical local structures meant sharecroppers and tenants, especially African Americans, would not necessarily be protected.

Another short-term measure in 1933 to pacify the farmers was the devaluation of the dollar to encourage exports and raise commodity prices. This was achieved by going off the gold standard and then forcing up the price of gold by the Federal Government buying it in large quantities. This was popular with militant farmer's organisations, although the long–term effects were probably negligible on farm prices. It was a typical FDR political initiative. Roosevelt defended it with the words '*We would have had an agrarian revolution in the country if we had not re-priced gold*'. One of Roosevelt's leading Brains Trust experts, Felix Frankfurter, thought it childish in economic terms but it was probably a political masterstroke in diffusing tension.

A much greater value to farmers in real terms was the Farm Credit Administration, which administered loans, and, with the passing of the *Farm Mortgage Refinancing Act* in January 1934, many farmers were helped with their debts by rescheduling them and avoiding foreclosures on indebted farms. The Tennessee Valley Authority (TVA) also helped many farming communities across the south-east of the USA by improving flood controls and providing cheap electricity (see page 109). Various measures did follow to help agriculture after 1933, not least the *Rural Electrification Act* of 1935, which aimed to provide electric power throughout the country. The Rural Electrification Agency provided low interest loans to rural cooperatives. These helped fund the coming of electricity to the more remote areas in which the big power companies had no interest. It also provided valuable lessons in cooperation and in the development of local democracy. People began to sense a purpose in contributing to local affairs. By 1939, 25 per cent of farming families were enjoying the benefit of electric power instead of the 20 per cent in 1933. By 1949, it was over 90 per cent.

Further problems and solutions

New problems afflicted farming between 1933 and 1937 when drought and dry windstorms produced widespread soil erosion in Oklahoma, Kansas, northern Texas and eastern Colorado, an area named the 'dust bowl' by one reporter. The problem partly arose from attempts to increase acreage in the previous decades by removing hedges and trees, the natural obstacles to erosion. Up to 300,000 farmers simply decamped to the Pacific coast. The Federal Government responded with various initiatives to combat soil erosion and heighten conservation awareness. The *Soil Erosion Act* was passed in 1935 and the *Soil Conservation Act* in 1936. Farmers were paid for planting soil conserving grasses and legumes, thereby reducing the acreage of crops whose output were seen as too great. Once again the chief gainers tended to be the big producers, who were the chief recipients of Federal funds.

Longer-term planning often proved difficult because it did not sufficiently engage the farming interest. There was no pretence at solving the problem of how urban America could afford to buy what American farmers could produce. The spread of electrification in the farming communities did, however, increase the demand for consumer goods from the industrial areas and as prosperity slowly returned there, the capacity to purchase more agricultural products improved. The removal of Prohibition partly helped farming by increasing the demand for malt and enabling the wine industry of the Pacific Coast to develop. As with so much of the New Deal, the attempts to help agriculture were many and often confused but did eventually produce positive results, with rising farm incomes. By 1936 farm prices had risen by 66 per cent and farm income by 50 per cent. However, in that year, the Supreme Court declared the AAA unconstitutional (see Unit 7 page 137). The result was that a new, somewhat modified, Act was passed by Congress in 1938 which was to provide support to farmers by price support, brought about by fixed marketing quotas and allotted acreage.

Source K

The price of farm products began to rise, falteringly at first, from their low point in 1932, and had nearly doubled by 1937; and those farmers who weathered the storm began to prosper again, assisted by a flood of new programmes out of Washington – conservation programmes, electrification programmes, resettlement programmes. A divided Supreme Court, in one of the worst decisions in its history, struck down the original *Agricultural Act* in January 1936 (US v Butler et al), but the essential parts were quickly re-enacted under the guise of a soil conservation law, and in 1938 the farm programme was put on a permanent footing by a new *AAA*. Washington having literally set its hand to the plough, would not look back.

From Hugh Brogan, *The Penguin History of the USA*, published 1999 (second edition)

The New Deal often led to a terrible waste of food in a time of scarcity, and it had a tendency to reward and favour the better-off farmers leading some to question its usefulness.

Source L

Despite all these programmes, the farm foreclosure rate remained high during the Great Depression, according to economist Lee Alston. He calculated that in 1931, 18.7 out of every 1,000 farms went into foreclosure. The foreclosure rate went up to 38.8 in 1933, but by 1937, it was only down to 18.1. Ever since the end of the US agricultural boom during World War I, there had been too many American farmers and this was still the case in the late 1930s. Until more farmers decided to pursue some other business, low farm income and high foreclosure rates seemed sure to persist.

From Jim Powell, *FDR's Folly*, published 2003

SKILLS BUILDER

Read Source K.

What is Brogan's view of the whole New Deal approach to farming?

SKILLS BUILDER

1. What is Powell's view of the New Deal's approach to farming in Source L. How does this differ from Brogan's?

2. Using Sources J, K and L and your own knowledge, how far do you agree with the view that the New Deal was essentially successful in dealing with the problems associated with agriculture?

Putting America back to work: recovery and relief

Roosevelt's policies to 'put America back to work' were heralded in his inaugural speech, but aroused controversy and wide differences of opinion. It is important to be aware of the context in which the policies were developed and the constraints under which he operated. The economy had been shattered in the slump. Roosevelt felt that in order to facilitate recovery he required the active cooperation of the business community, just as in the agriculture measures the administration sought the support of the wealthier farmers. The logic of this view is clear, but it did leave the government vulnerable to the charge that many of the proposals reflected vested interests. Ray Moley, a member of the Brains Trust explained the point very clearly:

> 'Large concentrations of economic power were inevitable; they were the product of economic efficiency; to break them up by anti-trust measures would be futile and retrogressive.'

Roosevelt was determined to save the American system of capitalism, not to replace it with something else. He was also conservative when it came to government spending. On the 10 March 1933, in the first week of his Presidency, he made his views clear:

> 'Too often liberal governments have been wrecked on the rocks of loose fiscal policy.'

His choice of Lewis Douglas as Budget Secretary indicated the President's determination to exercise control of spending and it was made clear that the budget deficit of 4.6 per cent of GNP in Hoover's final year was not acceptable. Clearly the Roosevelt administration had no intention of embarking on a spending bonanza.

There was, however, a feeling that the scale of the election victory (57 per cent of the popular vote) gave Roosevelt both the opportunity and responsibility to introduce fundamental change, and that Roosevelt was in office to curb the power of 'big ownership' and ensure a more just distribution of the national income. The words of his inaugural speech seemed to suggest that he felt the United States had been let down by the established financial and business communities. Many, therefore, expected action on this front. The central question was much clearer than the answer. Was recovery going to be achieved by maintaining the principles of the Free Market or was massive state intervention required? Even the business community was divided on this issue with some calling for massive State investment and others demanding that Central Government reduce its role to allow the economy the freedom to recover.

In March 1933 Roosevelt's Administration debated these issues but they did not have the time to weigh everything up and, even if they had, it is difficult to see how an effective consensus could have been arrived at. Roosevelt had to act and members of congress had ratcheted up the pressure by proposing a 30-hour working week and job sharing to combat unemployment. Roosevelt was against their proposals as he felt it could reduce purchasing power still further. Roosevelt's answer was to charge his advisors to come up with immediate proposals. Not surprisingly these measures showed signs of the haste with which they were produced.

Proposed measures

Reformers believed that proper recovery depended on healthy competition and that the development of cartels and large corporations would lead to dominance of the market and, before long, exploitation and higher prices. On the other hand, jobs were needed immediately and large-scale recovery would depend on Roosevelt and his advisors working with the business community. The President took a pragmatic line, basically trying anything which might work and have sufficient support in Congress to be carried. The centrepiece of the Administration's efforts was the *National Industrial Recovery Act* (*NIRA*) which established two crucial organizations: the **National Recovery Administration** (NRA) and the Public Works Administration.

The NRA focused on stressing cooperation in the USA's hour of crisis: emphasising that all sections of society could and must work together. The slogan 'we play our part' makes this clear. The NRA had many objectives but central was the desire to restore purchasing power and avoid excessive cut-throat competition. It appeared to give something to everyone, always a potentially dangerous formula. Larger businesses would benefit from the suspension of anti-trust legislation but many, such as Judge Brandeis of the Supreme Court, felt this was a betrayal of the spirit of freedom and competition that should be 'the American way'. Workers would benefit from the right to collective bargaining, enshrined in **Section 7a**, although some argued this led to too much power developing in the large unions who did not always have regard for the individual. Perhaps most significantly codes were established to regulate prices, working conditions and agree minimum wages. The remit of the agency excluded agricultural workers and domestic servants.

The principles sounded fine and were illustrated in a powerful and imaginative advertising campaign. The Blue Eagle badge of the NRA became a symbol of the national effort the administration was demanding. A two-and-a-half-minute propaganda film, with the inimitable gravelly voice of Jimmy Durante extolling the virtues of the NRA, was made and widely distributed. The choice of General Hugh Johnson as head of the NRA fitted in with the intention of the organisation. Johnson had enormous energy and embarked on an evangelical-style campaign, which covered 90 per cent of the nation's industrial capacity. A total of 541 codes were established but, well intentioned as they might be, they began to cause problems. The aim of the codes was to satisfy workers and at the same time guarantee bosses a fair profit, in other words, something for everybody. In practice, it created a muddled bureaucracy with some codes having a damaging effect on initiative and industrial growth. Many employers were delighted when the NRA was struck down by the Supreme Court in a famous case in 1935 (See Unit 7 page 137).

Definitions

National Recovery Administration

This body was created by the *National Industrial Recovery Act* was charged with creating legally binding industry-wide codes regulating wages, prices and competition. 541 codes were drafted.

Section 7a

Section 7a of the *National Industrial Recovery Act* obliged management to engage in good-faith collective bargaining with workers. It was therefore designed to assist trade union power and was much resented by some employers.

Source M

6.1 The Blue Eagle of the NRA. Henry Ford referred to this as 'Roosevelt's buzzard'.

Source N

The end of NRA was certainly not the only factor in the recovery that began in the summer of 1935, but it is beyond argument that the most sustained period of economic advance under the New Deal took place in the two years after the Blue Eagle was laid to rest.

From Richards Hofstadter, *The American Political Tradition*, published 1962

The Public Works Administration formed the second arm of the NRA. The fact that two agencies, with two very different administrators, were set up suggests a lack of coherence, which many commentators felt then and since was one of the central weaknesses of the New Deal. The PWA was established in an atmosphere of crisis. It was well funded, with $3.3bn made available, but its record is regarded as mixed. The objective was simple; the execution far more complex. The administration was to provide funding for public works schemes, which would make a significant contribution to economic and social recovery. These schemes would involve road building, construction of dams, hospitals and schools. This would improve the infrastructure of the United States, boost the construction industry and put money into workers' pockets.

Roosevelt's choice of administrator is very interesting and significant. He rejected any thought of Hugh Johnson combining his responsibility for the NRA, with running the PWA as well. Instead, he appointed his Secretary of the Interior, Harold Ickes. Ickes was austere and incorruptible with a highly developed sense of responsibility over the spending of public money. He did not court headlines and authorised the spending of only

$110m in the first six months. He demanded value for money and recognised that worthwhile projects would often have a long 'lead in' time and that is was essential that schemes were properly planned, assessed and costed if they were to produce appropriate results.

The PWA, after its cautious start, began to develop significantly with Ickes emphasising the importance of carefully budgeted, realistic and value for money projects. Eventually it funded some 34,000 major construction schemes, employing tens of thousands of workers. One of their most high profile projects being the construction of the Triborough Bridge in New York.

Source O

Title 11 of the Act authorised an appropriation of $3.3b for the creation of public works projects. These were run by a Public Works Administration under the direction of the Secretary of the Interior, Harold Ickes, a crusty old progressive from Chicago. Under Ickes' careful management the pump priming activities of PWA were slow to get off the ground and later in the year the Civil Works Administration was created to provide work on short term projects that could be quickly implemented.

From D.K. Adams, *Franklin D Roosevelt and the New Deal*, published 1979

Perhaps the most famous of relief initiatives was the Tennessee Valley Authority (TVA), which was meant to be an example to be followed by seven other similar schemes all aimed at regenerating areas facing considerable social and economic distress. All the other projects floundered in Congress but the TVA took off and provides a revealing study of Roosevelt and his advisors working in harness with some very committed individuals. The scheme had its origins in a similar project developed during the First World War. The Republican Administrations had no time for it but Senator George Norris, a remarkable personality, would not let it go. Norris found in President Roosevelt someone with a personal commitment to conservation and a strong believer in the potential of public power resources to regenerate a region. They were both aware that the lack of electricity inhibited the mechanisation and diversification of agriculture in the Tennessee Valley region. The scheme had linked targets:

- 20 dams would be constructed to provide irrigation, flood control and electricity, (**The Great Dams**)
- agriculture would be transformed with the use of fertilizers, which would be manufactured in the region.

This project was only possible because of an injection of Federal funding and, although there was some opposition because of the **States Rights issue**, it transformed the region. Only 2 per cent of properties had electricity in 1932. By 1945 this had risen to 75 per cent. Average incomes in the area went up by 200 per cent between 1929 and 1949.

Definitions

States Rights issue
This is the ongoing theme In US history from the inception of the Constitution. It concerns the relationship of the individual states to the Federal Government in Washington. The high point of the debate was of course the American Civil War of 1861–65.

The Great Dams
A series of dams built across the great rivers in the USA. They became symbols of American development and it is interesting that Alfred Hitchcock's wish to have his gang of saboteurs blow one up in the 1941 film *Saboteur* was quickly vetoed by the producers. Even critics of the New Deal, like Paul Johnson, tend to be complimentary about the TVA.

SKILLS BUILDER

How far does the success of the TVA, described in Source P, indicate that the thinking behind the New Deal was correct?

Source P

The Wilson Dam was used to provide vast quantities of cheap power to the fury of private sources, which had traditionally overcharged. The TVA rate was $2 to $2.75 a Kw-hour against a national average of $5.5. This began the industrial and agricultural transformation of a huge area. It was also a spectacular piece of engineering – the flood control system is so well designed that the turbulent Tennessee River can be shut off instantly like a tap. The project thus received intense national and international coverage, all of it favourable, which persuaded many that state-capitalism worked and that it was all FDR's idea.

From Paul Johnson, *A History of the American People*, published 1997

The Civilian Conservation Corps was very close to Roosevelt's heart. Cynics might say that his regular visits to CCC camps were perfect photo opportunities but there is no doubt that the President was genuinely proud of this initiative. The basic idea was very simple. Young men between the ages of 17 and 24 (later 28) were recruited to work in national forests and parks and get involved in a range of projects such as:

- reforesting denuded slopes
- cutting breaks to prevent fires
- building roads
- working in soil conservation
- taking part in irrigation and flood control schemes.

By 1935 over half a million men were enrolled in over 2,000 camps. They were paid 30 dollars a month, of which 25 dollars was sent back to their families and they lived a hearty life under military-style discipline.

Opponents of the scheme declared that it was a ruse, and that money was being wasted on temporary jobs, which generally only lasted six months. Supporters of the scheme, including the future President Johnson who had some involvement in running a camp in Texas, said it gave the young men a great experience, which helped to instill discipline, teamwork and above all a sense of purpose. Roosevelt, as we have discussed already, was alarmed at the prospect of young men going straight from college to the breadline and was convinced that the CCC was not a government handout. The young men had to work hard for their measure of relief.

The *Federal Emergency Relief Act* (*FERA*) was introduced in May 1933. Roosevelt put Harry Hopkins, who had administered his relief programme in New York State, in charge. Hopkins was allocated a budget of $500m and the intention was to provide help for the unemployed. The relief would involve half of the federal fund being spent directly, and the remaining $250m on the basis of one dollar for every three spent by a particular State. The majority of States cooperated and a vast number of projects got underway, especially in the construction industry.

However, there were some State Governors who objected to what was being done, Governor Talmadge of Georgia being especially vitriolic, who suggested that a dose of castor oil would be more appropriate medicine than a handout. Overall, the most significant contribution of *FERA* was that it established that central government recognised that it should take responsibility for social welfare and try to work in partnership with the states. The agency faced an overwhelming case load, which often led to unfavourable news coverage, again a study of Time magazine editions illustrates this clearly, but real progress was made, not least in the focus in many States on the issue of adult literacy.

The Civil Works Administration (CWA) was, like so much of the New Deal, introduced in a hurry to supplement the other agencies. The relief agencies were making some progress, but there was real apprehension, as the winter of 1933 approached, that not enough had been done and this would be exposed by the suffering that harsh weather conditions would bring. This agency was initially set up in November 1933 to create jobs for this winter period and had an initial budget of $400m but it soon went way beyond this. Within six weeks, it was spending more than $200m a month and Budget Director Lewis Douglas was beginning to alert the President about his concerns.

The Agency certainly put people to work but there was the feeling that a significant proportion of the posts created were, what was derisively termed, 'boondoggles'. In other words, they had no purpose. This criticism particularly antagonised Harold Ickes at the Public Works Administration. The CWA was used by many opponents of Roosevelt as evidence that his initiatives lacked coherence and an overall strategy. To a large extent this argument can be sustained but it needs to be decided whether the positives outweighed the negatives or vice versa. Roosevelt himself was worried that its vast expenditure would become permanent and prevent real recovery, so it was wound up in March 1934.

After two years of the New Deal there were serious concerns that it was not fundamentally working, that it had brought about some improvement but real recovery still was a long way off, as the following extract makes clear.

Source Q

Between 1933 and 1934, as a result of the New Deal, national income rose by one quarter, unemployment dropped by 2 million, and factory wages rose. Still national income was only slightly more than half of what it had been in 1929, 10 million workers were without jobs, and almost twice that many people were at least partially dependent on relief. Furthermore the recovery was stalled. Secretary of the Treasury, Henry Morgenthau, Jr. frankly admitted that 'we are not making any headway'.

From The American Social History Project, *Who Built America?* Volume II, published 1992

SKILLS BUILDER

Using Sources N, P and Q and your own knowledge, how far do you agree with the view that the New Deal in its first two years was marked more by failure than success?

A new measure appeared in April 1935, the *Emergency Relief Appropriation Act*. It added a new body, the Works Progress Administration (WPA) to existing agencies like the CCC and PWA. It was placed under Harry Hopkins who had managed the CWA until it was terminated in March 1934. The WPA was, for a time, the chief conduit for relief. Part was spent directly on federal projects and part through grants to the states. It was carefully allocated in order to strengthen the local Democratic Party machines, like that of Tom Prendergast in Kansas City. Hopkins' philosophy was very clear and he seemed, despite often chronic ill health, to have unbounded enthusiasm. He was sharp witted and noted for his vulgar profanities when provoked, which was fairly frequently. However, Hopkins had a very traditional attitude to the implementation of relief:

> '*Give a man dole and you sink his body and destroy his spirit. Give him a job and pay him and you save both his body and his spirit.*'

He was granted a budget of $4bn and began to allocate it with relish. By 1943 he had spent over $11bn on war relief employing 8 million Americans. In seven years WPA was responsible for 2,500 hospitals, 6,000 schools and 570,000 miles of roads. Over two million people were employed on WPA schemes within six months, and the achievements over the length of its existence were massive. For instance, 1,000 airfields were constructed and 8,000 schools either built or renovated. However, the schemes only employed one third of those who needed work and deliberately offered lower wages than the private sector, because they were primarily relief schemes. The range of initiatives that Hopkins fostered is, however, very impressive and often imaginative. Agencies were established, for example, for the arts and for writers. The theatre it encouraged helped develop the talent, for instance, of Orson Wells. The music agencies were also highly successful, sponsoring 38 symphony orchestras. It had had a Negro division, inspired by the black rights activist, Mary McLeod Bethune. The First Lady, Eleanor Roosevelt, relished her involvement with these schemes.

The *Emergency Relief Appropriation Act* (1935) also led to the setting up of other relief agencies amongst them the Resettlement Agency. This was set up with a dream of creating garden cities to provide a different life for the poor. However, only three of these were established and even these were not on the scale envisaged. The agency also loaned funds to smaller farmers and, again, had great plans to provide a fresh start but, due mainly to budgetary cutbacks in 1938, only 4,441 families resettled.

Relief related to housing

The administration introduced the Home Owners Refinancing Corporation (1933) and offered lower rates of interest over an extended borrowing period. Many wrote to Roosevelt at the White House thanking him for saving their homes. The Federal Housing Administration (1934) offered government backed insurance on long-term mortgages. This helped many families and also gave a necessary boost to the construction industry.

A small gesture was made towards public housing programmes in the *Wagner-Steagall National Housing Act* of 1937. In 1938 The Federal National Mortgage Association, generally known as Fannie Mae was established. Its role was to ease the trade in mortgages across the whole country, and make possible shifts in capital from one area to another that the generally small and local savings and loan societies (called building societies in Great Britain) could not do. However, the verdict on these measures is not universally positive. Many felt that white Americans living in the suburbs were the main beneficiaries, while the low income or unemployed of the inner cities, often members of ethnic minorities, did not benefit. Nevertheless, its importance to the future shape of the United States should not be underestimated. It massively boosted home ownership over the following thirty years, as the following source makes clear.

Source R

In the flood of acronyms the New Deal produced, it is easy to miss the fact that its most successful and enduring component was the new deal it offered with respect to housing. By radically increasing the opportunity for Americans to own their own homes, the Roosevelt administration pioneered the idea of a property owning democracy. It proved to be the perfect antidote to red revolution.

From Niall Ferguson, *The Ascent of Money*, published 2008

SKILLS BUILDER

How far do you agree with Niall Ferguson, in Source R, that the most successful part of the New Deal was what it offered in respect to housing?

Discussion point

Read Source S.

Can you find any inconsistencies in what Roosevelt was saying?

Was there a second New Deal 1935–38?

Many writers like the eminent New Deal historian Arthur Schlesinger Jr., believed that there was a second New Deal with a distinct identity. It consisted of a radical programme of reform hinted at by the President in his January 1935 State of the Union address:

Source S

We find our population suffering from old inequalities, little changed by past sporadic remedies. In spite of our efforts and in spite of our talk we have not weeded out the over-privileged and we have not effectively lifted up the under-privileged. Both of these manifestations of injustice have retarded happiness. No wise man has any intention of destroying what is known as the 'profit motive', because by the profit motive we mean the right by work to earn a decent livelihood for ourselves and our families. We have, however, a clear mandate from the people, that Americans must forswear that conception of the acquisition of wealth, which, through excessive profits, creates undue private power over private affairs and, to our misfortune, over public affairs as well. In building toward this end we do not destroy ambition, nor do we seek to divide our wealth into equal shares on stated occasions. We continue to recognize the greater ability of some to earn more than others. But we do assert that the ambition of the individual to obtain for him and his a proper security, a reasonable leisure, and a decent living throughout life is an ambition to be preferred to the appetite for great wealth and great power.

From Roosevelt's State of the Union Address, January 1935

More recent analysts like David Kennedy, have begun to blur the distinction and put the changes of 1935 into a broader context. They have also indicated a degree of continuity in Roosevelt's approach. He was still an ardent supporter of the balanced budget and concerned with making the American way work rather than charting a new direction. Equally there was still a lack of coherence about the reforms as they often reflected the attitudes and personalities of the very varied members of Roosevelt's team. The cautious approach of Harold Ickes as head of the PWA was very different to the full throttle bustle of Harry Hopkins at the WPA.

As always, Roosevelt was a responsive politician sensitive to shifting pressures and moods. Various factors had come together to spark new initiatives. The Democratic victories in the mid-term elections in 1934 strengthened the activist/radical wing of the Democratic Party leading to a demand for more reform. A host of new Democratic congressmen were eager to make their mark. On the other hand there was a solid group of conservative Democrats from the South East who could not be ignored. Roosevelt was to prove a past master at maneuvering between the two groups. There was the impact of what have been described as 'nostrum peddling demagogues' (see Unit 7 pages 133–135). Roosevelt became increasingly concerned about the views expressed by, and the support building up for, Huey Long, the Senator for Louisiana and a possible challenger for the nomination for the 1936 election.

Other critics from what might be broadly described as a left-wing perspective were Father Coughlin and Dr Townsend. These are all dealt with more fully in Unit 7. The President was a shrewd enough politician to recognise that there was a potential challenge to his re-election chances. Polls suggested that Long, even as the third Party candidate could well have an impact on the Democratic vote for Roosevelt in November 1936. In short, the President needed to 'steal their thunder'. The following extract points up a crucial meeting involving most of the great and the good of the New Deal – progressive Senators like Norris and La Follette, Wallace and Ickes, members of Roosevelt's cabinet and members of his Brains Trust, like Niles and Frankfurter.

SKILLS BUILDER

In your judgement, do Sources S and T indicate that there was or was not a second New Deal?

Source T

On the evening of May 14th 1935, The President met in the White House with Senators Borah, Costigen, Johnson, La Follette, Norris, and Wheeler, as well as Ickes, Wallace, Frankfurter and Boston think tank director David Niles (who had suggested such a meeting). The senators expressed their concern that the administration seemed to be running out of steam and that Long was making inroads. They generally felt that it would be impossible to placate the business community and urged the President to re-charge The New Deal.

From Conrad Black, *Franklin Delano Roosevelt: Champion of Freedom*, published 2000

The Supreme Court

The reservations of the Supreme Court about the constitutional legitimacy of much New Deal legislation led to some unravelling. The President was forced to recast some of his policies. In particular, there was the need to replace the NRA after the Supreme Court judgement in May 1935 (see Unit 7 page 137). The striking down of the *AAA* by the same body in 1936 added to Roosevelt's sense of outrage with conservative forces. There is also the possibility that Roosevelt was becoming increasingly frustrated with the bankers and the business community, blaming them for the failure of the economy to recover. He began to refer to them as 'economic royalists' even though he denied in one speech that he 'breakfasted on a diet of grilled businessmen'. The President began to speak out against the business community, but it is important to measure words against actions. Roosevelt never lost his underlying conservatism in his stewardship of the national economy. Ray Moley, a key figure amongst Roosevelt's advisors, expressed his concerns about the direction the Administration appeared to be moving at least in its public utterances: *'Class appeal represented a damaging radicalism. This was a smokescreen and covered a rejection of real planning'.*

Table 6.1 Outline of Measures of 1935–38

Date	Act/Organisation	Purpose
April 1935	*Emergency Relief Appropriations Act*	Created Works Progress Administration (WPA) to provide public works for unemployed.
May 1935	*Rural Electrification Act*	To provide low cost loans in order to encourage spreading of electric power to rural America.
June 1935	*National Youth Administration*	Jobs and training for 16 to 25 year-olds. Developed a Negro Bureau.
July 1935	*National Labor Relations Act* (known as the *Wagner Act*)	To guarantee rights of collective bargaining and outlaw anti-union practices.
August 1935	*Revenue Act*	Aimed at a fairer distribution of the tax burden.
August 1935	*Social Security Act*	A programme involving both Federal and some State Government to provide pensions and unemployment benefit.
August 1935	*Public Utility Holding Company Act*	Aimed to restrict power of great holding companies.
August 1937	*Wagner–Steagall Act*	Establishes US Housing Authority.
Feb 1938	*Agricultural Adjustment Act*	A replacement for the previous agricultural subsidy policies that had been declared unconstitutional.
June 1938	*Fair Labor Standards Act*	Introduces a minimum wage.

Moley, writing in the 1950s, felt that Roosevelt had been guilty of political dishonesty: *'Simulating righteous indignation'* without satisfying it, and producing reforms that represented *'a confused compromise'*. This is a significant judgement from one so close to FDR. Whatever the motivation for the new spate of legislation, it is impossible to deny its importance.

Some of the measures dealing with agriculture and relief have already been covered in earlier sections, but the three great measures of 1935, the *National Labor Relations Act*, the *National Revenue Act* and the *Social Security Act* need analysis and assessment.

Labour relations

Labour relations at the beginning of the 1930s were heavily loaded in favour of the employers. Conditions in factories, and other industrial workplaces like the mines and steel mills, were sometimes dictatorial and although some workers were often well paid, notably by the large automobile companies, their rights were severely circumscribed. The initiative for reform did not come from the Administration. Roosevelt was largely a spectator to the work that took place in Congress and in the determination of individual union leaders to change things. A number of congressmen, led by the Democratic senator for New York, Robert F. Wagner, believed fundamental reform of industrial relations was essential. It would provide greater stability and also, by putting a fair wage in people's pockets, help stimulate long-term recovery.

The *National Labor Act* was in part a response to the striking down of the NRA in 1935 by the Supreme Court. The NRA had encouraged the formation and growth of unions under the famous or infamous section 7a (see page 107). Senator Wagner took the opportunity to push through Congress a more radically pro-Union piece of legislation. Roosevelt had been initially half-hearted but the actions of the Supreme Court infuriated him (see Unit 7 pages 137–139) and he decided to back Wagner. The Act created a National Labor Relations Board. The idea was to force employers to recognise trade unions if workers in a plant requested it, and to recognise just one union as the representative of the workers, if indicated by a majority ballot of the workers in a plant or factory. This, in Great Britain, was known as the closed shop. It was and is the subject of some controversy as to its fairness in terms of the freedom of the individual worker who could be compelled to join a union against his will. It gave a powerful boost to the unions who had already grown significantly since 1933 and demonstrated considerable militancy in strikes in 1933–35. There had been a wave of unrest and no fewer than 2,000 strikes throughout the United States. In Minneapolis a four-month strike by truck drivers involved pitched battles in the streets and the declaration of martial law. In 1933 there had been just over two million union members; by 1938 there were almost nine million.

The *Wagner Act* became known as 'Magna Carta of the labour force'. It brought democracy into the workplace by establishing a National Labor

Relations Board, which would supervise free elections on union representation and guarantee the right to collective bargaining. The pattern established by the *Wagner Act* was followed by subsequent legislation. Notably the *Guffey–Snyder Act* of 1937, which brought fairer labour standards to the coal industry and *Fair Labor Standards Act* of 1938, which prohibited child labour, established the forty-hour week and the minimum wage.

What did the Wagner Act do?

- Prohibited companies from firing union members.
- Created the Labor Relation Board which soon developed a reputation as being fair minded in negotiation.
- Empowered the NLRB to conduct secret ballots to determine if workers wanted union representation.
- Strengthened the process of free collective bargaining.

The *Wagner Act* and the later measures did not apply to anyone outside inter-state commerce which meant that large numbers of African Americans, Mexican Americans and women who were concentrated in agriculture service and domestic work were not covered.

Although Roosevelt played a limited part in the forming of this legislation, it brought great benefits to the Administration and provided the basis for a long and fruitful alliance between the Democratic Party and the labour movement. Wagner presented his case skillfully against very powerful opposition from conservative elements in Congress. Wagner argued that achieving better relations and beginning to correct the imbalance between profits and wages would help to achieve growth. The argument that stimulating consumption was essential to recovery was beginning to gain more support.

A group of determined union leaders had emerged in the 1930s. Their goals went beyond improving wages. They wished to provide basic civil liberties for workers, including the right to have union membership accepted. Although they campaigned strongly it is important to stress that they did not have an agenda including revolution. John L. Lewis of the United Mine Workers of America, played a particularly important part in this development. He boosted membership of his Union from 150,000 in 1933 to half a million by 1936. The traditional policy of the American Federation of Labor (AFL) had been to organise workers by craft, but this had led to a vast number of small unions who were often arguing with each other and certainly not presenting a united front to the employers. In 1934 leaders like Lewis began to argue for whole-industry unions. The AFL was reluctant to reform itself but Lewis proved very determined and created the Congress of Industrial Organisation (CIO). Its aim, according to Lewis, was simple:

'To achieve economic freedom and industrial democracy.'

The new unions demanded a fair return for their labour, and a voice in improving working conditions. Lewis was an excellent orator and adept at using the radio. In the mid-1930s it was clear that working men were determined to 'have a voice'. In 1936, the auto workers began to make very effective use of the sit-in. To prevent employers simply bringing in new workers, the employees downed tools but stayed in the factory. In February 1937, General Motors agreed to negotiate and by 1941 even Henry Ford accepted, with extreme reluctance, that organised unions and collective bargaining was here to stay. Employers began to realise that strong unions were not the end of capitalism.

In fact, Lewis himself had feared that the smaller mineworkers union of 1933 was more vulnerable to communist take over than the giant he had created by the late-1930s. There was bitter conflict in the steel industry and in 1937 police fired on striking workers in Chicago killing ten people. However, union membership increased and by 1940 the leaders of the CIO could say: '*We could go to our bosses and talk to them like men rather than slaves*'.

The CIO believed strongly that the Federal Government had a role in fostering better industrial relations. They believed a fairer society would be a more prosperous society. Developments during and after the Second World War began to prove this to be true. The famous photograph below illustrates the bitter, and often violent, conflict that pervaded the industrial scene in the 1930s.

Source U

6.2 Richard T. Frankensteen (second right), organizer for United Auto Workers receiving a savage beating outside Ford Motor Company plant in Dearborn, Michigan, 1937. The incident arose from attempts to unionise Ford's plants and the strong-arm resistance meted out to the union organisers by the Ford Service Department (security).

Some historians are less than enthusiastic about the encouragement of unions and see it as one of the fundamental causes for the persistence of high unemployment.

Discussion Point

Look at Source U.

If union organisers received such beatings, how do you explain the growth in union membership at his time?

Source V

One of the most famous Roosevelt phrases in history, almost as famous as 'fear itself' was Roosevelt's boast that he would promulgate 'bold persistent experimentation'. But Roosevelt's commitment to experimentation itself created fear. And many Americans knew this at the time. In autumn 1937, the New York Times delivered its analysis of the economy's downturn: 'The cause is attributed by some to taxation and alleged federal curbs on industry; by others to the demoralisation caused by strikes.' Both the taxes and the strikes were the result of Roosevelt policy; the strikes had been made possible by the Wagner Act the year before. As scholars have long noted, the high wages generated by New Deal legislation helped those workers who earned them. But the inflexibility of those wages prevented companies from hiring additional workers. Hence the persistent shortage of jobs in the latter part of the 1930s.

From Amity Shlaes, *The Forgotten Man: A New History of The Depression*, published *2007*

A partial welfare state?

The other major measure of what has been characterised as the Second New Deal, was the *Social Security Act*, passed in June 1935. Here was the beginning of a partial welfare state, brought in 30 to 50 years after similar developments in Germany and Great Britain, the two other leading industrial powers in the world. It was funded by contributions from employers and employees and it provided small payments to the aged, the unemployed and dependents of wage earners who had died.

The limitations of the reform were obvious and disappointed many radical reformers. The Federal Government had no financial responsibility. Unemployment insurance was funded by a payroll tax. It is important to emphasise that because of the contributory element payment for pensions would not be forthcoming until 1940. There was no health insurance scheme, because the authorities did not wish to go against existing insurance arrangements. Roosevelt refused to allow direct taxes to fund the measures. They had to be self-financing. There was real concern about the size of the Federal budget and the need to get it under control. He was already concerned at the level of Federal spending and the deficit it was creating. They did not extend to farmers or domestic servants, two groups who had been particular victims of the Depression. The reforms were often delegated to States and this led to variation in arrangements and levels of payment. Some historical commentators choose to emphasise the limitations of the reform.

Source W

Welfare legislation was large in hopes generated but often pitifully small in actual benefits (pensions between 10 and 85 dollars a month, unemployment benefit of a maximum of 18 dollars a week and only for 16 weeks). It hardly represented a social revolution. None of the welfare programmes 'significantly redistributed the wealth of the country'.

From Paul K. Conkin, *The New Deal*, published 1969

However, the reforms should not be brushed aside in an outpouring of cynicism. They did set some important precedents and established the principle of Federal responsibility. Roosevelt had a track record of introducing reforms in New York State and these included old age benefits and unemployment insurance. He had resolved to bring these forward on to the national stage, pushed on by radical critics like Huey Long and Dr Townsend. Some historians see the end result as being a fundamental break with past traditions of individual responsibility.

SKILLS BUILDER

In what ways do sources W and X differ in their assessments of the *Social Security Act* of 1935? What might explain these differences?

Source X

The social security act represented a major step toward the government's responsibility for improving social and economic ills. Government now acknowledged its obligation to provide a minimum standard of economic security for those least able to help themselves: the poor, the sick, the elderly, children and the unemployed. The act represented a fundamental break with traditional elitist notions that blamed the poor and the unemployed for their condition; it became the foundation for a partial welfare state that protected all citizens.

From The American Social History Project, *Who Built America* Vol II, published 1992

Taxation and the Roosevelt recession

In 1935, and again during the election year of 1936, Roosevelt upped the attacks on the super-rich. Roosevelt, like Hoover, was much concerned with over-spending and felt that the Federal budget should be in balance. Neither he nor his advisers had accepted or understood Keynes's ideas of deficit spending to overcome recession. Certainly Federal spending had increased since 1933 but so had taxation, most of it regressive which hit the low income families through indirect taxes rather than the rich through increased direct taxes. Now in 1935, FDR introduced a Wealth Tax Bill, which it was claimed would strike at the rich. There was to be an increase in the corporate tax rate and taxation of large inheritances as well as a new excess profits tax. There were bitter debates in Congress and the original proposals were watered down. The Act, as it finally emerged to gain

Presidential approval, added a modest $250 million to Federal income, not enough to balance the budget but enough to elicit howls of protest from the rich, which was probably Roosevelt's intention. He could appear to be more radical than he really was. In the Presidential election of 1936 he was comfortably re-elected (see Unit 7). As David Kennedy has pointed out, Roosevelt's verbal attacks on the super-rich did not so much add insult to injury as substitute insult for injury.

After Roosevelt's successful re-election in November 1936, there was an increasing concern to reduce the gap between Federal spending and income – and the results were savage cutbacks in spending on relief. The result was a sharp rise in unemployment in 1937–38 and the onset of what has been described as the Roosevelt recession. The stock market collapsed again by 30 per cent in the autumn of 1937 and unemployment rose from six to ten million in the spring of 1938. Many of the hard earned gains of the last four years seemed to be disappearing. The whole New Deal could be portrayed as a failure. The causes of this fresh disaster have been much debated, as with so much to do with the New Deal. Those sympathetic to the New Deal, and on the left of the political spectrum, have tended to see the cause as being simply a result of the Treasury cutting spending too much too soon. The following extract from the British historian Hugh Brogan reflects this point of view.

This viewpoint can be nicely contrasted with that in Source V:

Source Y

The men closest to the President at that moment – Henry Morgenthau, the Secretary of the Treasury, for example – were orthodox financiers and economists who had managed to convince themselves, in the middle of a just barely convalescent economy, that the United States was in serious danger of inflation and that it was essential to balance the federal budget at last. They persuaded their chief, and he began to run down the spending programmes, at just the moment when the new social security taxes were taking large amounts of purchasing power out of the market. The result should have been foreseen: the industrial recovery was cut off suddenly, factories once more began to close and the number of unemployed leaped upwards.

From Hugh Brogan, *The Penguin History of the USA*, 1999 (second edition)

SKILLS BUILDER

1. Compare and contrast the explanations offered in Sources V and Y as to the reasons for the economic downturn in 1937–38.

2. What do the two extracts suggest are the political sympathies of their respective authors?

Curing a sick economy

There is widespread agreement that the New Deal did not cure a sick economy. Clearly at one extreme are those like Amity Shlaes (see Source V in this unit on page 119) and Jim Powell (see Unit 5 Source E on page 70) who hold that Roosevelt's policies actually worked against recovery and prolonged the Depression. But without going this far, mainstream historians of the New Deal often agree with David M. Kennedy who writes in his chapter 'What the New Deal Did': *'It might be well to begin by recognizing what the New Deal did not do, in addition to its conspicuous failure to produce economic recovery'.*

Fiona Venn in her more succinct study writes:

Source Z

The sharp downturn during the Roosevelt recession marred the economic reputation of the New Deal. It was the Second World War, rather than the New Deal itself, which achieved many of the economic goals of the Administration and secured acceptance of government economic management.

From Fiona Venn, *The New Deal*, published 1998

Paul Johnson makes the point more fully:

Source AA

The truth is, the recovery was slow and feeble. The only good year was 1937, when unemployment at 14.3% dipped below 8 million; but by the end of the year the economy was in freefall again – the fastest fall so far recorded – and unemployment was at 19% in 1938. In 1937 production briefly passed 1929 levels but slipped below again. The real recovery came only after the Labor Day weekend of September 1939, when news of the war in Europe plunged the New York Stock Exchange into a joyful confusion which finally wiped out the traces but not the memory of October 1929. Two years later, with America on the brink of war itself, the dollar value of production finally passed the 1929 levels for good.

From Paul Johnson, *A History of the American People*, published 1997

SKILLS BUILDER

How far do Sources Z and AA agree in their assessment of the economic impact of the New Deal?

War in Europe in September 1939 was a boon to US industry. Roosevelt assisted the process by persuading Congress to amend the *Neutrality Act* of 1935, which had banned the sale of arms and munitions to any powers at war. Under new legislation in 1939, Great Britain and France could now buy weapons as long as they transported them in their own ships. Both placed large orders in the USA. By 1940 there were orders for 10,800 aircraft and 13,000 aeroplane engines, amongst many other products. This was a huge stimulus to the US economy, and more was to come as the US began to re-arm itself. In July 1940, Roosevelt signed a bill from Congress vastly increasing the US Navy at a cost of $4 billion. Plans were set in place to produce 50,000 combat planes a year. By October 1940, Congress had voted $17 billion for defense. The outbreak of war itself finally put pay to the Depression absorbing all the unemployed by 1943. The impact of this on US economy and society is more fully detailed in Unit 8 on pages 141–163.

The social impact of the New Deal

One of the most interesting features of the Roosevelt Presidency was the emergence of the First Lady as a personality on the American political scene. Eleanor Roosevelt was a strong-willed character with a very clear set of values. These were perhaps never better illustrated than when she, with the active support of Harold Ickes, the Secretary of the Interior, arranged for the black contralto Marian Anderson to perform a concert in front of the Lincoln memorial at Easter 1939. The singer had previously been denied access to the Constitution Hall by the Daughters of the American Republic. This was a significant and very moving occasion, but it is difficult to resist the conclusion that much of the treatment of race and gender issues in the 1930s was higher on symbolism and promises than it was on the delivery of positive and constructive legislation.

African Americans and the New Deal

The New Deal produced no legislation that explicitly benefited African Americans. Even the Anti-Lynching Bills introduced in 1934 and 1937 got no backing from the President and floundered in Congress. The citizens of Owensboro, Kentucky staged the last public hanging in the United States, where Rainey Bethea had been convicted of killing a young white girl. About 20,000 people attended the execution and it was reported that some had attempted to strip the corpse for souvenirs. It was clear that the relief agencies did not treat African Americans fairly. They were not admitted into the CCC, and the NRA allowed them to be paid less than white people. They had lost out under the *AAA*, which did not really assist sharecroppers and poor tenant farmers, many of whom were black.

Some have put this down to politics. Roosevelt needed the support of the Southern Democrats and he allowed them to influence his actions. As long as white Southern Democrats like Pat Harrison and Joe Robinson ruled the Senate, Roosevelt was not prepared to put other legislation at risk. However, civil rights and racial justice never headed the list of the New Deal's priorities. The United States was still a country in which a black actress, Hattie McDaniel, could win an Oscar for her performance in 'Gone with the Wind' but a few months previously had been denied access to its premiere in Atlanta.

There is little doubt that black voters began to swing to the Democrats in the Northern cities. In 1932, Roosevelt held 4 out of 15 constituencies in the main cities. By 1940 this was all 15. A lot of this is put down to the perception of Roosevelt as a decent man who cared for the little man, whether black or white, and was doing his best. It is also important to register the positive acts of Harry Hopkins and Harold Ickes who both abhorred racism. It is significant that they both worked for the appointment of Mary McLeod Bethune, who proved to be a very effective head of the Negro division of the National Youth Administration.

Source BB

The Administration did not do enough to tackle the historic pattern of bigotry and discrimination, segregation and disenfranchisement, which relegated the blacks to inferior public facilities and stopped them from having a voice.

From M. Parrish, *Anxious Decades: America in Prosperity and Depression*, published 1992

However the criticisms made in Source BB need assessing in the light of the points made in Source CC, before a balanced judgement is made.

Source CC

The New Deal won a huge Negro following and broke the traditional link between black voters and the Republican Party. In 1932 nearly three quarters of blacks had voted Republican: in 1936 over three quarters voted Democratic. This was mainly because of the benefits blacks received from New Deal relief and recovery programmes. By 1935 nearly 30% of all black families were on relief – three times the proportion of whites; by 1939 over a million blacks held WPA jobs; about a third of all federal housing went to blacks; federal funds went into black schools, colleges and hospitals.

From Maldwyn A. Jones, *The Limits of Liberty*, published 1995 (second edition)

American Indians

There were 330,000 American Indians whose prospects had grown increasingly bleak. Readers of Dee Brown's haunting *Bury my Heart at Wounded Knee* will be aware of their extreme suffering in the 19th century. They endured poverty, a low level of educational provision and poor health care. The *Dawes Act* of 1887 had removed the legal rights of the tribes. The Indians were given the vote in 1924 but there seemed to be very little hope of substantive improvements.

John Collier was appointed Commissioner for Indian Affairs in 1933. He had lived among the Pueblo Indians for many years and respected and valued them. He had a vision of restoring tribal life and reviving their spiritual values. He also did much practical work on behalf of the American Indians. He squeezed all he could out of the relief agencies for better schools, hospitals and important irrigation schemes. The CCC recruited 12,000 American Indians. However, there were Native Americans with doubts about Collier's programme, accusing him of planning to transform reservations into living museums and to treat Native Americans as exotic people cut off from modern life. This is, perhaps, a harsh judgement on a very committed and well-intentioned figure. In the end the Administration came up with a compromise in the *Indian Reorganization Act* of 1934. It halted further sales of tribal lands but put the brakes on the grand schemes for cultural revival. Perhaps this was a characteristic example of the pragmatism that many felt was an abiding feature of the New Deal.

Culture and the arts

Reference was made at the beginning of this section to a concert promoted by Eleanor Roosevelt, and music and the arts in general were great beneficiaries of the New Deal as Source DD indicates.

Discussion Point

Do you agree with the view that pragmatism was the one abiding feature of the New Deal?

Source DD

The various artistic and cultural employment programs of the WPA are excellent examples of how relief provided more than employment ... At its peak the Federal Writer's project employed some 6,000 journalists, poets, novelists and PhDs of one sort or another; unknowns worked on the same payroll if not side by side, with John Steinbeck, Vardis Fisher, and Conrad Aitkin. The $46 million expended on art – that is, painting and sculpture – by the WPA in 1936–37 exceeded the artistic budget of any country outside the totalitarian orbit – and there art was frankly propagandistic. ... During the first fifteen months of the Federal Music Project, some fifty million people heard live concerts; in the first year of the WPA Theater, sixty million in thirty states saw performances with weekly attendance running to half a million.

From Carl N. Deglar, *Out of Our Past: The Forces That Shaped Modern America*, published 1959

SKILLS BUILDER

How does Source DD seek to indicate that the scale of the impact of the New Deal on art and culture was enormous?

Whatever the long term effects on culture in the USA, and this is difficult to assess and measure, it did win over to the Democrat party the artistic and intellectual elite who now formed an influential part of the great political coalition that Roosevelt's New Deal had created.

The overall impact of the New Deal

The New Deal left a huge impact on the USA, both in the physical form of dams, buildings, highways and bridges and it also had a massive psychological and political legacy. An impression was created of a dynamic government saving the nation. In Great Britain it came to be widely believed, after the Second World War, that an activist President had rescued the USA from economic catastrophe while cautious Conservative politicians in Great Britain had largely failed. This perception was largely untrue. Great Britain had recovered somewhat better than the USA by 1938. As the section above makes clear, the renewed slump in 1938 hardly justifies claims that recovery had in fact been achieved. It is important to understand what the New Deal did not do. It failed to bring about recovery. It failed to redistribute national income. The relative shares of national wealth were essentially the same in 1940 as in 1930 or even 1920. Although the scale and scope of the Federal Government increased with a significant increase in the number of Federal employees, there was no real challenge to private ownership. No significant state-owned enterprises emerged in New Deal America. Some important groups appeared to be neglected as has been indicated throughout the unit and as Source EE makes clear.

Source EE

Upon black Americans the Depression had a catastrophic effect. In the rural South where most of them lived, blacks were more dependent than whites on cotton, the crop hardest hit by the Depression. New Deal agricultural policies compounded Negro miseries; the AAA in particular displaced many Negro tenants and croppers. New Deal agencies generally discriminated against blacks. The NRA all but excluded them from skilled jobs and adopted discriminatory wage rates; the CCC operated segregated camps; the TVA set up all-white model towns. Roosevelt proved unresponsive to demands for Negro civil rights; unwilling to antagonise the Southern Democrats whose support he needed, he even refused to endorse a federal anti-lynching bill. Nonetheless the New Deal won a huge Negro following and broke the traditional link between black voters and the Republican Party. This was mainly because of the benefits blacks received from New Deal relief and recovery programmes.

From Maldwyn A. Jones, *The Limits of Liberty*, published 1999 (second edition)

Yet, for all its limitations, the impact was enormous:

SKILLS BUILDER

'The New Deal reinforced the American social and economic system by extending security to all.'

How far do you agree with this opinion? Explain your answer using the evidence of sources EE, FF and GG and your own knowledge of the issues relating to the controversy.

Source FF

In the flood of acronyms the New Deal produced, it is easy to miss the fact that its most successful and enduring component was the new deal it offered with respect to housing. By radically increasing the opportunity for Americans to own their own homes, the Roosevelt administration pioneered the idea of a property owning democracy. It proved to be the perfect antidote to red revolution.

From Niall Ferguson, *The Ascent of Money*, published 2008

Even the neglected black Americans gained much in terms of relief and welfare payments and proof of this was the revolution in their voting habits. Traditionally they had been Republican, the party of the North who had freed the slaves. Now increasingly they identified with the Democratic Party of Roosevelt and the New Deal. The New Deal had massively extended security for all groups from bankers to trade unionists and from prosperous farmers to unemployed blacks. The result was the saving of American Democracy as Roosevelt had intended.

Source GG

Above all the New Deal gave to countless Americans who had never had much of it, a sense of security, and with it a sense of having a stake in their country. And it did it all without shredding the American Constitution or sundering the American people. At a time when despair and alienation were prostrating other peoples under the heel of dictatorship, that was no small accomplishment

From David M. Kennedy, *Freedom From Fear: The American People in Depression and War*, published 1999.

Unit summary

What have you learned in this unit?

You have examined many aspects of the New Deal relating initially to the personality and politics of Roosevelt and then the evolution and impact of his policies as they affected banking, farming, relief of the unemployed and the recovery of industry. You have considered the apparent increase in radicalism in 1935, often referred to as the Second New Deal, and its positive and negative impacts. The unit, through many examples, has indicated the range of controversies generated on almost all aspects of the New Deal. Almost all aspects have been vigorously extolled and held up as models of statesmanship and just as vigorously damned as examples of incoherence and incompetence.

What skills have you used in this unit?

You have been asked to assess various secondary sources and to identify the varying interpretations that they represent. You have been invited to compare these interpretations and weigh them in terms of the evidence they produce in the case they attempt to make and also weigh them against your own knowledge, which may either support or contradict the case being made in the source. There is clearly a wide range of interpretations offered resting on the prejudices and political vantage points of the writers and exactly where and when they chose to focus their research.

Exam style question

This is the style of question you will find appearing on the examination paper as a Section B question.

'The New Deal had a very positive impact on the economy and society of the United States.'

How far do you agree with this opinion? Explain your answer using the evidence of sources HH, II and JJ and your own knowledge of the issues relating to the controversy.

Source HH

Upon black Americans the Depression had a catastrophic effect. In the rural South where most of them lived, blacks were more dependent than whites on cotton, the crop hardest hit by the Depression. New Deal agricultural policies compounded Negro miseries; the AAA in particular displaced many Negro tenants and croppers. New Deal agencies generally discriminated against blacks. The NRA all but excluded them from skilled jobs and adopted discriminatory wage rates; the CCC operated segregated camps; the TVA set up all-white model towns. Roosevelt proved unresponsive to demands for Negro civil rights; unwilling to antagonise the Southern Democrats whose support he needed, he even refused to endorse a federal anti-lynching bill

From Maldwyn A. Jones, *The Limits of Liberty*, published 1995 (second edition)

Source II

Yet the New Deal relief programmes were invaluable. They salvaged the lives of tens of millions from utter misery and hopelessness, endowed the country with a vast infrastructure, and re-vitalised much of the environment at bargain cost. Those still unemployed were to be sustained by Social Security and absorbed by eventual general economic recovery.

From Conrad Black, *Franklin Delano Roosevelt: Champion of Freedom*, published 2003

Source JJ

The Wilson Dam was used to provide vast quantities of cheap power to the fury of private sources, which had traditionally overcharged. The TVA rate was $2 to $2.75 a Kw-hour against a national average of $5.5. This began the industrial and agricultural transformation of a huge area. It was also a spectacular piece of engineering – the flood control system is so well designed that the turbulent Tennessee River can be shut off instantly like a tap. The project thus received intense national and international coverage, all of it favourable, which persuaded many that state-capitalism worked and that it was all FDR's idea.

From Paul Johnson, *A History of the American People*, published 1997

Exam tips

- *Plan* your answer before you start. You can use the advice about planning and structure which is given at the end of Unit 2 on pages 23–24.
- You will need to *analyse* throughout the response, supporting your arguments with well chosen own knowledge.
- Be very sure you know what '*view*' is being expressed in all three sources.

You should show that you understand the nature of the *debate* which lies at the heart of the question.

- *Cross-reference* between the sources by focusing on support and challenge.

Use your *wider knowledge* both to reinforce and to challenge the points derived from the sources. The view of Source HH, which is negative as far as the impact of the New Deal on black Americans is concerned, can be challenged by reference to the shift in black American voting habits in favour of the Democrats. Other issues not referred to in the sources can be raised such as culture and the arts.

- *Synthesise* the arguments and points presented in the sources into your analysis.
- Present a *substantiated judgement* as to the validity of the stated view and/or any alternatives in the light of your understanding of the issues of interpretation and controversy.

Source KK

6.3 A poster produced on behalf of the Works Progress Administration (WPA) in 1935.

RESEARCH TOPIC

How effectively do you feel the poster in Source KK captures what the WPA was seeking to achieve?

Find other examples of posters and artwork designed to promote other aspects of the New Deal. What message does each of these posters try to get across?

7 Opposition to Roosevelt and the New Deal

What is this unit about?

This unit offers a study of the opposition to the reforms introduced by the Roosevelt Administration to the end of 1941, when the United States entered the Second World War. It seeks to assess their impact in the shaping of the New Deal. Roosevelt and the New Deal were attacked from all sides; from the left who felt that he was going too slowly and too cautiously in reforming the United States and from the right, who felt that he was being too sweeping in his reforms and undermining traditional American values of self-reliance. Most histories of opposition to the New Deal tend to focus on the Supreme Court's decisions of 1935–36, which threatened to undermine the whole legislative programme. These decisions can be seen as part of the attack from the right in so far as the majority on the Supreme Court were adopting a conservative position in challenging the new powers taken by the Federal Government. As was made clear in Unit 6, the New Deal did not fundamentally alter the distribution of wealth or substitute state enterprise for free-enterprise. It tried to bolster the existing system by extending security to all or at least most groups. This Roosevelt hoped would turn radicals and potential revolutionaries into the supporters of the 'American way of life'.

In this unit you will:

- explore the nature and extent of opposition to the New Deal
- understand the reasons for the Supreme Court's opposition
- examine the impact opposition had on the delivery of the New Deal.

Key questions

- Who opposed the New Deal from the right wing and from the left wing perspectives?
- How successful was opposition to the New Deal?
- What was the Supreme Court controversy?
- In what ways and to what extent did opposition shape the New Deal?

Timeline

1932	Nov	Roosevelt elected by a landslide
1933	Mar	Roosevelt's Inauguration
1934		Congressional elections reinforce radical Democrats
	Aug	American Liberty League founded
		Father Charles E. Coughlin founds National Union for Social Justice
		Senator Huey P. Long launches Share our Wealth campaign

1935	May	Supreme Court declares *National Industrial Recovery Act* unconstitutional
	Sep	Huey Long assassinated
1936	Jan	Supreme Court judgement undermines the legitimacy of *AAA*
	Mar	Supreme Court undermines the legality of the Guffey *Bituminous Coal Conservation Act*
	Apr	Supreme Court invalidates minimum wage legislation in New York State
	Nov	Roosevelt wins second term with a landslide
1937	Feb	Roosevelt announces Supreme Court alteration scheme
		Massive opposition in Congress develops to reform scheme
	Mar	Supreme Court upholds minimum wage in Washington State
	Apr	Supreme Court uphold the *Wagner Act*
	Jul	Death of Democrat majority Senate leader
		Reform of Supreme Court dropped
1938	Feb	Anti-lynching law defeated
	Jun	*Fair Labor Standards Act* – Minimum Wage (last of New Deal legislation)
		Roosevelt begins campaign against conservative Democrats
	Nov	Congressional elections – victory for southern conservatives
1939	Jan	Roosevelt's State of the Union Message focused on foreign policy
	Sep	War in Europe
1940	Jun	Rearmament begins in USA
	Nov	Roosevelt re-elected for unprecedented third term
1941	Dec	USA enters Second World War

Threats from the Left and Right

Roosevelt faced threats from both the left and right wings of the political spectrum. However, until 1937–38 he appeared to have been more concerned by his opponents on the left, whom he felt were threatening to undermine free enterprise and the basic political and social structure of the USA. In this sense Roosevelt was a conservative and like the aristocratic Whigs in Great Britain in the 1830s trying to 'reform that he might preserve'.

The Threat from the Left

Source A

7.1 Strikers and police clash in San Francisco, July 1934.

1933 witnessed an explosion of protests from militant farming groups and violent strikes amongst groups of workers. The moderate union leader, William Green, president of the **American Federation of Labor** (AFL) had commented in August 1932 that unless orderly and constructive reform was carried out *'we shall be swept aside by a tide of revolt'*. A journalist, hired by the Federal Government to report on social conditions in Pennsylvania, reported in 1933 that *'vast numbers of workers were right on the edge and it wouldn't take much to make Communists out of them'*. In Toledo, Ohio, a full-scale battle developed in the summer of 1933 as a result of a strike at Electric Auto Lite. The National Guard was called out and two strikers were killed. In 1934, there were violent clashes in Minneapolis, Minnesota, resulting in deaths and many wounded as a result of police gunfire. In San Francisco, in July of the same year, a general strike developed with widespread violent clashes as the photograph above indicates. Many of the strikes indicated the growing influence of political extremists as the AFL feared.

The American Communist Party had polled a record 102,000 votes in 1932, admittedly far behind the 22.8 million for Roosevelt, or even the 884,000 vote for Norman Thomas, the Socialist Party leader. There were about 30,000 Communist party members by 1934. They were a very small minority, but the fear of many moderates was that the failure of the New Deal to bring about a dramatic improvement would lead to a surge of

Definition

American Federation of Labor (AFL)

Originally founded by 13 craft unions in 1886. More unions joined later and by 1920 it had 3,250,000 members but it remained largely an interest group for skilled workers. It was moderate in politics and kept a distance from the Socialist Party. An increasing number of members felt that it should encourage unionisation in semi-skilled or unskilled mass production workers. Supporters of this idea formed the Committee for Industrial Organisation (CIO). These were expelled from the AFL in 1936 and formed a rival organisation until 1955 when they reunited with the AFL.

support. In 1934 there was a surge of support for various disparate individuals and groups offering radical solutions to America's problems. If one charismatic figure could pull the underlying discontent into a mass movement, then at the very least Roosevelt's re-election in 1936 would be threatened. At the worst, the American political system might be overturned.

Growing radicalism

In fact, it was not political parties like the Communists, or even the Socialists, who garnered mass followings but a series of maverick individuals who achieved quite remarkable levels of support. In California, the novelist Upton Sinclair stood in 1934 as a Democrat for the position of Governor. He espoused a very radical platform, much to the embarrassment of mainstream Democrats and Roosevelt himself. Sinclair termed his programme EPIC, End Poverty in California. It was almost a revolutionary socialist programme, with its demand for a radical redistribution of wealth, and state ownership of economic activities to provide employment for the unemployed. Sinclair was made the subject of an effective smear campaign organised by the Hollywood film mogul, Louis B. Mayer. Roosevelt very obviously did not offer support and Sinclair lost to a Republican, but he still polled 870,000 votes. This indicated just how popular radical solutions were becoming in 'the land of the brave and the free'.

California was also the home for another example of this growing radicalism. If Upton Sinclair was a rather exotic politician from whom wild and woolly populist politics might be expected, Dr Francis Townsend was eminently respectable but his scheme for large old age pensions was very radical and proved massively popular. Only 28 states had any kind of old-age pensions with a range of $8 to $30 per month. Townsend proposed, in 1933, that all persons over 60 years old should be given $200 a month on condition that they spent it. The idea was that not only would it enrich a poverty stricken group, but also put money into the economy and thus stimulate jobs. Throughout 1934, Townsend clubs were founded to push the idea and by 1935 they had a membership of over half a million across the country. The generous pensions were to be paid for by a 2 per cent sales tax. It was largely based on guesswork that was hopelessly wrong and massive taxation would have been necessary to fund the project, but the popular response showed the national appetite for radical solutions.

National opposition

Source B

7.2 Father Charles E. Coughlin, the radio priest, speaking at a rally in Cleveland prior to the Ohio primary, May 1936.

Across the country in Detroit, another manifestation of the same yearning for dramatic change appeared in the shape, or to be more accurate, the voice of Father Charles Edward Coughlin. Coughlin was a Canadian by birth and a Roman Catholic priest by calling. He was possessed of a powerful weapon in the form of an exceptionally pleasing and reassuring voice. The development of radio gave his voice the power to sway millions. He had begun broadcasting in the mid-1920s appealing for money to keep a religious shrine going. In the Depression he turned increasingly to politics denouncing bankers and Herbert Hoover. Initially, he was an ardent supporter of Roosevelt and the New Deal but by late 1934, he was becoming increasingly critical, feeling that Roosevelt had not really taken on the banks and was in reality in the pocket of Wall Street. There was also a touch of anti-Semitism that crept into his radio sermons. Jews were prominent in banking and there were prominent Jews in Roosevelt's inner circle, such as Morgenthau, the Secretary to the Treasury, and Felix Frankfurter, a prominent member of Roosevelt's Brains Trust. At the end of 1934, Coughlin founded The National Union for Social Justice to promote the careers of political candidates who would attack Wall Street and promote the redistribution of wealth. Roosevelt initially tried to keep Coughlin's support by using prominent Roman Catholic Democrats like Joseph Kennedy as intermediaries, but the breach was permanent and growing. The Administration turned, then, to ridiculing the Radio Priest. Coughlin's ego and self-belief led him on to see himself as saviour of the

USA and in 1936 he founded a magazine '*Social Justice*' which contained increasingly virulent attacks on the Jews and Roosevelt. The president was described as 'Franklin Double-Crossing Roosevelt', the great betrayer and liar. In September 1936, he referred to Roosevelt as 'anti-God' and implied assassination could be justified. Coughlin's abuse became so virulent that the Church authorities intervened and forced a reluctant apology from the radio priest. He remained a critic and his influence was not finally broken until the beginning of the Second World War.

The most dangerous of all the critics of the New Deal, who attacked it for its moderation, and the most serious political threat to Roosevelt, was an extraordinary individual from the southern state of Louisiana, Huey Long. Here was a man who might pull all the resentment and discontent together and emerge as a candidate of the Left in the 1936 Presidential election. He had charisma and political clout and once elected Senator, soon established himself as a notable figure in Washington. In 1932, he campaigned for Roosevelt and the New Deal but by 1934 was increasingly disappointed with the slow pace of reform and broke with Roosevelt. He saw himself as an obvious replacement able to rally radical America.

In February 1934, he established a national 'Share our Wealth Society'. It promised every family a homestead allowance of $5,000 and a minimum annual income of $2,500. This was to be paid for by taxation of the rich and confiscation of all fortunes over five million dollars. As with Townsend's scheme the figures did not add up, but details like this were of little concern to the Louisiana Kingfish, as Long was known. By 1935, Long had become a national challenger to Roosevelt. Share Our Wealth Clubs had multiplied at a frightening rate until there were estimated to be eight million members in 2,000 clubs. Long was attacked by Roosevelt's close associates and **Federal patronage** cut off from Long's Louisiana political machine. Long could give back as much and more in terms of the abuse he received. It was very unlikely that he would be able to take the Democratic nomination from Roosevelt in 1936, but it was estimated that standing as a third party candidate he might get 12 per cent of the vote, enough to deny Roosevelt victory over the Republicans. Once again, as on so many other occasions, Roosevelt was lucky. On 8 September 1935, a slim white-suited man wearing glasses stepped from behind a marble pillar in the capitol building of Long's home state and fired a single shot at 'The Kingfish'. The assassin, a doctor, died seconds later, his body riddled with 61 shots from Long's bodyguards. Huey Long died thirty hours later.

Definition

Federal patronage

An important element in the US political system was the relationship of the Federal Government to the political parties in the various states. A Democratic President would seek to help a state Democratic Party Organisation, especially if it had played a big role in delivering votes in the presidential election. Federal jobs, money and contracts would be distributed through the local party machine enabling it to bind citizens to it. (See the section in Unit 6 on Tom Prendergast of Missouri, page 96.)

SKILLS BUILDER

Why was Huey Long regarded by the White House as such a dangerous threat to Roosevelt?

Why might he be considered more dangerous than the other individuals mentioned here as radical critics?

Biography

Huey Pierce Long (1893–1935)

Elected Governor of Louisiana in 1928, the year Roosevelt was elected Governor of New York, their backgrounds could not have been more different, as Long often pointed out. Instead of the silver spoons and gentility that had graced Roosevelt's childhood, Long came from one of the poorest states in the Union, where 20 per cent of white people were illiterate as were an even larger proportion of the large black community. He spoke for the poor white farmers amongst whom he was born in 1893. By brains and willpower, he secured a college education and set up as a lawyer where he was notable for his public speaking skills. As a candidate for governor of Louisiana, he campaigned against both the political elite of New Orleans and the Standard Oil Company who effectively controlled the state, and won on a populist platform of increased public spending to be paid for by taxing the rich and the oil companies. He delivered on his promises, and in 1931 became Senator for Louisiana but still retained control of the state through nominees and associates. His hold on the state was based on a mixture of genuine popularity, bribery and intimidation.

The impact of radical opposition

Some historians have accepted the judgement of Roosevelt's son, Elliott Roosevelt, when he wrote that the major measures of 1935, usually described as the Second New Deal, were *'designed to cut the ground from under the demagogues'*. This was clearly one factor and in the case of the *Wealth Tax Act* probably a major factor. But as far as the other major measures, the *Social Security Act*, the *Wagner Act* and the major overhaul of relief projects, many other things came into play: Roosevelt's frustration with employers and bankers, pressure from the new Democratic intake into Congress in 1934, and the growing strength of the Unions. Roosevelt had long had sympathy with the idea of extending social security provision and all the measures fitted in with his approach of extending security to all and thereby stabilising the rocking boat that was the USA.

The threat from the Right and the business community

While a growing army of radical critics assailed the President in 1934 for doing too little, there was an increasing vocal number of critics on the right who felt that he was doing too much. The extension of federal power seemed to these critics to be undermining traditional American virtues of self-help and personal initiative according to these. In the summer of 1934, the American Liberty League was set up *'to foster the right to work, earn, save and acquire property and to preserve the ownership and lawful use of property'.* It included some prominent Democrats, like the ex-Presidential candidate Al Smith, but the money came from big business: Du Pont (chemicals) Edward Hutton (Foods), Alfred Sloan (General Motors) and N Miller (United States Steel). It also had close links to Wall Street and the financial sector. J.P. Morgan, the giant of the banking world, was so angry with Roosevelt that guests were warned by Morgan's staff not to mention the President's name in Morgan's presence for fear of raising the banker's blood pressure. In general, the opponents of the New Deal in the business

Definition

Public Utility Holding Company Act

A measure passed in August 1935, which gave the Federal Government powers to eliminate holding companies which controlled numerous public utilities and could not demonstrate that they contributed to the efficiency of the industry. The big concession to critics of the Act was that the burden of proof before abolition was shifted to the Federal Government who had to demonstrate that the holding company worked against the efficiency of the industry.

community came from the traditional manufacturing sectors and many of the new high tech and service industries backed Roosevelt and retained close links to the White House. The keenest opponents were often the ones who felt most threatened by government regulation and the rise of unions for the semi-skilled and production line workers. The opposition was particularly bitter to the attempt by the Administration to regulate Public Utilities that controlled, for example, electricity generation and water supply. There was a massive lobbying campaign to get Congress to reject the **Public Utility Holding Company Act** and in the end Roosevelt, on Frankfurter's advice, had to compromise and tone down some of the clauses to meet the demands of the giant holding companies who were threatened by the Act.

The same thing happened with the *Revenue Act* of 1935 (*Wealth Tax Act*). The proposed highest levy on incomes was cut back from 79 per cent to 75 per cent and inheritance tax dropped altogether. Many southern conservative Democrats joined with Republicans in Congress to water down the radicalism of the measure. Not surprisingly, the Wagner *National Labor Relations Act* attracted bitter opposition. The American Chamber of Commerce and the National Association of Manufacturers campaigned bitterly against the *Wagner Act*. To many of America's richest citizens, Roosevelt was a 'traitor to his class'. He was denounced as a communist or socialist and almost no insulting adjective was too extreme to precede these two words. Some southern Democrat Senators feared the effects on manufacturing in the low wage-paying southern states if unions were strengthened. The Act's passage was largely due to the brilliance of Senator Wagner and his oratorical and tactical skills. Roosevelt himself was lukewarm, anxious not to upset his southern colleagues on an issue for which he cared little. In general, the conservative opposition was less effective than might have been expected because of the radical nature of the Congress elected in 1934, and the prevailing trend of radicalism in public opinion. Roosevelt could always play the card of his moderation: if some degree of radical reform was not passed far worse could follow. The bogeyman in the shape of Huey Long was quite useful in frightening the right and forcing concessions from them.

The abuse the President received from the right was useful in bolstering Roosevelt's credentials with left-wing Democrats and the poor and disadvantaged in general. Clearly the bitterness of his critics ultimately did Roosevelt no harm and may have done him much good. He won the 1936 Presidential election by a record margin, carrying every state except Vermont and Maine. He faced a moderate Republican in Alfred Landon of Kansas. It was significant that the Republican right-wingers did not dare put up one of their number. The only hope of the Republicans was that a candidate like Huey Long might attract sufficient radical votes from Roosevelt to ensure victory for Landon. However Long's death in 1935 removed this threat to Roosevelt. The Republicans were also crushed in the elections to the Senate and the House of Representatives. The Democrats totally dominated the new Congress in 1937 with 77 to 19 in the Senate and 328 to 107 in the House.

The challenge from the Supreme Court

The most effective challenge to the New Deal came not from Congress, but from the third branch of the Federal Government, the Supreme Court (see Unit 1 pages 11–12). The Supreme Court was the guardian of the Constitution and the arbitrator between the component parts of the US system of government, for example, between the rights of the individual states and the Federal Government or between President and Congress. There were nine Supreme Court Justices. All but one had been appointed by Republican Presidents, and their average age was 71. The eldest was Louis Brandeis at 80, but strangely enough he was one of the few liberals on the court, sympathetic to Roosevelt. Two others were inclined to some degree of sympathy but four, known as the '**Four Horsemen of the Apocalypse**', were very conservative and thoroughly opposed to the New Deal and all its works. Everything tended to turn on the Chief Justice, Charles Evans Hughes, former Secretary of State under Coolidge and Harding, and who was inclined to hold the balance of power in the Court.

Early in 1935, the Court declared by eight to one that some provisions relating to the *National Industrial Recovery Act*, which had given the President powers to prohibit interstate shipments of petrol in certain circumstances, was unconstitutional. They argued that Congress could not delegate such powers to the President. On 27 May 1935, the Court delivered a series of devastating judgements, calling into question fundamental aspects of the New Deal. The most famous struck at the NRA (see Unit 6 page 107), with its famed blue eagle badge. Delivered by nine to zero, in the case of Schechter Poultry Corps vs. United States, the Court found that Congress had again delegated too much power to the President and Congress itself could not regulate the slaughter of Kosher chickens, because its powers only related to interstate commerce and the 'sick' chickens in question were to be sold within the state. It was the end of the NRA and its multitude of regulations.

In January 1936, the Court, by six to three, undermined the legality of the *Agricultural Adjustment Act* by arguing that the Federal Government had infringed on the legitimate powers of the individual states to regulate. In March of the same year, they threw out an Act to regulate coal production as being beyond Federal competence. A few weeks later, they went even further by invalidating a New York State Law establishing a minimum wage in the state. The Court found by five to four that the idea of a minimum wage infringed the principle of freedom of contract. Thus, by mid-1936, the powers of President, Congress and even the individual states had all been called into question. It raised the important issue of whether government could tackle the fundamental economic and social problems thrown up by the Depression. Roosevelt was furious.

SKILLS BUILDER

Roosevelt's New Deal was a real threat to the traditional American business model.

To what extent do you agree with this view?

Definition

Four Horsemen of the Apocalypse
Part of the vision of the end of the world, described in the Book of Revelation. Four horsemen appear on four differently coloured horses. The riders are Pestilence, War, Famine and Death. They are not omens of good times to follow.

SKILLS BUILDER

1. Draw up a grid showing the different cases and the differing grounds on which the Supreme Court struck down New Deal legislation.

2. Which, in your judgement, was the most damning decision?

The impact of opposition from the Right and Roosevelt's response

In November 1936, Roosevelt won a stunning re-election victory, with 60 per cent of the popular votes cast compared to 36 per cent for his Republican rival, Alfred Landon. He swept the states' electoral votes with a total of 523 to 8 for Landon. His popularity and authority had reached new heights and now seemed the time to settle with the Supreme Court. Roosevelt had been increasingly embittered by opposition from the right and determined to act. At the time of the Schecter case, in 1935, his **Attorney General** Homer Cummings had said *I tell you Mr President, they mean to destroy us. We will have to find a way to get rid of the present membership of the Supreme Court'.*

Eventually, in 1937, Roosevelt and his closest advisers came up with a scheme to shift the balance in the Supreme Court. Roosevelt proposed that he be allowed to nominate up to six more justices, one for every serving justice over seventy years old. The justification given to Congress and the public was the need to rejuvenate the Court and increase its efficiency. This was not convincing. The oldest Justice was in fact a Liberal, and as Chief Justice Hughes pointed out, six more justices to consult with and argue with would slow things up rather than expedite matters. Roosevelt, in fact, handled it badly. He failed to consult in advance with Congressional leaders and the first most of them had heard of the plan was on its official announcement on 5 Feb 1937. Even his Vice-President was lukewarm. Many traditional liberal allies like Senator Wheeler of Montana opposed the scheme, which soon became known as the 'Court Packing Plan'. Wheeler, like many Americans, saw the Court as the essential defender of liberty. Southern conservative Democrats were appalled, fearing a new more liberal Court would open the floodgates to liberal decisions relating to black civil rights. The general public, who had just voted for Roosevelt in such numbers, were suspicious of a President becoming too big for his boots and removing a traditional obstacle to government abuse of power. Roosevelt had given no public warnings of his intentions towards the Supreme Court during the election campaign. The proposal became mired on the floor of the Senate and the strain of pushing the bill through brought about the death of the Democrat majority leader Senator Robinson of Arkansas.

The behaviour of the Supreme Court in 1937 also undermined the case for change. The two 'swing' justices, as Hughes and Roberts were known, since they were not firmly in either the liberal or conservative camp, now joined with the liberal three to deliver a series of judgements reaffirming the New Deal and the powers of the Federal Government and state governments to intervene. Hughes and Roberts were anxious to defuse the situation and get the Supreme Court to step back from what was turning into a bitter party political conflict. Having overturned the New York minimum wage in the Tipaldo case of 1936, the Court, now in the case of West Coast Hotel vs. Parish, affirmed the minimum wage in Washington State.

It was not legally consistent, but it was politically smart. In other judgements, the Court upheld the *Wagner Act* of 1935 and the *Social*

Security Act of 1935, the twin pillars of the so-called 'Second New Deal'. In May of 1937 one of the most rabid of the conservative justices, Van Devanter, announced his retirement, allowing Roosevelt to insert one of his nominees in his place. The unpopularity of his proposals and the fact that it now no longer seemed as necessary, led Roosevelt reluctantly to drop his Court Reform Package apart from some minor proposals affecting lower tier Federal Courts.

Who had won? On the surface it was a victory for Roosevelt. He had won the battle with the Supreme Court and the New Deal was safe. The Supreme Court from now on accepted an enhanced role for the Federal Government and this amounted to something of a constitutional revolution. On the other hand, Roosevelt had lost popularity and lost his hold on Congress, which he never regained. The ramshackle alliance, which constituted the Democrat Party and which had pushed through such a mass of legislation between 1933 and 1935 was at an end. Conservative rural America reasserted itself and a blocking alliance of northern Republicans and southern Democrats brought the New Deal grinding to a halt in 1937–38. The *Housing Act* of 1937 was 'a weak measure' in David Kennedy's words. The proposals to create seven little TVAs had to be dropped and, as indicated in Unit 6, pages 123 and 126, an *Anti-Lynching Bill* failed to get through, despite the overwhelming evidence of injustice and abuse in the South.

SKILLS BUILDER

1. Look at the timeline for Unit 6 (pages 91–92) and the pattern of legislation achieved. Relate this in a diagram to the chronology of the pattern of opposition described in this unit.

2. To what extent, in your view, did the Supreme Court radically change the New Deal?

Opposition in Congress

It is worth remembering that rural America formed a majority in Congress, with 54 out of 96 Senators and 225 out of 435 representatives in the Lower House coming from predominantly rural areas. When Roosevelt summoned a special session of Congress in November 1937, to push through various measures that had been pushed aside by the Supreme Court reform debates earlier in the year there was a real contrast to the Special Session of 1933 (see Unit 6). Now, in contrast to the large number of measures of the Hundred Days, agreed in 1933, nothing was achieved. Not a single measure proposed by the President got through. A group of Senators and Congressmen issued a 'Conservative Manifesto', demanding lower taxes, an end to strikes and warning of the dangers of creating a dependency culture through social security.

Roosevelt was determined to carry the fight to the enemy, and in the congressional elections of 1938 tried to unseat various conservative

SKILLS BUILDER

Why, in your view, did the New Deal come to an end?

Use all the information in this unit to reach a conclusion.

Democratic Senators in the South, Iowa and Indiana, and replace them with liberals more favourable to his programme. He failed almost totally. The downturn in the economy, known as the 'Roosevelt recession' (see Unit 6 page 120) undermined his prestige. The White House had tried to remove five Democratic Senators who had been up for re-election but failed to do so. All five returned triumphantly to Washington. In addition, the Republicans gained eight Senate seats and doubled their representation in the House. The New Deal was finished.

Unit summary

What have you learned in this unit?

You have been introduced to the varied range of opponents to the New Deal, firstly those who felt that it did not go far enough and charged Roosevelt with timidity. Here were both groups such as the small Communist Party and prominent figures who enjoyed wide popularity like Huey Long. You have also encountered those who felt the New Deal was transforming the United States too much. The crucial battle between the White House and the Supreme Court has figured prominently. You should be aware of what the differing impacts of opposition from both right and left had been.

What skills have you used in this unit?

You have understood the reasons why various groups and individuals opposed the New Deal. You have prioritised the seriousness of the threats posed to the New Deal, and you have reached judgements about the impact these threats had on the New Deal. Finally, you have come to supported conclusions about why the New Deal came to an end.

Exam style question

This is the style of question you will find appearing on the examination paper as a Section A question.

How far do you agree that Roosevelt's response to the challenges from the Supreme Court to the New Deal was a mistaken over-reaction?

Exam tips

You have read, at the end of earlier units, how to approach these traditional history essays. To reiterate:

- planning is crucial, as is the structuring of your paragraphs.

To answer this specific question, you need to:

- define 'Roosevelt's response' and 'the challenges from the Supreme Court to the New Deal'
- debate 'over-reaction' and 'mistaken' and find arguments on both sides in the case of both words.

Finally, you must offer a clear evaluation in terms of evaluating 'how far'.

RESEARCH TOPIC

Explore in detail one of the key Supreme Court decisions that threatened the New Deal. Try to understand the issues involved and why a majority of the Supreme Court took the decision they did. If it is one where some justices dissented try to understand why. The minority also published their reasoning, as well as the majority.

Understanding the division of opinion will give you a real insight into the US Constitution and will be excellent training if you have any ambitions in terms of studying law in Great Britain.

8 The Second World War and its aftermath to 1954

What is this unit about?

This unit focuses on the impact of the Second World War on the United States. The war brought about a huge growth in federal intervention in the economy and the machinery of government. The machinery of government had to be expanded and overhauled to cope with the demands of war. The economy was given an enormous injection of capital by the vast spending the conflict generated. The United States spent $320bn on the war, and 15 million men and over 300,000 women served in the armed forces. The scale of government activity dwarfed that of the New Deal. The worries about a balanced budget and the evils of deficit spending were forgotten. Yet it is important to remember that traditional American business interests and philosophy still had a central role.

The war brought with it both the demand for and the opportunity to provide social reforms. As a result the war accelerated major changes in United States society, which will be illustrated and assessed, and an increase in the power and prestige of Federal Government in general. The war clearly affected the way people lived and their standard of living. Both the immediate and the longer-term effects post-war will be studied. This unit will also examine the roots of the Red Scare and anti-communism, which manifested itself after 1945, and the particularly virulent form it took in McCarthyism between 1950 and 1954. The impact of the hysteria on US society and politics will be assessed.

In this unit you will:

- assess the impact the growth of Federal intervention in the American economy had on American people's perception of the Federal Government
- understand the changes the war made to the lives of the American people
- examine the nature of the Red Scare.

Key questions

- What evidence is there that the Second World War made fundamental changes to the balance of political power in the United States?
- Did the Second World War succeed where the New Deal had failed and lay the basis of post-war prosperity?
- Why were the forces of political intolerance so significant in the decade after the end of the Second World War?

Timeline

1939	**Sep**	Outbreak of war in Europe
	Nov	*Neutrality Acts* modified to allow 'cash and carry' sales of war materials
1940	**Nov**	Roosevelt elected for an unprecedented third term
1941	**Mar**	*Lend-Lease Act* gives the President powers to aid Great Britain and later the USSR
	7 Dec	Japanese bomb Pearl Harbor
	9 Dec	Germany declares war on USA
1943	**Jan**	Pentagon building completed
1944	**Nov**	Roosevelt wins a fourth term as President with Harry S. Truman as Vice President
1945	**Apr**	Roosevelt dies and Truman takes over as President
	May	End of the war in Europe
	Sep	End of the war in Asia
1947	**Mar**	Federal Loyalty Boards established in response to the Red Scare
1948	**Nov**	Truman unexpectedly wins re-election
1949	**Aug**	Soviet Union explodes atomic bomb
	Oct	China comes under communist control
1950	**Feb**	McCarthy launches his anti-communist campaign
	June	Outbreak of war in Korea
1952	**Nov**	Eisenhower wins as first Republican president since Hoover
1954	**Dec**	McCarthy censured by the Senate

What impact did the war have on the machinery of government?

The machinery of government had not been able to cope with the demands of implementing New Deal legislation leading President Roosevelt to expand White House staff and establish the Executive Office of the President in the teeth of opposition from Congress. It was clear that many, including members of the Democratic Party, had reservations about the development of Presidential power but the war bore all such reservations away and created a vastly more powerful Presidency and enlarged Federal Government.

The demands of the Second World War intensified the pressures for more Federal and Presidential activity that had been such a feature of the 1930s.

New agencies multiplied in order to cope. The *War Powers Act* granted Roosevelt unprecedented authority to lead the nation in a total war. There was the need to coordinate the government, the economy and the military. The construction of the **Pentagon** complex symbolised this very clearly.

Various new federal agencies were created such as the **Office of Price Administration** to manage the wartime economy. They increased the number of Federal employees considerably and led to a dramatic increase in the role of central government in the economy and society. However, it is important to note that the President's relationship with Congress was still a material factor and that some New Deal agencies disappeared such as the CCC, the NYA and the WPA.

The role of the Office of Production Management, later the War Production Board (WPB), was crucial. It allocated materials, limited some production of civilian goods and issued contracts. It was headed by two leading corporate executives, Donald Nelson, the president of Sears, and Charles E. Wilson, the president of General Electric. This was to be typical of much of the USA's approach to running the war. The business community and the Federal Government entered into a close and productive relationship. The Office of Price Administration rationed scarce products and introduced price and rent controls to guard against inflation. Rationing affected a range of items, such as gasoline (petrol), coffee, sugar, butter, cheese and meat. The role of Federal Government in helping to create a fairer society was being extended.

The war involved a massive increase in Federal expenditure. In 1940 the total Federal Budget had been $5.3bn of which a mere $1.9bn was spent on defence. By 1944, the year of peak spending, the total was $97.2bn, of which just over $90bn was on the war. This increase inevitably led to a revolution in revenue collection. The taxation system, which Roosevelt had begun to reform in the 1930s, needed fundamental revision. In 1940, four million Americans paid income tax – by 1945 this had risen to 40 million. Personal taxes were raised on a very steep graduated scale, with the highest rate of taxation on the very rich reaching 94 per cent. There was, too a 90 per cent excess profits tax and corporate income tax was raised to 40 per cent. Some 41 per cent of the cost of the war was paid for out of taxation compared to only 33 per cent in the First World War.

Definitions

Pentagon
A centralised military HQ ordered by Roosevelt in 1941. It was completed in January 1943. There are 17 miles of corridors but the five-sided shape was chosen so that no two offices are more than twenty minutes walk away from one another.

Office of Price Administration
This was set up in April 1941 to control prices, with limited powers granted by Congress, but its powers were much strengthened in October 1942. It proved very effective thereafter in preventing inflation. By the end of the war it had 73,000 paid employees.

SKILLS BUILDER

In what ways, and why, was the machinery of government strengthened because of the war?

What impact did the Second World War have on the United States economy?

8.1 Propaganda poster issued by the US government during the Second World War.

Roosevelt had cut the size of the already small US Army in 1933. With less than 140,000 men, it was considerably smaller than the forces that Belgium mobilised against Germany in 1940. In 1937, the USA spent only 1.5 per cent of its National Income on defence compared to over 20 per cent in Germany, Japan and the USSR. However, Roosevelt had long been suspicious of Nazi Germany and saw it as a threat to American interests. But American isolationism was strong, and amongst people and politicians there was no desire to repeat the experience of the First World War. Roosevelt realised that practical politics meant respecting the significant opposition to a more proactive foreign policy and a great rearmament programme. Those opposed to greater involvement had several persuasive and influential leaders and spokesmen, notably the aviator Charles Lindbergh. In the Presidential election of 1940, Roosevelt made it very clear that, although he did not intend to send 'our boys' into another war, the United States could not stand back from the international situation. The *Neutrality Acts* of 1935 and 1937, forbidding the sale of any war material to any belligerent were a major obstacle to aiding France and Great Britain. These were modified in November 1939, with great difficulty on Roosevelt's part, to allow any nation to buy arms on a cash and carry basis. There could be no US loans to Great Britain and the goods had to be transported in British ships.

Nevertheless, it was an important first step, and the huge orders were placed by Great Britain and France helped to revive the US economy, as well as their own war effort. With the further slackening of restrictions in 1940 and 1941, Roosevelt made it clear that the United States must be: *'The great arsenal of democracy'*. US rearmament also began to get underway. This gave a massive boost to production, especially on the West Coast.

The decision to re-arm was taken in 1940 as the world situation seemed more ominous, and Germany and Japan appeared to be heading for the domination of Europe and Asia respectively. The USA decided to create an army of a million men – double the size of the navy – already the second biggest in the world, and increase the air force to 7,800 combat aircrafts. The strain on any other nation's economy would have been enormous. However, although the USA produced six million more tons of steel a year than Germany, German steel plants were working flat out, whereas two-thirds of US steel plants were idle. In other words, the USA had massive spare capacity, which to the horror of Germany and Japan, rapidly became utilised.

The Japanese attack on the United States Pacific Fleet in Pearl Harbor, as the eminent British journalist and broadcaster, Alistair Cooke explained *'Deflated isolationism with a single thrust'*. Two days later, Hitler made things even easier for Roosevelt by declaring war on the USA. The United States landmass was not vulnerable to enemy air attack, and so was able confidently to embark on becoming the great workshop of the war. The stimulation of wartime production breathed new life into virtually every sector of the economy of the United States. In 1941, unemployment was still hovering around 14 per cent. By 1943 it was 2 per cent. The gross national product of the country grew from $91 billion to $214 billion by 1945. These indicators alone point to fundamental change. Certainly a great need for flexibility manifested itself during the war. Private manufacturers who had previously made cars, now produced tanks, and plant designed for manufacturing fridges turned out munitions.

The demands of war led to vast government investment in technology. Leaving aside direct military programmes, which will be examined separately, there are numerous examples of investment in new methods of production. The best example is perhaps the development of synthetic rubber; 51 new plants were constructed, which provided a huge number of jobs, but also changed the United States from being the world's largest importer of crude rubber into the world's largest exporter of synthetic rubber. Military production also created millions of jobs. Over two million people moved to California during the war and significant numbers gained employment in the aircraft and naval production centres of the northwest, especially in Seattle and Portland. However, it is important to emphasise that it was not all change. The central role of the business community was protected and even reinforced. Roosevelt made a series of speeches emphasising the need for cooperation between the Administration and business leaders. The words of Stimson, Roosevelt's Secretary for War, sum this up well: *'If you are going to win a war in a capitalist society you had better let business make money out of the process'.* The government guaranteed profits and in certain circumstances wrote off tax demands. Companies who were involved in extensive retooling to prepare for military production, gained significant tax breaks. The largest ten corporations in the country were awarded two-thirds of war production contracts.

SKILLS BUILDER

1. What were the economic advantages to the USA, of supporting the Allied cause?
2. Why, in the end, did the USA go to war instead of simply supporting the Allies with goods and money?

Gearing up industry for war: shipbuilding and the aircraft industry

Henry Kaiser, who had already made a name for himself as the builder of the South Coulee Dam, put his mind to the problem of providing vast numbers of heavy-duty military transport ships. Kaiser's experience in modern technology paid off and the design of the Liberty Ship was the result. The ship became the workhorse of both the United States and British Merchant Navies. It was 440 feet long and could pack in 3,000 Jeeps and 440 tanks, plus other equipment. The shipbuilding industry as a whole adapted to the ruthless demands of mass production for war.

Alistair Cooke described visiting one of Kaiser's production centres and seeing the interchangeable parts all laid out with their numbers. The assembling was done by a vast army of workers using welding techniques. The speed of production was extraordinary, with Kaiser boasting that he could produce a Liberty ship in four days. This was true, but very carefully staged for publicity. Even so, the normal production time of seventeen days was mightily impressive. Kaiser fully deserved his nickname of 'Sir Launchalot'.

Henry Ford was responsible for the world's largest aircraft factory at Willow Run, which grew up in what had been empty prairie fields. An assembly line, over 1,600 metres long, was constructed. Source B shows the scale of production and gives an indication of the application of methods of mass production to military objectives. By 1944 ten bombers a day were being built. A car averaged 15,000 parts to be assembled into the finished product. A B24 bomber, on the other hand, had 30,000 major parts and, with smaller parts, 1,550,000 in total.

In addition to aircraft Ford produced a vast range of other military hardware. The Ford Corporation alone produced more military equipment during the war than the whole of Italy. Other companies used the same mass production techniques as Ford.

Source B

8.2 The Douglas Plant in El Segundo, California, turning out dive-bombers, August 1943.

In 1939, the USA had produced only 2,000 aircraft, yet by 1942 the USA was building 47,000 aircraft and 24,000 tanks. When compared to 27,000 aircrafts and 11,000 tanks by the Axis, it shows how the United States was already out-producing the combined Axis forces of Germany, Italy and Japan in war materials. The rapid rise in output was replicated throughout American industry. By 1944, the USA had produced:

- 96,318 aircraft compared to 67,987 by the Axis
- 2,247 warships compared to 437 Axis ships
- 600,000 army trucks compared to just 88,000 by the Axis powers
- 16 major naval vessels to every one built by Japan.

In addition to rearming and equipping its own vast forces, the USA transferred billions of dollars worth of material to Great Britain and the USSR, and it was not always direct war material that went to the USA's allies.

- Great Britain's farming benefited enormously by the arrival of US-built tractors.
- Russia received 956,000 miles of telephone cable, 35,000 radio transmitters and 380,000 field telephones.
- The Red Army of the USSR was increasingly transported and supplied by US vehicles in the form of 200,000 Studebaker trucks, 151,000 light trucks and 77,900 Jeeps.

This rise in output happened far more quickly than anybody anticipated, and was a truly staggering testimony to the productive genius of US enterprise and organisational abilities.

Many historians have asserted with much truth that it was not 'Dr New Deal' but rather 'Dr Second World War' that played the biggest part in the economic recovery.

The social and economic historian James T. Patterson sums up the situation very clearly:

'The massive expenditure triggered by the war ended the Depression and stimulated an economic boom that brought prosperity. It doubled industrial output and created 17 million jobs. It increased corporate profits by 70 per cent. It raised real wages by 50 per cent.'

SKILLS BUILDER

Why was the USA able to produce so much war material so quickly?

Government spending had proved to be the key to recovery. It generated demand and over-tight control of the money supply was abandoned. American ingenuity and energy were released with an explosive force that was to blow away Hitler's regime in Europe and end Japan's pretensions to rule Asia.

What impact did the Second World War have on US society?

In general, most of the results of war were positive. The most dramatic change was the collapse of unemployment from nine million out of work in 1940, to only 780,000 in September 1943. The number of women in work grew by 50 per cent, increasing the income that families enjoyed. There was also some switch to greater equality in the distribution of income; earnings in the bottom fifth of society rose by 68 per cent, but their share of national income only rose from 4 per cent to 5 per cent. The richest 5 per cent saw their share of national income drop from 26 per cent to 16 per cent, largely as a result of taxation. The chief gainers were the middle classes. There were new job opportunities created and this often linked with very significant demographic changes. Areas of the South were transformed with hundreds of thousands of sharecroppers and poor tenant farmers leaving to seek a better life on the West Coast or in the Northern cities, where war industries provided well-paid jobs. A staggering 10 per cent of Americans moved state during the war, and 27 million (or 20 per cent) at least moved location. Over a million black people left the South to move to places like Detroit and work in the massive war industries.

By almost every measurable index living standards rose. Reference has already been made to the rise in wages. Farm incomes quadrupled. Despite rationing, most Americans ate and dressed better than before the war. The rationing was not as severe as in Great Britain and the deprivations of the Russian people were completely outside the experience of American civilians. Life expectancy increased by three years on average and for black people this increase was by five years. Infant mortality fell by a third. Earlier marriages and a soaring birth rate became a feature of the wartime USA, reversing the pattern of the Depression. The above social trends therefore produced a rapidly expanding population which more than offset the battle-deaths of 292,131.

The number of women in employment rose rapidly from 11 million to 20 million. Many women also moved from low paid to better paid jobs.

The numbers of female workers in the automobile industry rose from 5 per cent of the workforce in 1940 to 20 per cent in 1945. In electrical manufacturing it was 50 per cent by the end of the war. This led to a real struggle for equal pay. The Federal Government through the War Labor Board approved and encouraged equal pay, but the reality was that women tended to be paid at lower rates and male-dominated trade unions showed little enthusiasm for equalisation. Because of the numbers involved, the United Electrical Workers' Union was the exception in championing women's pay. It eventually, in 1945, won its case but the two big electric companies, Westinghouse and General Electric refused to comply with the War Labor Board's instructions on the grounds that the war had ended. To aid working mothers, the Federal Government built childcare centres, but many mothers refused to use them because of the cost and low quality of care, and most working women doubled up as workers and housewives.

The strengthening of trade unions

The war certainly strengthened the influence of union organisations. The CIO, in particular, grew considerably. Unions realised that they would benefit from working together and having a more united voice when working with both employers and the government. The Federal Government encouraged employers to recognise unions and this even happened in the case of Ford Motors, in stark contrast to their previous stance (see Unit 3, page 35). The unions responded by accepting the need for more industrial harmony. Strikes counted for well under 1 per cent of working days lost during the war. There was only one glaring exception, and this was the coal strike of 1943; President Roosevelt responded by legislating to provide himself with emergency powers to intervene if union action threatened the national interest. In the end, though, he had no need to use this power. The unions accepted the need for due moderation in wage claims and their members benefited, because there was more security of employment, a clear definition and acceptance of their rights and a number of other measures. More employers introduced paid holidays, health insurance and the desirability of better pensions. The improved industrial relations, by and large, continued after the war.

Race

The war brought together Americans from right across society. It exposed many issues and, especially in the military, evidence of discrimination and segregation was very clear. Many regiments were segregated and very few blacks were officers. There was even evidence that on occasions some found themselves being less well treated than Axis prisoners. There are several reports that African Americans were being forced to give up their seats to German and Italian prisoners of war when travelling on buses and trains and that German prisoners were fed in diners from which black people were excluded.

Black Americans made considerable material progress during the war, as the figures given above on migration and life expectancy indicate. Those

SKILLS BUILDER

1. How far did American women's lives change because of the war?
2. To what extent did the war benefit American women?

black people holding industrial jobs in 1939 averaged 40 per cent of the earnings of white workers doing similar jobs. By 1945 it was 60 per cent. Of all black people living in the southern states, 10 per cent moved north or west, but the movement was not without renewed examples of prejudice. White employees often went out on strike in protest at the employment of black workers. In June 1943, 25,000 white workers struck at Packard's engine plant in Detroit, when the management proposed to employ two black workers. Such actions were repeated in various northern localities.

Much is often made of the paradox of a racist USA denouncing racist Germany but such criticism is unfair. In the USA, the government condemned racial discrimination and sought to end it through such directives as *Executive Order 8802* (see below). Racist sentiment welled up from below and was not encouraged, as it was in Nazi Germany, by the government. There were alarming episodes outside the workplace, and in Detroit in the summer of 1943, 34 people – 29 of them black – were killed in brutal riots and street fighting. It served as a grim reminder that there was a very long way to go over the issue of Civil Rights.

The role of **Philip Randolph** is central to progress in Civil Rights, as is the development of the **National Association for the Advancement of Colored People** (NAACP) and Congress of Racial Equality (CORE). In 1941 Randolph planned a march on Washington, which caused concern to President Roosevelt and prompted him to act. The Administration issued *Executive Order 8802* in June 1941. This outlawed racial discrimination in defence industries and enabled tens of thousands of African Americans to get jobs during the war and in the defence industry as it continued to develop after the war. Roosevelt still did not go as far as Civil Rights campaigners wished but, to an extent, prepared the ground for President Truman's further reforms after the war.

The war made many African Americans recognise the essential irrationality of their position. They were part of a struggle against tyrannous and racist regimes, yet the position in the United States was deeply flawed. As one black serviceman, who had fought in Europe put it, as his ship sailed into New York harbour in 1945, *'I was a nigger again'*. The **Double V campaign** developed and pressure groups began to mobilise.

Definitions

National Association for the Advancement of Colored People

This organisation was formally set up in 1945. It recognised the feelings and aspirations of millions of servicemen who had high hopes for greater civil, political and social rights. It is significant to note that voter registration amongst African Americans went up from 2% to 12% between 1940 and 1947. While this was still a deeply unacceptable situation, there were at least glimmerings of movement. Changes were brought about in the military as the war progressed. For instance during the Battle of the Bulge, in 1944, segregation effectively broke down and in January 1945 the first formally integrated unit was established.

Double V campaign

This originated in a letter to a Pittsburgh newspaper calling for victory over the Axis abroad and victory over racial prejudice in the USA.

Biography

Philip Randolph 1889–1979

Philip Randolph was a union leader representing the Brotherhood of Sleeping Car Porters. His was a clear yet peaceful voice. He established the importance of expressing views clearly and in an organised way. He recognised the need for statements of discontent while also pointing the way forward. He wanted to bring home to the white community the importance of fairness and harmony in society. To a considerable extent it is possible to see the forerunners of many of the factors associated with Martin Luther King in the mid-1950s and later.

Randolph inspired others, notably **James Farmer** who set up the CORE in 1942. This developed the philosophy of clearly articulated but non-violent protest. A number of '**sit ins**' took place, anticipating campaigns after the war.

Post-war prosperity

The United States economy after the Second World War experienced a period of growth unprecedented not only in American history but in world history. It became a vibrant economy, based largely on consumer goods and experiencing living standards which would have been unimaginable in the 1930s. In 1947, despite possessing only 7 per cent of the world's population, the USA produced half the world's manufactured goods. It also accounted for 43 per cent of the world's electricity, 57 per cent of the world's steel and 62 per cent of the world's oil. Never had the world been so dominated by the economic muscle of one power. Its military and diplomatic position in the world reflected its economic strength. It was number one.

The curse of the 1930s, unemployment, had all but disappeared. In 1945 it stood at 1.9 per cent and although it rose to 4 per cent in a temporary slump in 1950, in all the eight years after the war there was less need for expenditure on social welfare provision, a lot more taxation revenue for the Federal and State governments and significant increase in consumer spending as people got used to having more money in their pockets. There was still poverty and deprivation, with 20 per cent of families living below the poverty line – one-third of homes having no running water and 40 per cent had no flushing toilets. However, even in this respect the USA compared favourably with war-torn Europe. By the end of the 1940s the average American enjoyed an income fifteen times greater than the average European. Even the poorest in the USA were rich by world standards. The per-capita income of Harlem – one of the poorer areas of New York City – ranked within the top five nations in the world and elsewhere. In poor rural areas such as Harlan County, Kentucky, two-thirds of homes would have televisions and three-fifths a car by the early 1950s. Many in Great Britain, in the same period, were living in homes without electricity or indoor lavatories.

The general picture was one of spreading affluence based on prosperous and developing electrical and automobile industries and a massive construction boom.

The construction industry had received a major boost during the war. There was especially dramatic development on the West Coast and the building of suburbs became characteristic of US cities and towns. Some enterprising builders, like Levitt and Sons in New York, made especially dramatic progress building tens of thousands of simply designed homes. There was the cheaper 'Cape Cod Box' house with four rooms and also a larger ranch-style home. A Bendix washing machine was usually thrown in to tempt potential buyers. The houses themselves were cheap to build and by the end of the 1950s, over 30 per cent of Americans lived in the suburbs. These tended to be overwhelmingly populated by white families.

Biography

James Farmer 1920–99
James Farmer was the son of a Texas theologian, the first black American to secure a PhD, and something of a child prodigy himself. He helped set up the Congress of Racial Equality (CORE) and remained a respected leader of the Civil Rights movement throughout the 1950s and 1960s, taking a leading part in the Freedom Ride of 1961.

Definition

Sit-ins
These were a favourite form of protest with black protestors sitting in an area designated as 'whites only'.

SKILLS BUILDER

In what ways and why was the impact of the Second World War so positive on the USA?

Source C

8.3 An aerial view of Levittown, 1957. Just one of several suburban developments built by Levitt and Sons.

SKILLS BUILDER

How far did the post-war recovery benefit all sections of American society?

Table 8.1 US total car sales 1945–55

Year	Cars sold
1945	69,000
1946	2.1 million
1949	5.1 million
1955	7.9 million

The Automobile industry was a key indicator of economic performance and prosperity both before and after the Second World War. The higher the level of car sales the more prosperous the population was, and in the post-war years it rose dramatically.

By 1950 there were 40 million cars on the roads of the USA. As in the pre-war period, the spin-off effect was considerable, with boosts to the oil industry and highway construction. Car ownership determined the pattern of post-war life in many respects, both in terms of the development of suburbia and the growth of out-of-town shopping. Giant shopping malls and supermarkets made their appearance as a key component in the American way of life.

Technology had been given a great boost during the war with high levels of investment, notably in medicine. There were to be many spin-offs to whet the appetite of the consumer. For example, the period after the war brought the long playing record and the Polaroid camera. The frozen food industry expanded as more and more families invested in refrigerators, as the item entered the price range of what they could afford. The sale of household appliances went up five times. Luxury goods and the inessentials that are the hallmark of an affluent consumer society multiplied. In 1952, for example, Americans spent $255m on chewing gum and $23m on mouthwash.

The baby boom was both a cause and consequence of incredible prosperity. It was perhaps the most amazing social trend of the post-war era. In 1946, there were 3.4 million babies born. Between 1946 and 1964, 76.4 million babies were born. This formed 40 per cent of the population. This encouraged the development of a dynamic juvenile market. For instance, each infant was reckoned to be worth $800 to the producers of baby and child products.

The basis of this prosperity is clearly multi-causal. As indicated above, technology encouraged by the war played a large part. The New Deal helped by increasing security for all groups. The growth of a unionised workforce ensured a prosperous blue-collar working class of consumers. Wages were high. There was a spate of strikes in 1946, which led employers and many Republicans to argue that the *Wagner Act* had shifted power too much in the unions' favour. The 1946 congressional elections saw a massive swing to the Republicans and Congress passed the **Taft–Hartley Act** curbing union powers.

Truman vetoed the Act but Congress immediately re-passed it with a sufficient majority to override the presidential veto. Thereafter employers and unions tended to work sensibly together and there was no return to the embittered trench warfare of the inter-war years. The deal signed in 1948 between Charles E. Wilson, President of General Motors and Walter Reuther, the head of the UAW (United Automobile Workers), was a model for other industries. Reuther got job security and wage increases linked to sales and productivity, and automatic cost of living rises for his members. In return the company got a 'no strikes' agreement. Both sides were the winners.

There is no doubt that Federal Government spending was also a key factor. Deliberately aimed to prevent a post-war recession and avoid the bitterness of the Bonus Marchers of 1932, the *Serviceman's Readjustment Act*, better known as the *G.I. Bill* was passed in 1944. It showed a vastly different approach to the veterans than that shown at the end of the First World War. Cash benefits were offered which facilitated educational opportunities and the government guaranteed home loans with which veterans could become homeowners. This had a great effect in promoting the housing boom referred to above, but also helped to stimulate the economy in general. Federal expenditure of $95 billion in 1945 shrank to $36.5 billion in 1948, an inevitable outcome of the ending of the Second World War. The latter figure still dwarfed the pre-war level of $9.4 billion. The growing confrontation with the Soviet Union, which became known as the Cold War, fuelled a renewed weapons production and expansion with notable developments around Seattle, in Southern California and in the Rocky Mountain states. The projects focused on the developments of aircraft and missile systems. Military expenditure, which had fallen to 4 per cent of GNP in 1948, rose to 14 per cent by 1953. Even with the ending of the Korean War in that year, federal expenditure on armaments remained far above the levels of the 1930s.

Partly, the boom was an inevitable product of the great shake out that the slump caused. Poverty-stricken sharecroppers gave up their smallholdings and became an industrial workforce. Old inefficient coal mines and textile

Definition

Taft–Hartley Act
It outlawed the closed shop and secondary picketing, and made unions liable in law for broken contracts. Unions had to abide by a sixty-day cooling off period before striking. Unions also had to make public their financial statements. The Act was in part a response to permeation of some unions by racketeers, and a growing fear of communist influence. Many of the clauses became a model for those in Great Britain, who wished to control union power, and passed into British law in the 1980s.

SKILLS BUILDER

The basis of America's post-war prosperity was multi-causal.

Design a spider diagram or flowchart that shows how a number of factors linked together to create this prosperity.

factories collapsed. Slumps are the essential engines of progress. Like a forest fire it destroyed old wood and allowed new to grow from the ashes.

The Red Scare and McCarthyism

If the Cold War contributed to prosperity it was also responsible for another notable feature of post-war America, the Red Scare and the hysteria which became known as McCarthyism.

Source D

"Fire!"

8.4 A cartoon by Herbert Block called 'Fire!', published in the *Washington Post* on 4 March 1954. It is perhaps the most famous pictorial depiction of some of the extreme behaviour engendered by the impact of the Red Scare.

It is very important to appreciate that the Red Scare, and the furore it provoked, predated the emergence of Senator McCarthy. There was some justification for the anti-communist hysteria, or the 'Red Scare', whose roots were many and varied. There had been serious Soviet penetration of the USA in the 1930s and early 1940s. In 1941, we now know there had been 221 Soviet agents in the USA reporting back to NKVD, the Soviet secret police, and more Soviet Army Intelligence agents reporting back to the Red Army. Stalin knew more about the top secret Manhattan Project to build the atom bomb than Truman did as Vice-President of the USA. In the late 1930s and during the war, the Roosevelt administration had been somewhat over-relaxed at the degree of penetration by Soviet agents. Today it is often portrayed as some figment of the right-wing press and media with little basis in reality. George Keenan, a perceptive and, on the whole, balanced member of the State Department described the penetration of US government services in his memoirs as *'not a figment of imagination'* and *'not trivial in proportions'*.

The defection of a cypher clerk, Igor Gouzenko, from the Soviet Embassy in Ottawa in September 1945 led to a rash of information revealing communist infiltration. It highlighted the leaking of vital secrets to the Soviets, especially information on atom bomb development. As the wartime alliance with Russia broke down in 1945–46, it became clear that there was a new totalitarian regime in that country, which might threaten the USA in particular, and liberal democracy in general. During the war the appalling Human Rights record of the Soviet Union under Stalin tended to be forgotten. In terms of sheer brutality and the creation of human misery it is worth remembering that there was little to choose between the Soviet regime and that of Adolf Hitler. It just happened that as Hitler had attacked Russia, Russia came in on the Allied side. With peace came the growing awareness that here was a regime which treated its own people with barbarity and in terms of foreign policy it needed treating with extreme suspicion.

The House Un-American Activities Committee (HUAC) was set up in 1938 to deal with the possibility of subversion by Nazi sympathisers. President Roosevelt's Administration dealt with threats on advice of J. Edgar Hoover's **FBI**. The investigations by the FBI into communist subversion and penetration of government were stepped up on Truman's orders and in March 1947 the President issued *Executive Order 9835*, which established the Federal Loyalty Boards. The phrasing of the legislation provided scope for the anti-Reds to operate. It led to the scrutinising of the personal lives and political beliefs of not only government workers but many private individuals as well. The investigators had to find 'reasonable grounds' to suspect individuals and they often did so. Presumption of innocence sometimes appeared redundant and between 1947 and 1951 over 3,000 government employees were forced to resign and over 300 were dismissed. As many as 39 states backed up this process by passing their own anti-subversion regulations.

HUAC or 'The Committee,' as it was often referred to, began to extend its activities and its initial question, *'Are you now, or have you ever been, a member of the Communist Party?'* was uttered with chilling frequency. Its chairman, John Rankin of Mississippi, was likened by many on the Left to a Nazi leader. It is important to recognise that Joe McCarthy was not the only one to be cast as a devil during the Red Scare. The committee wanted a higher profile for its activities, and between 1947 and 1951 it targeted Hollywood. During the Second World War many pro-Russian films had extolled the virtues of the Russian character and there were many working there with clear left-wing and even communist sympathies. This was now deemed to be a threat and there was the feeling that the film industry had been infiltrated. Some performers spoke out against the pressure and persecution, notably the actor Frederic March: *'Who's next? Is it your minister who will be told what he can say in the pulpit? This hysteria reaches into every American city and town'.*

The Republican Party lost five successive Presidential elections, the defeat in 1948 being a particular shock, and they were hungry to regain power. In 1946, they had enjoyed a massive success in congressional elections and held clear majorities in both Houses of Congress. Emphasising the communist threat, and the hitherto rather relaxed attitude of the Democratic Administration, might pay rich political dividends. In other words party politics added to the gathering momentum behind the Red Scare. The young Republican congressman from California, Richard Nixon, gained a national reputation by pursuing a suspected communist agent in the State Department, Alger Hiss.

However it is important to realise that there were many genuine communist sympathisers and they did pose a real threat. Events played a big part in developing fear of communism. The 'loss of China' to communists led by Mao Zedong in 1949 was blamed on weak minded individuals by the right-wing press and the so-called **China Lobby**. Although anything but weak-minded, Truman's leading foreign policy advisers, Marshall and Acheson, were described as such by their critics. The explosion of a Soviet atomic bomb in 1949, long before they were expected to develop one, seemed to confirm the fears that there were traitors at the heart of government. In reality, communist espionage had aided the Russians as a series of high profile trials in the 1950s made clear.

In some senses, the Red Scare was not such an aberration and could be placed in a broader context of United States history. The playwright, Arthur Miller, a notable left-wing intellectual, who resisted the committee, later expressed his feelings in his play *The Crucible*, which tried to draw a parallel between the Red Scare of his lifetime and the events in 17th century Massachusetts during the Salem witch trials of 1692. There is some irony in the fact that the behaviour of the Soviet security forces accorded much more closely with the physical persecution Miller portrayed than did the US authorities, although he does fairly capture some of the irrational public hysteria present in the USA. The Red Scare at the end of the First World War (see Unit 4, pages 56–59) had displayed many of the features of this latest Red Scare.

In the Second World War there were examples of wartime patriotism leading to paranoia and the consequent violation of civil liberties, most notably the treatment of Japanese Americans. Thousands had been forcibly moved from the West Coast to camps in the interior in 1941–42. Was a fear of internal subversion endemic to the United States part of the psychology of small town communities? Was it a phenomenon of a free populist press? Many influential figures in the media stoked the flames. The newspapers and journals owned by **William Randolph Hearst** were enthusiastic backers of the work of 'The Committee' and pressed for action against the Reds.

McCarthysm: the immediate background

Alger Hiss was a well-connected diplomat in the State Department and a personal friend of Dean Acheson, the Secretary of State. Hiss had been supplying the Soviets with diplomatic secrets at the time of the Yalta conference in February 1945 and before. The truth of this was not to be confirmed until the opening of Soviet records in the 1990s. In 1948, he had been accused of treachery by a self-confessed Communist. Hiss made a series of denials and was prosecuted for perjury – lying under oath. At a trial in 1949, the jury could not reach a verdict, but after a second trial he was found guilty in January 1950. This gave a powerful boost to the Red Scare phenomena. Most other Soviet agents had been rounded up between 1945 and 1950 by the FBI. As indicated above, Truman's government had tightened up with increased loyalty tests and some would say excessive security precautions in 1947–48. In this sense, the real threat was over by the time McCarthy got into the act. However, the final Hiss verdict, the

Source E

8.5 A protestor at an anti-communist demonstration during the Rosenberg trial in 1951 (see pages 160–162 for details on this trial).

new awareness that Russia had an atomic bomb and the fact that China had been 'lost' to communism, all created a mounting hysteria in 1950s America, which it found difficult to resist.

Within days of Hiss being convicted, Klaus Fuchs, a German-born British scientist who had worked on the Manhattan Project to develop atomic weapons at Los Alamos, was sentenced in Great Britain for leaking atomic secrets to the Soviets. The Hiss case, and linked events like Fuchs, allowed Republicans to implicate the reigning Democrats in *'the Communist conspiracy'*. The attacks reached to the highest levels of Truman's administration: Acheson himself was repeatedly attacked, as was General Marshall, the Secretary of Defence who was the other great prop to Truman in the conduct of foreign policy.

McCarthyism: the reality

One of the least impressive members of the Senate was to give Truman cause for real concern from 1950 onwards and magnify the Red Scare to ludicrous proportions. In the process his career was to illustrate the power of public opinion and the press. Senator Joseph McCarthy of Wisconsin had been voted the worst Senator by press correspondents serving in Washington. He had few political friends, even within his own Republican Party. In 1950, however, a dinner companion suggested that he might raise his profile by launching a campaign against communist infiltration of the government. As one journalist pointed out, Joe McCarthy knew little about communism and could not tell Karl Marx from Groucho Marx (an American comedian and film star). However, McCarthy was not one to let ignorance stand in the way of a good idea, as can be seen from Source F.

The 205 communists in the State Department was not a random number picked out of thin air, as is sometimes suggested. The US Secretary of State before Dean Acheson, James Byrnes, had admitted to a Congressman that there were 285 alleged security risks in the State Department. 79 had been fired, leaving 206. McCarthy suffered from faulty arithmetic and reached a total of 205.

Over the next few weeks more speeches followed. The numbers changed but not the message. Although no evidence was produced, the public began gradually to take notice and the smears started to have an effect. Some fellow Republicans and even some Democrats in the Senate and House began to lend support to McCarthy's campaign. Joseph Kennedy, the Democratic Senator for Massachusetts and his up-and-coming young congressman son, John F. Kennedy, were sympathetic; they had a large number of anti-communist Catholic constituents. Many American Catholics had relatives in Eastern Europe in Hungary and Poland, now under Soviet control and were bitterly opposed to the Soviet Union. John F. Kennedy explained to an audience *'The **pinks** betrayed US policy in China ... McCarthy may have something'.*

What McCarthy had, apparently, was a list, which varied in number, of traitors at the heart of the United States Government, notably in the State

Source F

I have here in my hand a list of 205 people that were known to the Secretary of State as being members of the Communist Party and who nevertheless are still working and shaping the policy of the State Department.

From a speech made by McCarthy on 9 February 1950 at a meeting in Wheeling, West Virginia

SKILLS BUILDER

How far do you agree that McCarthy was simply doing his duty and responding to the legitimate fear of the majority of Americans?

Definition

Pinks or 'pinkoes'

A derogatory nickname given to those liberals who if not Communists themselves were suspected of being soft on Communists or mildly sympathetic.

Department. McCarthy appeared to possess animal cunning and a highly developed instinct for publicity. He used the press and radio stations to great effect, and seemed to be able to trigger paranoia in many ordinary Americans, who were fundamentally ignorant of the world but had heard of the evil dictator Stalin and knew that he now had the fearsome atomic bomb. After Republican election gains in Congress in November 1950, the anti-communist rhetoric increased. It was the obvious party political weapon with which to embarrass the Democratic Administration of Truman. McCarthy became the leading figure, rather overshadowing HUAC. Eventually, in 1953, he assumed the chairmanship of a hitherto unimportant Senate committee set up to scrutinise government activity at all levels, and with his flare for publicity made it the centre of the drive against 'commies'. The meetings degenerated into witch-hunts, where the constitutional rights of citizens were ignored and those pleading the 5th Amendment, the right to silence, were treated as though they had made an admission of guilt.

Source H

8.6 Senator McCarthy outlining details of Communist Party organisation to the HUAC.

The international and political context was crucial to his success. Events in Korea, such as the humiliating defeat of US forces by the Chinese Army in the Winter of 1950–51 and the subsequent dismissal of General Macarthur,

Biography

Ethel and Julius Rosenberg

In 1951 the Rosenbergs were accused of passing atomic secrets to the Soviet Union. They admitted communist sympathies, but refused to cooperate with the authorities. They were executed in June 1953 for treason.

increased the unpopularity of the Truman Administration and especially Dean Acheson. The Korean War seemed to indicate that the Cold War was becoming much hotter. American boys were now dying fighting Communists. Fresh hysteria was provided by the arrest and conviction of **Ethel and Julius Rosenberg**, spies who seemed to prove that the Communists had been able to breach American security. In September 1950, the conservative bloc in Congress demonstrated its contempt for Truman's loyalty programme by passing the *Internal Security Act* over a Presidential veto. This Act subjected private citizens to much more direct political surveillance.

The Republican victories in the presidential election of November 1952 in the shape of General Eisenhower, and Republican gains in Congress, initially confirmed McCarthy's influence still further and McCarthy began to launch wider and wilder campaigns. He was firmly warned off going for the CIA, the USA's new and expanding intelligence agency and he then mistakenly began to mount a campaign to prove there was disloyalty at the heart of the United States Army. This contributed to his downfall. McCarthy had inadvertently mobilised against himself the force and prestige of President Eisenhower, who was furious at McCarthy's increasingly hysterical accusations against his beloved Army. Perhaps even more significantly, the Army hearings were televised and large audiences were increasingly alienated by McCarthy's bullying treatment of witnesses

Source I

A cartoon of Joe McCarthy by Herbert Block, published in May 1954.

called before his Senate Committee. McCarthy was also damaged when it emerged that his assistant, a 25-year-old lawyer, Roy Cohn, had tried to use his influence with the Army to secure favours for his boyfriend, David Schine, who was a conscripted soldier. McCarthy's hold on the public withered and political friends deserted him. He was formally censured by the Senate in December 1954. McCarthy, always a hard drinker, declined into increasing alcoholism. He died in 1957.

The importance of the Red Scare and McCarthyism

At one level McCarthyism was simply political froth created by the media. Eisenhower said as much to a close friend in 1953: *'We have here a figure who owes his entire prominence and influence in today's life to the publicity media of the nation. Now these same media are looking around for someone to knock off the creature of their own making.'*

McCarthy was essentially a cartoon villain who seized his moment to achieve national prominence. It suited the Republicans in control of both Houses, but deeply resentful of Truman's narrow and unexpected presidential victory in 1948, to use the Red Scare against the Democrats. McCarthy, with few real friends even in his own party, took the opportunity to attract attention to himself and win party support. It brought him a popularity and coverage he had never had before.

Circumstances conspired to keep him in the popular eye. The fear triggered by the Soviet possession of an atomic bomb, and the revelation that spies had helped the Russians get it, was an essential backdrop to his performance. So was the Korean War, which began in June 1950 and eventually ended in stalemate in 1953. It is no accident that once the war ended and a Republican was installed in the White House, McCarthy's days were numbered. The press withdrew their favour and he sank into alcoholic oblivion.

The broader Red Scare from 1946 onwards, had a more widespread and more lasting impact. The stupidities and bogus claims of McCarthy after 1950 have had the effect of concealing, or leading people to forget the very real threat that did exist of communist penetration into various important aspects of American government. The Red Scare virtually eliminated Soviet Agents, and may have even gone too far in purging the State Department, so that only **Cold War hawks** were left. Those moderate officials who would have preferred a more nuanced response to the communist threat, which was real, were now silenced. This was to have considerable impact on US policy in Vietnam which tended to follow the more aggressive route espoused by the hawks.

On domestic policies, the Red Scare had a longer-term impact. It harmed the Civil Rights movement, as many of the 1930s activists on behalf of improved rights for black Americans had been associated with, or were actual members of, the Communist Party. It now became an easy charge for southern conservatives to make that any reformers were communist

SKILLS BUILDER

1. What factors explain Senator McCarthy's fall from prominence?

2. To what extent would you agree that McCarthy was a creation of the media?

Definition

Cold War hawks

Those who believed that the only way to deal with Soviet aggression was to meet it with equal aggression. The ultimate hawk was probably General Curtis Le May, the head of the US Air Force in the 1950s. The opponents of the hawks, who favoured a more conciliatory approach, were christened 'doves'.

sympathisers. It had a real impact on American unions. The *Taft–Hartley Act* of 1947 (see page 153) required union leaders to take an oath that they were not Communists. American unions developed very much as patriotic anti-communist organisations. This development was, of course, very much aided by the growing prosperity of the USA. Capitalist America seemed infinitely preferable to most workers to the drab, deprived Soviet Union.

Clearly some suffered during the Red Scare. Many government employees, with only limited connections with, or sympathies for, communism lost their jobs. Some actors and directors in Hollywood were blacklisted by the studios, and consequently had their careers blighted. Nevertheless, it is important to realise that this period of fear and paranoia is not in any way comparable to the purges in the Soviet Union. The victims in the USA were measured in hundreds, not hundreds of thousands, and the worst that happened was loss of jobs. The Rosenbergs, for example, were executed for spying but only after due process of law. Alger Hiss received a five-year prison sentence for perjury. He was lucky not to be given more in view of his genuine treason.

Conclusion

By 1954, the United States was still in the early years of an economic boom, which was to last to the 1970s. Ordinary people were to enjoy living standards and a lifestyle new to the planet. It was centred round home ownership, the automobile and the television. It was to be a more private world than the one of the early 20th century. Travel and entertainment were increasingly undertaken with the family not the general public. The railways declined and bus services were for the urban poor. It is little wonder that communism or even socialism made little headway in the United States. Bill Levitt, the entrepreneur who did so much to fashion the new sub-urban America said *'No man who owns his own house and lot can be a Communist. He has too much to do'*.

The United Automobile Worker's leader, Walter Reuther, famously traded insults with the Soviet leader Nikita Khrushchev at a meeting in San Francisco in 1959. At one point Reuther tossed across the table to the Soviet leader a list of American wage rates *'How can we say these people are wage slaves exploited by capitalism, making these kind of wages in America? How can he say they have nothing to lose but their chains?'* Reuther had a point. The traditional American working class were disappearing in a blaze of prosperity and little wonder they showed a deep suspicion of communism and its Russian patron. It was the contrast in lifestyles between the bleak, oppressive world of the Soviet Union and North American freedom and prosperity that had led Igor Gouzenko to defect in Ottawa and trigger the Red Scare.

Yet there were powerful fault lines in American society, which – in some ways – prosperity made harder to tolerate. The great curse of racial disharmony remained to blight the American dream. Hundreds of thousands of black Americans had moved from their traditional places of servitude in the South and now filled the great cities of the North and West. Roosevelt had been able to do little in terms of legislation. Truman had ended segregation in the Army but the southern block of conservative Democrats in Congress frustrated attempts to go further. However, it was in May 1954 that a significant advance occurred. The agent of this development was the Supreme Court. In the important case of Brown versus the Board of Education of Topeka, the court unanimously ruled that segregated schools contravened the Constitution. Here was the opening scene in the great drama of the Civil Rights movement which over the next 15 years was to finally address, if not cure, the racial divide.

Unit summary

What have you learned in this unit?

You have been introduced to the dramatic impact of the war on the US economy and society. The enormous scale of the productive achievement has been outlined and the consequent social changes sketched. The continuing economic advance after the war has been presented in outline and some of the reasons for this suggested. Finally the post-war phenomena of the Red Scare and McCarthyism were described and some of the reasons for them suggested.

What skills have you used in this unit?

You have discussed a number of issues and weighed factors against each other to come to a conclusion. You have answered a number of questions that are central to this topic and you have used your analytical skills to explain the impact of the Second World War on the USA.

Exam style question

'Although the Red Scare was exploited by self-seeking individuals it was rooted in a very real threat to the USA.'

How far do you agree with these judgements?

Exam Tips

In answering this take note of all the general advice given earlier on writing responses to traditional history essays (see pages 23–24).

In this case remember that this is essentially a causal question and offers an explanation of the 'the Red Scare', namely 'a real threat to the USA', which needs debating.

You are clearly expected to deal with Joseph McCarthy and possibly other individuals who might be considered as causes. Don't feel obliged to agree with the proposition but do find arguments on both sides.

RESEARCH TOPIC

The Red Scare dominated American society for a number of years.

Research one person who was subjected to McCarthy's investigation and reach a conclusion as to whether the investigation was justified or not.

What was the impact of the enquiries on that individual, and the society or industry to which s/he belonged?

Thematic review: making a substantiated judgement on an issue or interpretation

The topic you have studied in this book covers a long period of time. It is, therefore, important to stand back and review the period as a whole. This unit has been looking at the nature of change and the factors that have caused tension as well as those that have reduced it. The concepts of change and continuity and cause and consequence have underpinned the focus of this study. You need to be asking yourself not only what happened but why it happened and why it happened when it did and not earlier or later. Change is brought about by a range of factors but you should be asking yourself which factor is the most important. What is the role of each factor and how do they work in combination to produce the events that occurred? Were any events critical turning points in the period as a whole? Thematic review questions, spanning the whole time period, will help to focus your thinking. These are the thematic review questions that relate to *The United States, 1917–54: Boom, Bust and Recovery*. You can probably think of more, but these are the key ones to start you off working in this way.

- How far did the power of the Federal Government increase in these years?

- How far and in what ways was traditional, protestant, rural America challenged in these years?

- How far was US society marked by increasing conflict over race and immigration?

- How far did new technology transform the USA in these years?

- How far was the USA transformed by war and the threat of war in these years?

Choose one of these thematic review questions that you plan to answer. Working through this section will make much more sense if you have an actual question in mind.

Answering a thematic review question

There are two key approaches to answering a thematic review question: select and deploy.

Select You need to select appropriate material from sources and your own knowledge.

Deploy You need to deploy what you have selected so that you answer the question in as direct a way as possible.

Unpacking 'select'

All of the thematic review questions are asking you to provide evaluation in order to reach a substantiated judgement. They ask 'How far …?', 'To what extent …?', 'How significant …?', which means that you will have to weigh up the evidence given by the interpretations you have selected. You will, therefore, have to select interpretations that give you a range of differing perspectives. For example, referring to three perspectives that agree with each other will severely limit your opportunity to discuss, debate and evaluate. You will need to select interpretations that pull in different directions so that you can weigh up the evidence that they use and its value. This will help you reach a reasoned, supported conclusion.

Now go ahead.

(i) Look back through this book and select the sources that you think will give you the appropriate range of balance in terms of interpretations.

(ii) Make notes of the knowledge you will need to use to contextualise the sources and create an argument.

You can't, of course, simply use the sources in an answer to illustrate points and provide proof that an interpretation or argument is valid without assessing the value of the interpretation and the evidence it highlights. You, therefore, need to evaluate the sources you have selected and use that evaluation to create the argument you will be making when you answer the question. You have already had practice of doing this, but here is a reminder of some of the questions you will need to ask of a source before you can turn it into evidence.

- What is the **thrust** of the interpretation? What does it say that relates to the question I am answering?

- What evidence is used in the **content** of the source to support its interpretation? What is the nature of the evidence that it is using?

- What is the **perspective** of the interpretation? Does it focus on individuals and their importance or the context within which they operated? Is it likely to be from the perspective of a Keynesian or a Monetarist? Has the background of the author influenced the interpretation? Is the date of publication significant? Was the author able to access the full range of sources for this topic?

- What material from your own knowledge supports the interpretation given?

- What material from your own knowledge leads you to modify, challenge or reject the interpretation given?

Now you have your selection of source material and own knowledge you need to think about it as a package. Does it do the job you want it to do? Does it supply you with enough evidence of different points of view so that you can show you have considered what weight the evidence will bear in reaching a reasoned, supported conclusion? In order to do this effectively you need to **cross-reference** the sources, showing where they support each other and where they differ. You should then provide an explanation of the differences and attempt to resolve them as part of your own argument. Can differences be explained by perspective, date of publication, nature of evidence used? What evidence gives your view more weight? This will be the key feature that makes your argument convincing.

Unpacking 'deploy'

The key to deploying material effectively is relevance. You must address the specific question asked and sustain your relevance throughout the answer. Always ask yourself, 'how does this paragraph take my answer further?' What are you trying to do that relates directly to the question? Make the relevance of your answer explicit at all stages. Do not rely on the reader to work out how your material might be relevant. If you find that a section of your answer does not relate to the specific focus of the question be ruthless and remove it. You may need the time and space for more relevant material.

You have already had a lot of practice in essay planning and writing, so this is just a reminder of the main things you need to bear in mind.

Plan

- Plan carefully how you are going to construct your answer and make out your case. Remember the saying 'Failure to plan is planning to fail'.

Structure

- Give your answer a clear, logical structure. It is always a good idea to examine the premise given in the statement in the question first. For example, in answering the question 'To what extent was the slump and depression a product of government policies?' it is advisable to assess the evidence that supports the importance of 'government policies' first before widening out your answer to consider other factors.

Introduction

- Give a brief outline of your argument and how you will develop it. Don't be tempted to 'set the scene' by giving a narrative description. Start as you mean to go on by focussing on the specific demands of the question and presenting your own argument in response to it.

The main body

- This section of your answer should be a series of paragraphs that develop your argument by assessing the evidence available. When considering an interpretation remember to provide evaluation by critical consideration of the evidence that relates to it.

Conclusion

- This should pull your case together to provide a reasoned summary of your overall argument. It is essential that you reach a reasoned judgement that addresses the specific question you have been asked to consider. Make sure that your conclusion links to your introduction. Is your argument sustained from beginning to end?

You do not, of course, have to respond to these thematic review questions by writing an essay on your own. You could work collaboratively with others, or use them to prepare for a class debate. Some websites provide opportunities to discuss and debate historical issues with students across the country and abroad. Whatever way you are going to use these thematic review questions, the approach will be the same: select, deploy and make it relevant.

Exam zone

Relax and prepare

Hot Tips: What other students have said.

From AS to A2 level

- A2 level History seems like a big step up at first with more demands made on independent reading and more complex source passages to cope with. However by the end of the first term I felt as if my written work had improved considerably.

- Start reading around the topics studied in class as early as possible. Reading helped me understand how historians present their arguments and use evidence.

- Studying the unit on Boom, Bust and Recovery helped my understanding of current affairs. I found listening to the news and reading newspapers reinforced my understanding of the topics we studied.

- There are now lots of History programmes on TV, even whole channels devoted to History. Although they vary in quality, it is always worth looking out for interesting programmes that relate to what you have studied.

- It is sometimes hard to tell which websites might be useful to look at but I have become better at ensuring I know who has produced the site so that I can evaluate its material. Many universities have useful websites.

- The more practise source based questions I attempted, the more confident I became and quite quickly I picked up the necessary style and technique required for success.

- Don't get flustered or panic. Ask your teacher if you are not sure. History teachers aren't that scary!

What I wish I had known at the start of the year

- I used the textbook a lot during the revision period to learn the key facts. I really wished that I had used it from the beginning of the course in order to consolidate my class notes.

- I wish that I had taken more time reading and noting other material such as the photocopied handouts issued by my teacher. Reading around the subject and undertaking independent research would have made my understanding more complete and made the whole topic more interesting.

- It helps if you annotate your notes and reading material as you do it. This makes your reading more active and therefore more useful.

- A Level History is not just about learning the relevant material but also developing the skills to use it effectively. I wished that I had spent more time throughout the year practising source questions to improve my style and technique.

- I wish I had paid more attention to the advice and comments made by my teacher on the written work I had done. This would have helped me to improve my scores throughout the year.

How to revise

- I started my revision by buying a new folder and some dividers. I put all my revision work into this folder and used the dividers to separate the different topics. I really took pride in my revision notes and made them as thorough and effective as I could manage.

- Before I started the revision process, I found it helpful to plan out my history revision. I used the Edexcel specification given to me by my teacher as a guideline of which topics to revise and I ticked off each one as I covered it.

- I found it useful to revise in short, sharp bursts. I would set myself a target of revising one particular topic in an hour and a half. I would spend one hour taking revision notes and then half an hour testing myself with a short practice question or a facts test.

- Planning answers to key questions is helpful because it saves time later.

- I found it useful to always include some practice work in my revision. If I could get that work to my teacher to mark all the better, but just attempting questions to time helped me improve my technique.

- Sometimes I found it helpful to revise with a friend. We might spend 45 minutes revising by ourselves and then half an hour testing each other. Often we were able to sort out any problems between us and it was reassuring to see that someone else had the same worries and pressures at that time.

Refresh your memory: revision checklist

The following provides a useful list for checking the information you need to revise for your exam.

Unit 1: The USA in the early 20th century (General context)

- The differences between the Federal Government and the States.

- The different branches of the Federal Government – President, Congress and the Supreme Court.

- The key features of the economy of the USA.

Unit 2: The impact of the First World War (Section A Topic)

- What was the impact on the economy both pre-1917 and after the US declaration of war in April.

- The social consequences, e.g. Prohibition.

- The political consequences, e.g. the growth in power of the Federal Government, the enfranchisement of women.

Unit 3: The years of prosperity, 1919–29 (Section A Topic)

- Where was there growth and development – growth of suburbia, cars, consumer goods, electrical power, new forms of entertainment?

- The reasons for the economic growth – new technology, development of credit, advertising.

- The role of government in the economy – laissez faire but also protection.

- Winners – large number but also losers – agriculture, particularly share croppers, old industries, e.g. coal and textiles.

Unit 4: Political and social tensions, 1919–29 (Section A Topic)

- Religion and belief.

- The impact of Prohibition.

- Tensions over race and immigration.

- Women's suffrage and its impact.

Unit 5: The coming of slump and the Depression 1929–33 (Section B Controversy)

- The structural weaknesses in the US economy of the 1920s.

- The reasons for the Stock Market Crash of 1929 and its impact – Did it cause the Depression?

- The Banking Crisis – Why were so many US Banks vulnerable?

- The International dimension 1931–39.

- The response of Hoover and the Federal Government – too little or too much?

Unit 6: The New Deal and its impact (Section B Controversy)

- The nature Of the FDR administration and the New Deal.

- Dealing with the banking crisis1933–34.

- Dealing with the crisis in agriculture 1933–35.

- Dealing with unemployment and Industry 1933–35.

- The so-called Second New Deal 1935–38.
- Welfare, unions and restructuring of former measures.
- The impact of the New Deal in terms of reviving the economy, creating greater security, impact on race and gender issues.

Unit 7: Opposition to Roosevelt and the New Deal (Section A Topic)

- Opposition from the Left.
- Opposition from the Right.
- The Supreme Court and its impact.
- Roosevelt's responses to the Supreme Court.

Unit 8: The Second World War and its aftermath to 1954 (Section A Topic)

- The political, social and economic impacts of the Second World War on the USA.
- Post-war prosperity – Why?
- The Red Scare and McCarthy – distinguishing between the two. What were their effects?

This revision checklist is very knowledge-based. Don't forget that in Section B of the examination your skills in handling sources will also be tested.

Result

You have spent a lot of time working on plans and constructing answers to the (a) and (b) questions. So you now have a pretty good idea about how to plan an answer and write a response to the question on the examination paper. But what are the examiners looking for? And what marks will you get?

About the exam

As part of your A2 Level History course you are required to carry out a study in depth, in this instance *The United States, 1917–54: Boom, Bust and Recovery*. You will be required to gain a firm understanding of the chronology of the topic and of the key issues, problems and debates associated with it. You will also be required to explore the nature of challenges and conflict both within the period and relating to the societies and political systems studied, and will do this by working with secondary sources that provide differing views about historical controversies.

At the end of your A2 course you will take a written exam and you will need to answer two questions. The sources will be supplied with the paper.

- In Section A you will need to reach a substantiated judgement on an historical issue or problem. You will have a choice of two questions, and this question will be worth 30 marks.
- In Section B you will need to compare source material to explore an issue of historical debate, reaching a substantiated judgement using your own knowledge. There will be a choice of two questions and this question will be worth 40 marks.

The exam will last 2 hours. Make sure you plan your time carefully and allow enough time to answer both questions thoroughly.

Section A

These essay questions, from which you choose one to answer, will have an analytical focus that will require you to reach a substantiated judgement on a historical issue or problem. For example, questions are likely to be worded with the instruction 'how far/to what extent ...' and to be followed by either a statement or an interpretation that you are asked to weigh up.

Section B

In this section you will be provided with five or six secondary sources that total about 700–800 words. You will then have to answer one question from a choice of two. Each question will ask you to discuss two or three of the sources while exploring an issue of historical debate, and to reach a substantiated judgement based on the sources and your own knowledge.

Questions are likely to be worded with the instruction 'How far do you agree with the view that ...' You will also be instructed to 'Explain your answer using the sources and your own knowledge of the issues related to this controversy'.

Section A

What will you have to do, and what marks will you get for doing it?

This question tests your ability to recall, select and deploy information and your ability to understand key concepts and features. There are 30 marks available for this section. You will be working at one of five levels. Try to get as high up in the levels as you can.

Level 1

1–6 marks

- **You are able to** produce a series of simple statements.

Knowledge will be generalised with few examples. The answer will not be made relevant to the question.

Level 2

7–12 marks

- **You are able to** produce answers with some development using examples.

The range of examples is likely to be limited. There may be some attempt to link the material to the question but it will not be made explicit.

Level 3

13–18 marks

- **You are able to** produce an answer that shows an understanding of the question and what it is getting at.

The answer will, however, drift into irrelevance at times or be based on material which although developed in places is limited in its range.

Level 4

19–24 marks

- **You are able to** produce an analytical answer that shows a clear understanding of the focus of the question.

The answer is drawing out key points with detailed knowledge used to develop an argument. There may still be some drifting from the specific question or a lack of balance with some aspects dealt with briefly but the answer shows some attempt to evaluate the evidence used in the argument.

Level 5

25–30 marks

- **You are able to** produce a sustained analytical answer.

The answer is a well-structured argument that discusses the evidence used to support/reject/modify the statement in the question. The answer evaluates the evidence for the argument.

Now try this question

How far would you agree that new technological inventions underpinned the prosperity of the 1920s?

GUIDANCE NOTES

Remember that in order to weigh up a statement or interpretation you need to look at the following:

- Explain the statement/interpretation.
- Outline the evidence that could be used to support the statement/interpretation and discuss its validity.
- Outline the evidence that could be used to reject/modify the statement/interpretation and comment on its validity.
- Come to a developed, reasoned judgement that presents your own argument.

N.B. The best answers will show that they have thought seriously about the issue/problem and have a well-supported, reasoned argument of their own in relation to the question they have been asked.

This argument will be **sustained** i.e. be present from the introduction to the conclusion. Thus, especial care is needed when you write your introduction.

The argument will be based on sustained **critical evaluation** of the evidence. This will require the value of the evidence to be discussed rather than just provide a list of the evidence itself.

Now use the marking criteria to assess your response.

How did you do?

What could you have done to have achieved higher marks?

The examiners will not be nit-picking their way through your answer, ticking things off as they go. Rather, they will be looking to see which levels best fit your response and you should do the same when assessing your own responses.

Section B

What will you have to do, and what marks will you get for doing it?

This section tests your ability to recall, select and deploy information and to understand key concepts and features. This objective carries 16 marks. You are also being tested for your ability to analyse and evaluate differing interpretations in relation to their historical context. This objective carries 24 marks. Thus, Section B has a total of 40 marks. You will be working at one of five levels. Try to get as high up in the levels as you can. The examiners will be marking your answer using two sets of criteria: one for knowledge and structure, and one for knowledge of the controversy and setting the sources in the context of the controversy.

This is what the examiners will be looking for as they mark the ways in which you have selected and used your knowledge to answer the question:

Level 1

1–3 marks

- **You are able to** produce a series of simple statements.

Knowledge will be generalised with few examples. The answer will not be made relevant to the question. Links to the sources will be few or indirect.

Level 2

4–6 marks

- **You are able to** produce answers with some development using examples.

The range of examples is likely to be limited and this may be linked to the sources. There may be some attempt to link the material to the question but it will not be made explicit.

Level 3

7–10 marks

- **You are able to** produce an answer that shows an understanding of the question and what it is getting at.

There will be some links between own knowledge and the sources. The answer will, however, drift into irrelevance at times or be based on material which although developed in places is limited in its range.

Level 4

11–13 marks

- **You are able to** produce an analytical answer that shows a clear understanding of the focus of the question.

The answer is drawing out key points with detailed knowledge used to support analysis of the sources. There may still be some drifting from the specific question or a lack of balance with some aspects dealt with briefly but the answer shows some attempt to evaluate the evidence used in the argument

Level 5

14–16 marks

- **You are able to** produce a sustained analytical answer.

The answer is a well-structured argument that discusses the evidence used to support/reject/modify the statement in the question. The answer evaluates the evidence for the argument.

This is what examiners are looking for as they mark your source evaluation skills.

Level 1

1–4 marks

- **You are able to** understand the sources at face value and use them to identify points.

There will be no integration of the sources with each other or with own knowledge – they will be treated singly and separately – when coming to a conclusion.

Level 2

5–9 marks

- **You are able to** understand the sources and can use them to develop points relevant to the question.

There will be some linking together of the material from the sources. The answer will reach a judgement based on limited support from the sources.

Level 3

10–14 marks

- **You are able to** interpret the evidence from the sources drawing out key points from the evidence in the sources.

Develops points that both support and challenge the interpretation under discussion and shows an awareness of the nature of the debate that the interpretation relates to. The answer may well be unbalanced with not all aspects covered but there is a clear attempt to reach a reasoned answer supported by information and argument from the sources.

Level 4

15–19 marks

- **You are able to** interpret the sources with confidence, showing an understanding of the basis of the arguments offered in the sources.

Answers will relate the interpretations offered by the sources to their wider context by using own knowledge to discuss the arguments presented. Judgements will be reached that integrate the sources and own knowledge to support a well-developed and sustained argument.

Level 5

20–24 marks

- **You are able to** produce a sustained evaluation of the sources to present a fully-reasoned argument.

The interpretations offered by the sources are discussed and evaluated with the validity of the interpretation assessed by reference to own knowledge. Thus, sources and own knowledge are effectively integrated to address the full demands of the question.

Don't forget to take care with your English. The quality of your communication can be used by the examiner to decide which mark to give you within a level. Quality of communication is about more than spelling. It is about whether your answer is well-structured with paragraphs and clear sentences.

Now try this question

How far do you agree with the view that it was the Wall Street Crash of October 1929 that caused the Depression of the next few years?

Explain your answer, using the evidence of Sources 1, 2 and 3 and your own knowledge of the issues related to this controversy.

Source 1

Had the economy been fundamentally sound in 1929 the effect of the great stock market crash might have been small. Alternatively, the shock to confidence and loss of spending by those who were caught in the market might soon have worn off. But business in 1929 was not sound; on the contrary it was exceedingly fragile. It was vulnerable to the kind of blow it received from Wall Street. Those who have emphasised this vulnerability are obviously on strong ground. Yet when a greenhouse succumbs to a hailstorm something more than a purely passive role is normally attributed to the storm. One must accord a similar significance to the typhoon which blew out of lower Manhattan in October 1929.

From *The Great Crash 1929* by J.K. Galbraith, published 1954

Source 2

The agricultural sector, still critical within the overall American economy, had been weak since the early 1920s, as a glut of primary commodities on the world market caused prices to collapse. From an index of 217 in 1919 (based on 1910–14 as 100) prices had fallen to 148 in 1929. This again reduced the pool of customers for the mass production industries. Moreover the weakness of the rural economy had other implications for the United States as a whole. Having over-expanded in the 'golden age' caused by the First World war, many farmers found themselves in serious debt. Total farm mortgages in the United States rose from $6,700 million in 1920 to $9,400 million in 1925. This placed considerable strain upon the rural banking sector, which contained many of the smaller and more vulnerable banks in a system itself prone to difficulties.

From *The New Deal* by Fiona Venn, published 1998

Source 3

Much of the easy money found its way into the stock market and by 1928, a number of Federal Reserve officials had become concerned that the stock market speculation was out of hand. The discount rate was raised to 5 percent. In August 1929 this was raised to 6 percent. The October 1929 stock crash made clear that the Fed had overplayed its hand. The problem here, as always, was that it takes time for a change in Fed monetary policy to have an effect on the economy, and nobody knows in advance how big the effect might be. These Federal Reserve policies began a monetary contraction. As the contraction became more severe, it brought on a depression in output, employment and income. If nothing else had happened there would have been a depression because of the severe monetary contraction.

From *FDR's Folly* by Jim Powell, published 2003

GUIDANCE NOTES

These questions can be quite challenging to answer because they require you to integrate the sources with your own knowledge while discussing and making a reasoned judgement on an interpretation. The key features of a good answer will be:

- A discussion of the issues raised by the sources that shows a clear understanding of the arguments they present.
- An integration of sources with own knowledge. Own knowledge will be used to test the validity of the views expressed in the sources.
- Relevant discussion of all aspects of the controversy raised in the question.
- Come to a developed, reasoned judgement that presents your own argument in relation to the question.

As with answers in Section A the best answer will contain arguments that are **sustained** and include **critical evaluation** of the interpretation offered in the question.

Now use the marking criteria to assess your response.

How did you do?

What could you have done to have achieved higher marks?

The examiners will not be nit-picking their way through your answer, ticking things off as they go. Rather, they will be looking to see which levels best fit your response, and you should do the same when assessing your own responses.

How will I time my responses?

You have 2 hours to answer two questions. Both Section A and Section B give you a choice of questions.

Take some time, about five minutes, to read the paper carefully and think about your choice of questions.

The Section A question carries 30 marks and the Section B carries 40. You should therefore aim to spend more time on the Section B question, about 1 hour and 10 minutes, compared with about 50 minutes for Section A. Remember that this includes reading and planning time.

Always conclude each answer with your overall judgement so that your answer reads as a coherent response as a whole. This is important even if you find you have not got enough time to cover all aspects in the detail you wanted to.

You have now had a lot of practice in planning, writing and assessing your responses to the sort of questions you can expect to find on the examination paper. You are well prepared and you should be able to tackle the examination with confidence.

Good luck!

Bibliography

The American Social History Project, Who Built America? Volume II (1992)

Adams, D.K. (1979) *Franklin D. Roosevelt and The New Deal*

Allen, F.L. (1931) *Only Yesterday*

Badger, A.J. (1989) *The New Deal: The Depression Years 1933–40*

Black, C and Delano, F. (2000) *Franklin Delano Roosevelt: Champion of Freedom*

Brogan, H. (1999) *The Penguin History of the USA (Second Edition)*

Caro, R.A. (1981) *The Years of Lyndon Johnson; The Path To Power*

Conkin, P.K. (1969) *The New Deal*

Deglar, C.N. (1959) *Out of Our Past: The Forces That Shaped Modern America*

Evans, H. (1998) *The American Century*

Ferguson, N. (2008) *The Ascent of Money*

Ford, H. (1922) *My Life and Work*

Furnas J.C. (1974) *Great Times: an Informal History of the United States 1914–29*

Graubard, S. (2004) *The Presidents*

Hofstadter, R. (1962) *The American Political Tradition*

Johnson, P. (1997) *A History of the American People*

Jones, M.A. (1995) *The Limits of Liberty, (second edition)*

Josephson, M. (1934) *The Robber Barons*

Kennedy, D.M. (1999) *Freedom from Fear: The American people in Depression and War 1929–45*

Kindleberger, C.P. (1973) *The World in Depression, 1929–39*

McCullough, D. (1992) *Truman*

Middletown, R and H.L. (1929) *a study in Contemporary American Culture*

Moore, L. (2008) *'Anything Goes': A biography of the Roaring Twenties*

Parish, M.E. (1992) *Anxious Decades: America in Prosperity and Depression 1920–1941*

Powell, J. (2003) *FDR's Folly, How Roosevelt and His New Deal Prolonged the Great Depression*

Reynolds, D. (2009) *America: Empire of Liberty*

Shlaes, A. (2007) *The Forgotten Man: A New History of The Depression*

Tindell, G.B and Shi, David E. (1984) *America: A Narrative History Vol.II*

Venn, F. (1998) *The New Deal*

Walton, G and Rockoff, H. (2005) *A History of the American Economy*

Watkins, T.H. (1993) *'The Great Depression'*

Glossary

American Federation of Labor (AFL) Originally founded by 13 craft unions in 1886. More unions joined later and by 1920 it had 3,250,000 members but it remained largely an interest group for skilled workers. It was moderate in politics and kept a distance from the Socialist Party. An increasing number of members felt that it should encourage unionisation in semi-skilled or unskilled mass production workers. Supporters of this idea formed the Committee for Industrial Organisation (CIO). These were expelled from the AFL in 1936 and formed a rival organisation until 1955 when they reunited with the AFL.

Anti-Saloon League The Anti-Saloon League emphasised the links between drink and violence that became the staple scene of western films when disputes over a woman or cheating at cards resulted in a mass brawl. It had been founded in 1895 and drew much of its strength from women activists, many of whom felt that alcohol was often linked to their oppression. They had a formidable champion in the six-foot tall Carry Nation who even expressed her view in verse:

'Drink will make the dark, dark blot.

Like an adder it will sting

And at last to ruin bring

They who tarry at the drink'

The dream of temperance reformers was Prohibition.

Attorney General Chief law officer of the Federal Government and head of the Justice Department. The Attorney General is a member of the President's cabinet and appears for the President and his government in cases before the Supreme Court.

Bank failures This refers to banks closing their doors to custom and going out of business because they have lent out too much of their borrowed money and cannot get in money owed to them to pay back to the people who have invested in the bank.

Big Bull Market An expression used in share dealing, meaning a period when there are more buyers than sellers and share prices are rising.

Bolshevik A Communist or someone who is sympathetic to communist ideas.

Bolshevik seizure of power In February 1917 the Tsarist regime had been overthrown by a popular revolution. After six months of mounting chaos and continuing defeat in the First World War, a Marxist minority group, known as the Bolsheviks, under the leadership of VI Lenin, seized power in October and established 'a revolutionary dictatorship'. They won a brutal civil war, in which they were known as the Reds and their opponents as the Whites. Lenin and his colleagues saw their victory as merely the first step in the defeat of world capitalism. In reality, they had leashed on Russia a brutal and old-fashioned tyranny. Lenin killed more political opponents in the first year of his power than the last Tsar had in the whole of his 23-year reign.

Bootlegger These people were responsible for the illegal production and transportation and sale of intoxicants during Prohibition. Many showed great ingenuity in manufacturing 'medicinal alcohol' which exploited a loophole in the legislation. George Remus the self-styled 'King of the Bootleggers' was reckoned to be making 5 million dollars a year at one stage.

Brains Trust A group of academics that advised Roosevelt during his campaign in 1932, and he referred to as his 'privy council'. They continued to exercise influence when FDR took office. The New York Times christened it his 'Brains Trust' in September 1933. The founding member was Raymond Moley of Columbia University, and also two others from Columbia, Rexford Tugwell and Adolf A Berle. Vienna-born Felix Frankfurter, of Harvard Law School, was also important. The ideas of the group often conflicted and they in no ways monopolised policy formulation. They were a new feature in American public life and, as such, attracted media attention, which probably exaggerated their influence.

China Lobby This was a powerful group in the USA who supported the Chinese Nationalist leader Chiang Kai-shek (Jiang Jieshi) and felt that Truman's government should have done more to assist the Chinese Nationalists during the civil war. It included several Republican politicians and Henry Luce, the publisher of the influential Time and Life magazines.

China was the most populous state in the world and there had been strong connections with the USA since the Nationalists came to power in the 1920s. The USA had given extensive military help to China during the war.

Closed shop This was a business or company where a worker had to belong to a particular union or group of unions in order to be employed. It could be said to violate the freedom of the individual to choose whether to belong or not.

Cold War hawks These were those who believed that the only way to deal with Soviet aggression was to meet it with equal aggression. The ultimate hawk was probably General Curtis Le May, the head of the US Air Force in the 1950s. The opponents of the hawks, who favoured a more conciliatory approach, were christened 'doves'.

Consumer credit Alongside 'Hire Purchase', consumer credit was a vital innovation in stimulating demand for products. Customers were provided with credit, in reality a loan by a credit company which enabled them to have the article they desired immediately in return for a deposit and then a series of weekly or monthly payments, which of course included interest on the loan. In Great Britain it came to be known as the 'never-never' as final repayment seemed to take forever. The system worked well to everyone's advantage, as long as the purchaser retained his or her job and did not buy more than they could afford to repay.

Corporations Corporations are groups of people legally empowered to act as individuals. These 'companies' had evolved in Great Britain and Western Europe as capitalism developed and were commercially advantageous compared to privately owned individual family businesses.

Debtor/creditor nation In the 19th century there had been massive investment in the USA from Great Britain in particular. Many US businesses were partly or wholly owned by foreigners, largely British. This meant that more interest was paid from the USA than came in from US investments abroad thus making the USA a debtor nation. This was reversed as British investment in the USA was sold off and bought by American banks and citizens during the war and the USA became a creditor nation.

Democratic Party One of the two main political parties in the US. The Democratic Party was the more 'liberal' or left-wing of the two parties, although white members from the southern states were traditionally Democrat and anything but liberal or left-wing, being strongly opposed to black civil rights.

Devaluing Since the pound sterling was no longer tied to gold at a fixed rate, its international value fell in relation to the dollar. In 1925, Great Britain returned to the gold standard at the pre-war value, which gave a dollar parity of $4.76. In September 1931, it fell to $3.60.

Double V campaign This originated in a letter to a Pittsburgh newspaper calling for victory over the Axis abroad and victory over racial prejudice in the USA.

Draft A government order forcing people to join the armed forces in time of war, it was also known as conscription.

Economies of scale The benefits gained by a business by creating a larger scale of production e.g. it may be possible to secure discounts by buying raw materials in larger quantities.

Electoral College This is the group of people selected to vote for the President. Each state has the number of Electors that is equivalent to the number of members of the House of Representatives (determined on the basis of the population of the state) plus the number of Senators (two per state, irrespective of population).

FBI The Federal Government organisation responsible for checking inter-state crime and internal threats to US security. J. Edgar Hoover had been the director since its founding in 1924 and continued to head the bureau until his death in 1972. It was said he was too powerful for any president to remove.

Federal patronage An important element in the American political system was the relationship of the Federal Government to the political parties in the various states. A Democratic President would seek to help a state Democratic Party Organisation, especially if it had played a big role in delivering votes in the presidential election. Federal jobs, money and contracts would be distributed through the local party machine enabling it to bind citizens to it.

Foreclosures Foreclosures refers to banks who have lent money to farms or businesses on the security of the property and who are refusing to lend more or extend the period of the loan, taking over the property in compensation for the 'bad debt'.

Four Horsemen of the Apocalypse Part of the vision of the end of the world, described in the Book of Revelation. Four horsemen appear on four differently coloured horses. The riders are Pestilence, War, Famine and Death. They are not omens of good times to follow.

Gold Standard Currencies are given a fixed value in term of gold for which they can be exchanged. This gives stability and confidence in international trade. The *Gold Standard Act* of 1900 had fixed the dollar at $20.67 per ounce of gold.

Great Dams A series of dams built across the great rivers in the USA. They became symbols of American development and it is interesting that Alfred Hitchcock's wish to have his gang of saboteurs blow one up in the 1941 film Saboteur was quickly vetoed by the producers. Even critics of the New Deal, like Paul Johnson, tend to be complimentary about the TVA.

Gross Domestic Product (GDP) The total value of all the goods and services produced in a country.

Gross National Product (GNP) A measure of the total value of goods and services produced in a country and its overseas earnings. Divided by the number of people, GNP will give an approximate indication of the standard of living. It is a useful way of comparing the relative economic importance of different countries.

Hawley Smoot Tariff Act of 1930 This raised duties on a range of farming products and manufactured goods to an average level of 42%. It produced retaliation from other countries and even free-trade Britain adopted tariffs in 1931. It contributed to the downward spiral in world trade.

Insider dealing This involved the buying or selling of shares by those privy to crucial information on the company not available to the general public, e.g. it was subject to take over bid not yet publicised.

Ku Klux Klan Originally a terrorist secret society organised in the South after the Civil War that used violence and murder to promote its white supremacist beliefs. It was re-founded in 1915 in Georgia with the same white supremacist beliefs and same techniques of terror and violence.

Liberty bonds Like most combatants the USA paid for much of the war by borrowing off its own people. In return for their cash, citizens received a promisory piece of paper (bond) guaranteeing repayment and or a fixed rate of interest on the sum loaned. Such bonds could be traded and sold on or kept until the redemption date if there was one specified. Clearly foreign banks or wealthy individuals might buy such bonds.

Limited liability The principle of limited liability meant that only the assets put into the corporation by a shareholder were at risk in the event of bankruptcy and not other assets such as their corporations could therefore raise capital more easily than an individual.

Liquidity This refers to the availability of money. Interest rates reflect the dearness or cheapness of money. High interest rates mean dear money: it costs more to borrow and this can lead to a liquidity crisis (i.e. shortage of cash).

Marginal land This is land that is expensive to farm productively but can make a profit when food is in short supply.

Mass production This involves the use of standardised parts on an assembly production line. By using standardised parts that can be machine manufactured, economies of scale can be achieved and by moving materials continuously through the production process it is possible to speed up that process. Both these elements have the effect of making the process faster and also cheaper as unskilled and semi-skilled workers can be used rather than craftsmen.

National Association for the Advancement of Colored People This organisation was formally set up in 1945. It recognised the feelings and aspirations of millions of servicemen who had high hopes for greater civil, political and social rights. It is significant to note that voter registration amongst African Americans went up from 2% to 12% between 1940 and 1947. While this was still a deeply unacceptable situation, there were at least glimmerings of movement. Changes were brought about in the military as the war progressed. For instance during the Battle of the Bulge, in 1944, segregation effectively broke down and in January 1945 the first formally integrated unit was established.

National Recovery Administration This body was created by *National Industrial Recovery Act* was charged with creating legally binding industry-wide codes regulating wages, prices and competition. 541 codes were drafted.

Office of Price Administration This was set up in April 1941 to control prices, with limited powers granted by Congress, but its powers were much strengthened in October 1942. It proved very effective thereafter in preventing inflation. By the end of the war it had 73,000 paid employees.

On the margin This involved buying shares through a stockbroker without putting up the money for their purchase. The broker bought on your behalf and then when the stock rose, sold it, making a profit for the purchaser and money for himself through a commission. The banks charged up to 12% to underwrite the purchase i.e. to guarantee the stockbroker would not lose out. The system worked fine with everyone a winner while share prices were rising.

Paternalistic Meaning 'father-like', when used for employers it implies that while looking after the material concerns of their employees, there is generally an expectation that in return the employees will give them due respect.

Pentagon A centralised military HQ ordered by Roosevelt in 1941. It was completed in January 1943. There are 17 miles of corridors but the five sided shape was chosen so that no two offices are more than 20 minutes walk away from one another.

Pinks or 'pinkoes' A derogatory nickname given to those liberals who if not Communists themselves were suspected of being soft on Communists or mildly sympathetic.

Prohibition The banning of the sale of alcoholic drinks.

Protectionism This policy is one that restricts trade from abroad in order to limit competition.

Public Utility Holding Company Act A measure passed in August 1935, which gave the Federal Government powers to eliminate holding companies which controlled numerous public utilities and could not demonstrate that they contributed to the efficiency of the industry. The big concession to critics of the Act was that the burden of proof before abolition was shifted to the Federal Government who had to demonstrate that the holding company worked against the efficiency of the industry.

Real wages What the wages earned by a worker will buy. In other words, wages once the effects of inflation on purchasing power have been taken into account.

Reconstruction Finance Corporation An organisation established in 1932 to dispense federal funds and fight the recession.

Republican Party The Republicans were the party of big business and Western farmers. It was the party of Abraham Lincoln and associated with anti-slavery so if black people in the South could vote it was likely to be Republican. This was to change between the 1930s and 1960s with southern whites realigning with the Republicans and blacks becoming increasingly Democratic.

Salem In 1692 there were infamous witch trials in Massachusetts, when hysteria gripped the small community of Salem and led to the execution of 19 citizens as witches. These trials were made famous in the 1950s by Arthur Miller's play *The Crucible*.

Scientific management Seen as the brainchild of Frederick W. Taylor and deriving its name from his 1911 book *The Principles of Scientific Management*, he tried to establish a set of principles that would improve the efficiency of industry. The key to his method was careful observation of all components of a task. Based on these observations, standards could be established which laid down the way in which the task should be performed and the amount of time it should take. By following these principles productivity would be increased. Workers who carried out their tasks in good time would be rewarded with bonus payments; so the application of scientific management had the tendency to raise real wages for the workers involved, even though the pace of change in the nature of the work was sometimes very rapid.

Section 7a Section 7a of the *National Industrial Recovery Act* obliged management to engage in good-faith collective bargaining with workers. It was therefore designed to assist trade union power and was much resented by some employers.

Securities Exchange Commission Securities Exchange Commission had five members and its task was to administer the *Federal Securities Act* of 1933 and the *Securities Exchange Act* of 1934. It was given strong legal powers to enforce rules on stockbrokers, and in the process stopping the widespread practice of buying shares 'on the margin'.

Separation of the powers An important political concept developed in the 18th century which came from a French study of the English Constitution, which was in part misunderstood. It came to believe that the greater liberty present in England when compared to France arose from the separation of Royal power (the executive) from the law-making power of parliament (the legislature) and the judges (the judicial power). The framers of the US Constitution in 1787 rigidly applied these ideas.

Sharecroppers These were tenant farmers who paid part of their crops as rent to the land owner.

Sit-ins These were a favourite form of protest with black protestors sitting in an area designated as 'whites only'.

Speakeasy A place where illegal alcohol was sold and drunk.

States Rights issue This is the ongoing theme in US history from the inception of the Constitution. It concerns the relationship of the individual states to the Federal Government in Washington. The high point of the debate was of course the American Civil War of 1861–65.

Supreme Court One of the most distinctive features of the US Constitution is the Supreme Court.

This arose from the belief of the Founding Fathers in the doctrine of the separation of the powers. The Supreme Court was there as the guardian of the Constitution and as a permanent check on political abuse either by an over-powerful president or an over-enthusiastic democracy. The Supreme Court could pronounce an action by the President as unconstitutional and even overturn a law passed by Congress and approved by the President.

Taft-Hartley Act It outlawed the closed shop and secondary picketing, and made unions liable in law for broken contracts. Unions had to abide by a sixty day cooling off period before striking. Unions also had to make public their financial statements. The Act was in part a response to permeation of some unions by racketeers, and a growing fear of communist influence. Many of the clauses became a model for those in Great Britain, who wished to control union power and passed into British law in the 1980s.

Tariffs These are duties on imported goods which raise revenue for the government, but also have the effect of making foreign goods dearer and thereby encouraging consumers to buy locally produced goods. In this sense they are often referred to as 'protective' tariffs since they protect native industries and jobs. They have the disadvantage of raising prices to consumers and could cause other countries to retaliate by putting duties on exports.

Temperance Temperance was the abstention from drinking alcohol and had long been popular in the many protestant chapels of Great Britain and North America.

Underwriting This banking practice took a percentage of profits in return for guaranteeing that a stockbroker would not lose out on their 'on the margin' trading. The system worked fine with everyone a winner while share prices were rising.

Veto Latin for 'I forbid'. In constitutional terms the power given to an individual or group to stop a measure going through. The US President could stop a law he disapproved of, but this could be over-ridden by a two-thirds majority in both Houses of Congress. It can be a useful bargaining tool, the president threatening to veto a measure unless Congress lets through something else that the President favours.

Voluntarism The use of – or dependence on – voluntary contributions rather than government funds.

Weimar Germany Term used to describe the new Republican Germany established in 1919. The name comes from the town of Weimar where the new republican Constitution was drafted.

Index